Contemporary History in Context Series
Published in association with the Institute of Contemporary British History
General Editor: **Peter Catterall**, Director, Institute of Contemporary British History

What do they know of the contemporary, who only the contemporary know? How, without some historical context, can you tell whether what you are observing is genuinely novel, and how can you understand how it has developed? It was, not least, to guard against the unconscious and ahistorical Whiggery of much contemporary comment that this series was conceived. The series takes important events or historical debates from the post-war years and, by bringing new archival evidence and historical insights to bear, seeks to re-examine and reinterpret these matters. Most of the books will have a significant international dimension, dealing with diplomatic, economic or cultural relations across borders. in the process the object will be to challenge orthodoxies and to cast new light upon major aspects of post-war history.

Titles include:

Oliver Bange
THE EEC CRISIS OF 1963
Kennedy, Macmillan, de Gaulle and Adenauer in Conflict

Christopher Brady
UNITED STATES FOREIGN POLICY TOWARDS CAMBODIA, 1977–92

Peter Catterall and Sean McDougall (*editors*)
THE NORTHERN IRELAND QUESTION IN BRITISH POLITICS

Peter Catterall, Colin Seymour-Ure and Adrian Smith (*editors*)
NORTHCLIFFE'S LEGACY
Aspects of the British Popular Press, 1896–1996

Helen Fawcett and Rodney Lowe (*editors*)
WELFARE POLICY IN BRITAIN
The Road from 1945

Harriet Jones and Michael Kandiah (*editors*)
THE MYTH OF CONSENSUS
New Views on British History, 1945–64

Wolfram Kaiser
USING EUROPE, ABUSING THE EUROPEANS
Britain and European Integration, 1945–63

Keith Kyle
THE POLITICS OF THE INDEPENDENCE OF KENYA

D1448532

Spencer Mawby
CONTAINING GERMANY
Britain and the Arming of the Federal Republic

Jeffrey Pickering
BRITAIN'S WITHDRAWAL FROM EAST OF SUEZ
The Politics of Retrenchment

L. V. Scott
MACMILLAN, KENNEDY AND THE CUBAN MISSILE CRISIS
Political, Military and Intelligence Aspects

Paul Sharp
THATCHER'S DIPLOMACY
The Revival of British Foreign Policy

Contemporary History in Context
Series Standing Order ISBN 0–333–71470–9
(*outside North America only*)

You can receive future titles in this series as they are published by placing a standing order. Please contact your bookseller or, in case of difficulty, write to us at the address below with your name and address, the title of the series and the ISBN quoted above.

Customer Services Department, Macmillan Distribution Ltd, Houndmills, Basingstoke, Hampshire RG21 6XS, England

Northcliffe's Legacy

Aspects of the British Popular Press, 1896–1996

Edited by

Peter Catterall
Director
Institute of Contemporary British History

Colin Seymour-Ure
Professor of Government
University of Kent

Adrian Smith
Senior Lecturer in Historical Studies
University of Southampton New College

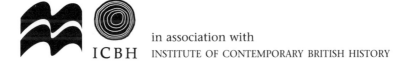

ICBH in association with
INSTITUTE OF CONTEMPORARY BRITISH HISTORY

First published in Great Britain 2000 by
MACMILLAN PRESS LTD
Houndmills, Basingstoke, Hampshire RG21 6XS and London
Companies and representatives throughout the world

A catalogue record for this book is available from the British Library.

ISBN 0–333–72011–3 hardcover
ISBN 0–333–91997–1 paperback

First published in the United States of America 2000 by
ST. MARTIN'S PRESS, INC.,
Scholarly and Reference Division,
175 Fifth Avenue, New York, N.Y. 10010

ISBN 0–312–23256–X

Library of Congress Cataloging-in-Publication Data
Northcliffe's legacy : aspects of the British popular press, 1896–1996 / edited by
Peter Catterall, Colin Seymour-Ure, Adrian Smith.
p. cm.
Papers of a conference held in 1996 at the Institute of Historical Research to mark
the centenary of the founding of the Daily Mail.
Issued in association with Institute of Contemporary British History.
Includes bibliographical references and index.
ISBN 0–312–23256–X (cloth)
1. Press—Great Britain—History—20th century—Congresses. 2. Northcliffe,
Alfred Harmsworth, Viscount, 1865–1922—Congresses. I. Catterall, Peter, 1961–
II. Seymour-Ure, Colin, 1938– III. Smith, Adrian, 1952– IV. Institute of
Contemporary British History.
PN5118 .N67   2000
072'.09'04—dc21

99–089311

This book is printed on paper suitable for recycling and made from fully managed and sustained
forest sources.

10   9   8   7   6   5   4   3   2   1
09   08   07   06   05   04   03   02   01   00

Printed and bound in Great Britain by
Antony Rowe Ltd, Chippenham, Wiltshire

Contents

General Editor's Foreword

One of the hazards it is the duty of the contemporary historian to warn against is the assumption that everything now is very different, is getting steadily better or, more frequently perhaps as far as people's views of the popular press are concerned, is getting steadily worse. The perils of such an approach are delineated here, not least in the final chapter on Maxwell's *Mirror*. As this collection of essays instead shows, an emphasis, for instance, on entertainment rather than hard news long pre-dated Rupert Murdoch's arrival in Wapping, even if changing public tastes gave the *Sun* more latitude in how it sought to entertain its readers. Nor was this emphasis a result of competition from broadcasting, deriving more as it did from a need to meet the requirements of the mass market which was already emerging in the decades of Northcliffe's pomp, even before the advent of the BBC. Meanwhile organisations like the BBC or early Channel 4, cushioned as they were by their particular funding regimes from the dictates of the market, did not entirely escape its influence and now, in the competitive world of current broadcasting, are increasingly exposed to it. BBC news managers talk openly of 'tabloid values' in an environment in which it is more important to record soundbites and set up artificial arguments than explore issues. Clearly Northcliffe's legacy extends beyond the bounds of print journalism. What are games shows and 'confessional' chat programmes but the newspaper stunts and titillation of yesteryear?

But how far is it Northcliffe's legacy? Despite the Napoleonic pretensions of 'the Chief', and the no less elevated views of themselves held by some of his successor proprietors, how far were he and they actually the movers and shakers of the popular press in the twentieth century? Were their organs, instead, shaped much more by perceptions of their potential readership?

This is not just a matter of the limits to which the personal foibles or sensibilities of proprietors can interfere with the running of their papers, as with the failed attempt of the Cadburys to drop racing news and other incitements to gambling from the *Daily News* before the First World War. It is about how far the contents of newspapers, including 'the news', is packaged for the readers – so that even if the information is new the way in which it is presented confirms what its readers already believe to be true about the world. In other words, is the popular press simply an artifice of its social milieu, to which it must constantly adapt or, like the *Daily Herald*, be condemned to die?

Some of the old newspapermen who attended the conference in 1996 which led to this book clearly had fairly detailed mental profiles of who their readers were and where their interests lay. Northcliffe himself saw his newspapers as the articulators of their readers' interests. It should be remembered, however, that he consequently saw their proprietor as the custodian of these interests. This was not a role the *Daily Herald*, hamstrung as it was by its party affiliation, was well-adapted to play. Proprietors like Beaverbrook, in contrast, could play at leading opinion, enjoying starring roles in the cartoons in their own newspapers. Similarly, though rather less ostentatiously, Murdoch's *Sun* has nailed its colours to the mast on matters like Europe. In contrast to Beaverbrook's noisy intra-party dissent, it has also been prepared to work closely and covertly with first Thatcher in the 1970s and 1980s and then Blair in the 1990s when the interests of particular political parties and those of its proprietor have happened to coincide.

This might perhaps reflect more limited room for manoeuvre for the modern proprietor. It is not just the rise of broadcasting that they have to contend with. Whereas Northcliffe could claim, rightly or wrongly, to represent readers' views, since 1937 and growing in importance in the postwar years, the opinion polls have claimed to reflect these views far more directly. It seems, under New Labour, more important than ever to try and ensure political management of the media, but influence in the other direction has been ceded, not least to focus groups and polls as alternative means of reflecting or massaging opinion.

There is, in any case, the question of whether campaigning efforts of any kind by popular newspapers have ever had much effect. The limited electoral effect of the *Sun* is after all legendary – as *Yes, Prime Minister* had it, *Sun* readers don't care who runs the country, 'as long as she's got big tits'. But it might be wrong to see this simply as apolitical apathy. In mid-century C.S. Lewis was suggesting instead in *That Hideous Strength* that readers of the popular press, tutored by the entertainment values of their newspapers to regard their 'hard news' contents with healthy scepticism, were in fact far more resistant to propaganda than the *bien-pensant* readers of the qualities. The relationships between newspapers and their readers is complex and cannot readily be recaptured by the simplistic content analysis that sometimes passes for scholarship in this area. One of the strengths of this book is the way in which this relationship instead provides one of the key themes running through the various chapters.

This book would never have happened without Colin Seymour-Ure. It was his suggestion that led to a conference at the Institute of Historical Research in 1996 to mark the centenary of the founding of the *Daily Mail*. As well as thanking all those who made this conference such a success, I ought to pay tribute to my other co-editor, Adrian Smith, whose energy, enthusiasm and persistence in dragging us back from other projects to complete this one was instrumental in ensuring that it would eventually see the light of day. As Colin suggests in his introduction, there is a need for more press history, not least to help us to understand better the relationship both between the press and our society and the press and other media. And, to return to the point I made in my opening sentence, without a historical dimension to this study, we cannot know whether what we see is novel, or understand how it has developed. This book, offering as it does a broad range of approaches and case studies, makes an important contribution to exploring and answering such questions.

PETER CATTERALL
London

Notes on the Contributors

Peter Catterall is Director of the Institute of Contemporary British History and Lecturer in History at Queen Mary & Westfield College, London. He has recently edited *The Making of Channel 4* (1999).

Jean Chalaby is Research Fellow at the Department of Sociology, London School of Economics. Author of *The Invention of Journalism* (1998) and *The De Gaulle Presidency and the Media* (forthcoming), he has published numerous articles on comparative journalism in leading European and American journals.

Chandrika Kaul has recently completed her doctoral research at Nuffield College, Oxford into British imperial politics and propaganda in the 1880s–1920s. She teaches imperial and media history at the University of Newcastle upon Tyne.

Siân Nicholas is lecturer in History at the University of Wales, Aberystwyth. She is the author of *The Echo of War: Home Front Propaganda and the Wartime BBC 1939–45* (1996).

Dilwyn Porter is Reader in History at University College, Worcester and a Research Fellow at the Business History Unit, London School of Economics. He is currently working on a history of the financial press in Britain.

Donald Read is Emeritus Professor of Modern English History at the University of Kent. His books include *Press and People: Opinion in Three English Cities 1790–1850* (1961) and *The Power of News: the History of Reuters* (2nd edn 1999). He was the President of the Historical Association 1985–88.

Colin Seymour-Ure is Professor of Government and former Dean of Social Sciences at the University of Kent at Canterbury. He has written on various aspects of media history, including *The British Press and Broadcasting since 1945* (2nd edn 1996).

Adrian Smith is Senior Lecturer in Historical Studies at University of Southampton New College, and has written widely on modern British history. He is the author of *The New Statesman: Portrait of a Political Weekly 1913–1931* (1996) and the forthcoming *In Search of 'Mick' Mannock – the Life and Politics of Major Edward Mannock VC MC DSO RFC/RAF*.

James Thomas is a tutor in history at the University of Wales, Swansea. He has recently completed a PhD thesis examining the treatment of the Labour Party in the British popular press in the twentieth century.

Peter Twaites is a professional studies tutor at the School of Journalism, Media and Cultural Studies, University of Wales, Cardiff. He was formerly a staff and freelance press photographer for national, regional and overseas newspapers and magazines for over thirty years. He has also been a freelance film cameraman, serving the BBC and ITV networks.

Introduction: Why Not More Press History?

The chapters of this book are by authors from a scatter of academic departments and disciplines. They originated in papers for a conference organised by the Institute of Contemporary British History and the University of Kent in 1996. 1996 should have been a noisy time in press history. It was the centenary of Alfred Harmsworth's foundation of the *Daily Mail*. This, more than any other single act, marked the beginning of the popular national daily press as we now know it. Ownership of the paper remains with the Harmsworths, neatly symbolising the continuity. Rival media, notably broadcasting, have influenced and been influenced by the press, but clearly they have not killed it. Daily, for persons and for institutions, the press helps recreate our society – our values and interests, our very knowledge of the world beyond our doors. Its influence is none the less for being generally immeasurable and all the more, during the period covered by this volume, for having no major competitor until the spread of television in the 1950s. Yet the 1996 landmark passed with little scholarly noise at all.

Why does modern press history fail to flourish in Britain? Why are there no press history institutes, no prestige annual lectures, no Pulitzer prizes? One possible answer is intellectual; others, more practical and decisive, are to do with the structure of academic work and the nature of news organisations.

The intellectual reason, in brief, is that questions about media typically turn out to be questions about something else. Newspapers are means not ends. What is at issue is their role in everything from the growth of violence, for example, to the outcome of elections, the

1

beginning of wars or changes in *haute couture*. Turned around, this means that a study of the press may form part of studies of the psychology of violence, the political science of voting behaviour, the dynamics of armed conflict, or the fashion industry. The very breadth of press content and readership (the ideal of 'all the news that's fit to print') makes the subjects with which press history may deal seemingly inexhaustible. Once one goes beyond the history of newspapers – their foundation, ownership, readership, organisation – the practice of press history has to be extremely selective, concentrating most obviously on such topics as the role of the press (and journalists) in politics. The skills of the political scientist will be needed, in this particular case, in addition to those of the historian. Scholars of press history are thus to be found in many departments apart from history: politics, international relations, sociology, languages, literature, economics, law, psychology; and in multidisciplinary places such as schools of journalism, communication studies or area studies.

But in most such departments press history arguably is marginalised. The academic world in Britain – and this is the point about structure – is simply not big or rich enough for it to be otherwise. There is no tradition of undergraduate journalism teaching, with staff researching as part of the job. Quite the opposite: the very idea used to seem flaky. Those universities (mostly polytechnics at the time), which tried to establish degrees some twenty years ago, found it hard to get the validating authority, the Council for National Academic Awards, to approve them. The problem, often, was precisely the lack of a core discipline of 'communications'.

Without teaching departments, there has been little impetus for graduate work and thus little scope for building a critical mass. Lacking an institutional base, a subject cannot easily attract research grant. Nor in Britain has there been a culture of private sector funding, to match even proportionately, say, the United States. There, of course, both the culture of higher education and the wider civic culture recognise the importance of studying the structures and methods of mass communication. Fittingly, in that sense, the most detailed study of British partly politics and the press has been written by an American, Stephen Koss.[1]

Much of all this has been changing in an academic world with four times as many (and much bigger) universities as thirty years ago. The former polytechnics, rightly seeing a gap in the prospectuses of the 'old' universities, have developed thriving media/communications schools. Nobody much wants to fund graduate students; but research funding has increased. History, however, has not been a priority. The new legitimacy of media research, from the fundor's point of view, rests principally on its relevance to policy, in an age when media are melting into one another and governments cannot escape having media policies. The focus is on the contemporary and on the skills of the social scientist. History has to be smuggled in as part of the context.

The third cause of the neglect of press history, and the most frustrating, has been the news industry itself. Why should an industry that makes a living sticking its feet into other people's doors be so incurious about its own attics? Explanations come easily to mind. Papers are obsessed with the present. Until very recently, their unions stuck rigidly to a typically British belief in learning on the job. The idea of news, and the twenty-four hour cycle, discourage excessive abstraction: events are preferably explained in terms of personalities, and facts 'speak for themselves'. The barons have not often run their papers for profit (which is not to say they have run them on purpose to make a loss), so some of them have certainly been philanthropic, including towards universities (the various Harmsworth chairs, for example). None, unfortunately, has chosen to patronise press history, though there are examples of support for particular scholars and projects (such as a recent Reuters Lectureship in Media History at the University of Kent).

The history that does come out of news organisations is often written by journalists themselves – even the institutional histories, such as that of *The Times* and David Ayerst's history of *The Guardian*. This has advantages. More or less by definition, their books are a good read, and often they are well researched. No undergraduate is going to be bored, either, by Matthew Engel's broader survey, *Tickle the Public*. Nor were they, in its day, by Francis Williams's *Dangerous Estate*. But much of this is not historians' history; still less are the autobiographies, which tend to be anecdotal and nostalgic, or many of the biographies.

The extent to which the weight of twentieth-century press history does not rest with the academic historian is emphasised by a contrast with broadcast history. Broadcast organisations have always had a sense of history, because they have always existed within the sphere of public policy. Broadcasting is engaged in a continuous internal dialogue about its forms and purposes. This is intrinsic, at the BBC, to its corporate identity and organisation; and, at the ITV channels, to their status as franchisees accountable to the Independent Television Commission.

For several decades this internal dialogue was private. (There were not even any public hearings before the reallocation of the ITV franchises in 1967.) The BBC was unhappy about, so to speak, random academics. But both BBC and ITV commissioned well-researched, multi-volume, official histories; and their archives are accessible. At the same time, and for the same reasons, there has been a varying dialogue between broadcasters and the public. This has been punctuated, during much of broadcasting's life, by periodic official inquiries every ten years or so, when large amounts of information entered the public record as part of the process of deciding where broadcasting should go next. Similarly, the public policy factor provided an impetus for the establishment of broadcasting research units in universities: for example, at Leicester, first, where the incentive was anxiety about audience effects; at Leeds, where the focus was TV and voting behaviour; and at Glasgow, where the emphasis was on content analysis and bias. All those centres expanded and began to acquire some historical depth.

It is fun spending other people's money. But why should public or private funds, including those of news organisations themselves, be spent on press history? There is a general answer based on the importance of the press in public and social life. But the broadcasting example provides a more specific answer, directed at the news organisations. Institutions which appear to exercise significant influence over public opinion and behaviour inevitably find themselves under suspicion and therefore scrutiny. There could be no better example than Rupert Murdoch. Politicians court him; for many people, he is a demon.

The case for newspaper organisations helping to fund press history, therefore, is that history can be a form of accountability, and it is in newspapers' own interests to show themselves publicly accountable. The accountability of the market place – the dominant form for British newspapers in the twentieth century – is certainly powerful. If readers shunned the *Sun* in droves when it invaded privacy, the *Sun* would soon stop doing so. But all that prevents politicians legislating against the press about such matters is an uneasy awareness, probably, that in meddling with newspapers, they meddle with an instrument of their own accountability. So if the press wishes to strengthen its defences against intervention, it could well find that one or two institutes of press history came cheap at the price.

Given that background, it is natural that the essays in this book cover a variety of topics. To entitle them *Northcliffe's Legacy* is to risk implying, wrongly, a synoptic view. But Northcliffe was a begetter, though not the onlie begetter; and the Napoleonic image in which he was sometimes portrayed invites discussion about what exactly his lasting impact is, seen from our vantage point one hundred years later. The first essay confronts this issue directly; while in the second Jean Chalaby analyses his skills and style specifically as a journalist, not a proprietor. Northcliffe, Seymour-Ure concludes in the first essay, encouraged people's expectations that newspapers will be entertaining and cheap, and that they will not be laying down a line dictated by partly bosses. But in return for the political freedom brought by advertising revenue, he loosened the ties of popular accountability, beyond a general responsiveness to market forces.

Central to the popular press was accessibility – the opportunity for readers to extend their reach, if not always their grasp. Thus Dilwyn Porter traces the development of financial news. The very first number of the *Daily Mail* had a column of 'Chat on 'Change'. Readers may not actually have had money to invest – but many of them aspired to, and succeeded, like the 'Sid' to whom TV advertisements offered privatised gas shares under Mrs Thatcher. Porter goes further, to explore how well in fact the investing public were served by the popular press. It is a most apt question. For sometimes the popular press is David, protecting its readers against the goliaths of the world; and sometimes the press itself is the problem, so that the reader needs a different kind of protector.

Chandrika Kaul takes the argument to the Empire. The *Mail*'s coverage of India, and Northcliffe's direct involvement, brought issues about self-government and independence into the realm of populist argument, beyond Westminster and Whitehall. Not only did this reflect the interests of the many readers with friends and relatives in the sub-continent: it introduced a new and complicating factor into the politics of the situation. Genuine discussions and policy initiatives became necessary, going further than the Montagu reforms of 1919, if a diehard coalition including Northcliffe was to be prevented from setting a fresh reactionary agenda.

The accessibility of which Peter Twaites writes is different again: the power pictures and the weasel claim that the camera never lies. Picture journalism preceded Northcliffe, and British photojournalism reached its apogee nearly twenty years after his death, in the period – so short in retrospect – of *Picture Post's* celebrity in the 1940s and 1950s. But the term 'graphic' is perfect for the visual content of popular journalism, for it encapsulates the shifting balance between pictures in the service of words and words in the service of pictures. In Northcliffe's own time, the story and the words were graphic. In the tabloids, later, the picture might take over. But the underlying values and objectives remained similar.

Reduced to essentials, the development of the popular press concerned the relationship between newspaper economics – what Northcliffe's henchman Kennedy Jones called journalism as a branch of commerce – and the non-financial purposes for which newspaper proprietors usually ran their papers. Adrian Smith's account of the *Daily Herald* between 1930 and 1964 is an excellent illustration of the potential tensions. By 1930 these were entrenched in the *Herald's* ownership structure. J.S. Elias, the printer, owned 51 per cent of the shares and was not interested in party journalism. The TUC, with 49 per cent, kept the paper on a firm Labour leash. The outcome was increasingly an official Labour 'pudding', compared with unofficial Labour 'sauce' in the tabloid *Daily Mirror*, as Cecil King put it. At length the cost proved too great. In a final irony the paper was sold to Rupert Murdoch, who turned it into the Thatcherite *Sun* (keeping the name adopted for a relaunch in 1964).

The same kind of tensions are explored in the essays by Donald Read and Siân Nicholas. As Nicholas's account of the press and broadcast news shows, the great worry about the new medium of broadcasting was economic: would independently collected radio news damage newspaper sales? But radio, as with many another medium, turned out to be complementary, not competitive. Read's story about Reuters has a more spectacular ending. For Reuters, the tension was not between profit and party politics but profit and 'service' – in this case the most 'complete' low-cost, British-based service of foreign news, provided by what was to be maintained as the leading agency in the world. Some of Reuters' overseas competitors had official subsidies, for governments had an interest in foreign news. Reuters was eventually owned by the press, and the general news service was frequently subsidised by the growing commercial and financial service. The owners never saw much profit. But then the explosive growth of the business in worldwide computerised financial information and trading transformed the agency's finances, and the tension between profit and service relaxed.

These various themes of newspaper economics, press partisanship, accessible content, proprietorial power and public accountability are brought together in the last essay by James Thomas. This is about Robert Maxwell's idiosyncratic and destructive proprietorship of the *Daily Mirror* between 1984 and 1991. Maxwell played up flamboyantly to the image of the autocratic and mercurial press baron, dealing on equal terms with party leaders in the currency of citizens as tabloid readers rather than as voters. Superficially he seemed an end-of-century heir to Northcliffe. But in substance (other than in physique, of which he had no shortage) he was no such thing, and his ownership collapsed in scandal. His death in the waters of the Azores, after an unexplained fall from his yacht, prevented him suffering the humiliation of exposure and the cruel confirmation that if anyone was Northcliffe's heir it was not he but Rupert Murdoch. Few twentieth-century newspaper dynasties have survived more than a generation. The Murdochs, like the Harmsworths, may prove an exception. But not the least fascinating aspect of press history is to watch a press baron build up his empire, enjoy it as an instrument of social or political leverage, and yield it in turn. Would that the barons' enjoyment extended more often to an active interest in the history of their industry.

Note

1 Stephen Koss, *The Rise and Fall of the Political Press in Britain*, 2 vols (London: Hamish Hamilton, 1981, 1984). See also his biography of the editor of the *Daily News*, A.G. Gardiner: *Fleet Street Radical* (London: Allen Lane, 1973).

1
Northcliffe's Legacy

Colin Seymour-Ure

Alfred Harmsworth, Lord Northcliffe, controlled at his peak a larger share of national newspaper circulation than Rupert Murdoch in the 1990s – and this at a time, before the First World War, when print had no competitors as a mass medium. No wonder politicians courted him. A.J. Balfour put him in the House of Lords (aged 40, in 1905), and Lloyd George tried to bottle him up during the First World War with minor government jobs. When he died in 1922, aged only 57, he lay in state like royalty in Westminster Abbey. To Lord Beaverbrook, a competitor, he was 'the greatest figure who ever strode down Fleet Street'. In many ways he was the model of the press baron: perceptive about popular likes and dislikes; audacious in business dealings; autocratic and mercurial in temperature and management style. He inspired grovelling affection in staff, or dislike. He liked being referred to as 'Chief', and he so signed himself with a big flourish.[1] Facing up to prime ministers, he claimed a popular authority based on his immense constituency of newspaper readers – which was independent of parliament and party and gave him, in his own mind, political power. 'The whole nation will think with us when we say the word', he asserted. At a lunch for seven thousand staff, to mark twenty-five years of the *Daily Mail*, he allowed a priest to give thanks for him 'guiding aright the destinies of this great Empire'. To his mother he was a dutiful son, heeding her matronly comments on his papers. Dying mad, he showed that touch of lunacy which signals genius even while marring it.

So in his own lifetime Northcliffe was very big indeed. But he died before the century was one quarter gone. We are bound to ask, how big has been his legacy? In a narrow sense, the answer is plain: his *Daily Mail*, whose foundation in 1896 inaugurated the era of a mass circulation national daily press, was the only such paper to remain in the same family ownership for the entire twentieth century.[2] But apart from that, was he, so to speak, all splash and no ripple? Or is his legacy still detectable in our millennial mix of multinational, multimedia conglomerates, seething in a world of electronic glut?

To answer those questions, we need first to review the changes with which Northcliffe was associated and to judge how far he was responsible for them. On the latter point, a conclusion can be baldly stated. The changes in the press were the result of substantial shifts in the economic and social structure of Britain. No one person, even in an industry that welcomes outsize individualists and tends to explain events in terms of personalities, could do more than steer them in particular ways. At most, Northcliffe gave a specific shape to changes which were likely to have happened anyway in some form or other.

The *Daily Mail* readership is an obvious illustration of the point. Northcliffe simply exploited first the potential of a large new class of literate readers for whom no one was yet providing an attractive, affordable, daily paper. Sunday papers had achieved mass circulations earlier. *Lloyd's Weekly News* sold 100000 in 1854, when most dailies sold fewer than ten thousand, and it reached one million in the *Daily Mail's* first year. The *Daily Mail* itself claimed an initial sale of 897215, settling down below that and briefly touching one million during the Boer War. These new readers were lower middle class, upwardly mobile, with increasing leisure and spending power to enlarge and satisfy their curiosity about the world. Northcliffe spotted especially the importance of appealing to women. He founded the *Daily Mirror* in 1903 not, as one might now expect, in order to hold a glass to the often grim conditions of the working class, but as a boudoir paper for – and produced by – women. The mass working-class readership, by contrast, would not be fully penetrated until the 1930s.

Large circulations depended on fast presses, quick-drying ink, special newspaper trains – all using technology that was equally available to Northcliffe's competitors. But Northcliffe's flair gave him the edge. The *Daily Mail* was the first to start printing an edition out of London – in Manchester (1900). In the same way, Northcliffe turned to advantage the economic and financial opportunities of his day. Fundamental to the success of the *Daily Mail* was a steady stream of advertising revenue. This enabled the paper to be billed as 'a penny newspaper for one halfpenny'. The appeal was both to purchasers' pockets and to their vanity. It made the product affordable and good value. At the same time it flattered the office readers that they were getting a paper at half the price their betters were probably paying. Revenue came from small ads, but also from consumer durables (such as bicycles and pianos) and branded goods. These latter fitted well with a nationally circulating paper, and they stimulated the development of advertising agencies.

The importance of advertising revenue can hardly be exaggerated. Northcliffe's contemporaries, such as Arthur Pearson's *Daily Express*, also mined the seam. Almost the entire newspaper business was thus transformed. The *Daily Mirror* was launched, for example, not simply because Northcliffe saw a readership among women, but because he saw a female advertising market. As one commentator argued, Northcliffe found journalism a profession and left it an industry. In the words of another, 'journalism had at last become a trade and journalists were in the employment of a publisher, not of a party nor of a rich man performing a party service by paying their salaries'.[3] Inside papers, control shifted from the editorial staff towards the management. Outside, papers could survive more realistically than before without dependence on a subsidy.

Reliance on advertising revenue put a new stress on circulation. Northcliffe and his brother Harold (Lord Rothermere) founded the Audit Bureau of Circulation, to give advertisers a reliable gauge of value for money. The *Daily Mail* was the first paper, too, in which people could buy shares. This made profitability a priority, for the purpose of paying dividends which, in turn, put a premium on advertising revenue and thence on circulation. None of that would have worked if people had not liked that they read. Northcliffe's most distinctive and creative contribution to the new daily press was arguably, therefore, his nose for the popular. Near the end of his life he contrasted the *Daily Mail* with its predecessors:

> You could search the Victorian papers in vain for any reference to changing fashions, for instance. You could not find in them anything that would help you to understand the personalities of

public men. We cannot get from them a clear and complete picture of the times in which they were published, as one could from the *Daily Mail*. Before that was published, journalism dealt only with a few aspects of life. What we did was to extend its purview to life as a whole.[4]

That is a classic summary. The *Daily Mail* reported the news – wars (an important selling point), the Empire, politics, crime, accidents, sport. But it was also full of chat and gossip, regaling readers with trivia about the great and famous, and thereby creating a spurious sense of knowingness and shared intimacy. A story in the first issue about 'our cycling MPs' gave a nudge that, in the saddle, 'public men' were plain folks like the rest of us. One headline, 'VERY ORDINARY PEOPLE OFTEN MISTAKEN FOR ROYALTY', took this idea to the extreme. Not only *were* royalty ordinary human beings: they were literally indistinguishable from the rest of us. In every *Daily Mail* reader lurked a prince or princess.

Thus did readers get a feeling for 'life as a whole'. As part of it they also got a magaziney confection of cookery and dressmaking tips, features and serial fiction – and advertisements in the same spirit. What they did not get, of course, was 'a clear and complete picture of the times'. The newspaper's world view, then as now, was an artificial construct, following rules of selection and presentation tacitly agreed between papers and readers. But Northcliffe's view was more exciting, entertaining and expansive than anyone else had offered, day in day out.

For all his flair, Northcliffe obviously did not invent popular journalism alone. Just as the economic and technical conditions for success were outside his control so too did he follow paths which others had explored in different kinds of publication. Many ideas about style and content came from the United States. The 'Interview', for instance, was invented around the time of the American Civil War. Northcliffe's business manager, Pomeroy Burton, was brought over from the *New York World*. Northcliffe gave him a big office. 'Big rooms means big ideas!', said Northcliffe.[5] Thomas Kenealy, the *Daily Mirror* editor (1904–15) who put the paper on its feet when the original team of women had failed (he said sacking them was like drowning kittens), trained in America. Other English forerunners included George Newnes, C. Arthur Pearson, W.T. Stead and T.P. O'Connor.

Newnes founded *Tit-Bits* (1881), a trivia magazine which made a fortune and survived at least into the 1960s. On it Northcliffe modelled *Answers* (1888, founded as *Answers To Correspondents*) which earned him the capital for his first ventures into daily journalism – notably the purchase and rapid revival of the derelict Conservative London *Evening News* in 1894. Pearson too, having trained on *Tit-Bits*, founded a profitable magazine – *Pearson's Weekly* – before starting the *Daily Express* (1900), which was the first paper to put news on the front page. Stead edited the London *Pall Mall Gazette*, a 'clubland' evening paper with a small but influential circulation. Stead was an ebullient compaigning journalist, chiefly celebrated for a sensational five-part series in 1895 on 'the Maiden Tribute of Modern Babylon'. Procuring a child prostitute, to expose the traffic in British children sold to continental brothels, Stead found himself convicted for abduction. Wonderful defiant photographs survive, showing him in a prison suit with arrows, such as convicts in *Beano* and *Dandy* used to wear.[6] O'Connor likewise edited a London evening paper, the *Star* (founded 1888), and he became a well known parliamentarian.

Northcliffe, lastly, benefited greatly from the business acumen of his brother Harold. They were a formidable duo, with yet more brothers in tow. Harold became Viscount Rothermere, and it is his own descendants, Northcliffe having died without legitimate heirs, who inherited the *Daily Mail* and its sister publications.

The legacy for the press

The part of Northcliffe's legacy which stares us daily in the face, then, is the specific character of the end-of-century newspaper's contents. Northcliffe's epitaph is Christopher Wren's: '*Si monumentum requiris, circumspice*' [If you want a monument, look about you]. A 'Page Three' breast does service for the dome of St Paul's. In a perceptive contemporary essay comparing Northcliffe and C.P. Scott, A.G. Gardiner, veteran editor of the *Daily News* argued that Northcliffe's outstanding achievement was his initial conception of the commercial possibilities of journalism – and then its triumphant translation into reality. He saw that 'what the democracy wanted was not instruction but amusement and thrills'.[7] (Scott, upright editor – even when riding his bicycle every day to work – of the [then]

Manchester Guardian, took the opposite view.) There is indeed a direct line from Northcliffe to the Murdoch *Sun*; and 'commercial possibilities' explain it. As Gardiner further pointed out, Northcliffe applied the lessons of magazine journalism, where he got his start, to daily papers. At every step in the development of newspaper content across the twentieth century, editors have responded to popular taste, in order to optimise sales and advertising revenue. In the process, naturally, they have also helped to shape taste. Thus it may not have occurred to readers that nudes could be printed to Page Three, but when they were, *Sun* readers certainly enjoyed them. Nudes are not news, in the historic sense of 'latest intelligence', yet they symbolise the extent to which the newspaper today (especially the tabloid) is a daily magazine, much of which is not particularly time-sensitive. This, in a simple sense, is due to Northcliffe and his imitators. Popular journalism, in Chalaby's telling phrase, is a discourse of seduction.[8]

This, then, is a legacy of barn door proportions, explicable in terms of newspaper and advertising industry economics. But what have been some of the other consequences, beyond this sensitivity to readers' likes and dislikes? Two at least are comparably large. One is the wedge which progressively drove apart the small and the mass circulation papers. Once commonly described as 'quality' and 'popular', this difference is now more familiar as 'broadsheet' and 'tabloid'. Northcliffe, his competitors and his successors, pumped up circulation in order to maximise advertising revenue and fund the increasing fixed costs of competition. 'Quality' papers could survive on much lower circulations: they could charge higher advertising rates, since their readers had more purchasing power. The extreme illustration, perhaps, is that the *Financial Times* could be profitable in 1960 on a circulation of 120 000, while the *News Chronicle* lost heavily with a circulation ten times greater. These simplicities were complicated in the last quarter of the century by the economics of concentration of ownership. The broadsheet/tabloid division was based on contrasting contents, style, readership patterns and circulation size. The last of these, at the century's end, was becoming much less sharp, since the *Daily Telegraph* and *The Times*, for example, approached or overtook the circulations respectively of the *Express* and the *Daily Star*.

The second large consequence was the development of a truly national press at the expense of the provincial press. The number of London-based national daily papers has remained remarkably constant across the century, at about ten or eleven, although the individual titles themselves have changed. But whereas, before the *Daily Mail*, the difference between a London paper's circulation and that of the papers in large provincial cities was not always huge, Northcliffe made it so. Across the nation, morning daily papers collapsed, from 43 to 25 between the Wars, and to fewer than 20 thereafter. By the end of the Second World War, the principal provincial market was for evening papers. A metropolitan/provincial pattern of morning papers was replaced by a 'national morning'/'provincial evening' pattern. Together with this went the combination of the evening and surviving morning papers into London-dominated 'chains' – following quite closely a classical economic model of market capitalism. With the diversification of media, the term 'chains' in turn fell out of use, as people became concerned with concentration of ownership more broadly.

The same developments, lastly, were associated with vastly increased difficulty in entering the newspaper market, especially on a national scale. No new national daily was started in the sixty years between the end of the First World War and the foundation in 1978 of the *Daily Star*, to exploit excess printing capacity. Even such an established title as the *Manchester Guardian* found the translation from a provincial to a London base, and to the national league, a risky business in the early 1960s. Entry became briefly affordable in the 1980s, when production costs were slashed by Rupert Murdoch's defeat of the production unions (with Eddie Shah's *Today* as pioneer). The *Independent*, launched in 1986, was initially a success. But the costs of competition in the recession of the early 1990s killed *Today* and emasculated the *Independent*.

Such were the logical consequences of a press made dependent on sales and advertising revenue. In the absence of significant government interference with the market, except during the Second World War and by partial limits on postwar press/broadcast concentration, today's press barons are Northcliffe's natural heirs. Their energies, egos, temperaments and management styles seem recognisably his. Like landowners sizing up the neighbouring estate, the barons circle endlessly round each others' properties, looking to improve their market position by takeover or investment. Broadcasting and electronics, of course, have made them multi-media barons of a type Northcliffe could never be. He died just as broadcasting was about to take off – and four years before the foundation of the BBC as a public corporation in 1926. He was excited by broadcasting, not least as a competitor. Had he lived longer, he would certainly have tried somehow to accommodate it.

The international dimension of media ownership in the last decades of the century similarly has an economic logic missing in Northcliffe's time. Apart from oddities like the continental *Daily Mail* (1905; printed in Paris and strong on the Riviera), Northcliffe's was a British empire. His fellow press barons might start life foreign, like Beaverbrook (Canadian) or the Astors (American), but once here, they stayed. A later Canadian, Roy Thomson, came – intitially to invest in ITV and then in the *Sunday Times* (1959) and *The Times* (1966) – but he never completely settled. Now the overseas entrepreneur, such as Murdoch or Conrad Black, is even less deeply immersed in the society which his media properties do so much to shape.

The legacy for the political system

The other consequence of Northcliffe's impact on publishing economics was the new scope for newspaper independence. It is an obvious truism that this was not economic independence: newspapers had to fight for their share of the overall level of advertising revenue in the economy, in order to survive. But it was a liberation from external subsidy and control. What, then, has been Northcliffe's legacy in this direction?

The position of many newspapers in the late nineteenth century is typified in Stephen Koss's remark about the Liberal *Daily News*: since 1873, 'proprietors had come and gone, prepared to sustain losses for the sake of the party and never pleasantly surprised to the contrary'.[9] Contrast the comment by Lloyd George on Northcliffe: 'He owed no allegiance to any party, so that every genuine party man deplored his paper. Most of them bought it and read what was in it and then damned it'.[10] Formal ownership of papers by parties was rare. Possibly the *Daily Herald* came closest, when controlled by the TUC and the Labour party between 1922 and 1929. But in the latter year losses forced the sale of a 51 per cent interest to the paper's printer, Odhams. The TUC kept the other 49 per cent – with control over policy. Even after 1945, the Editor of the *Daily Herald* had to account for his conduct of the paper to a closed session of the annual party conference. Usually, however, party control meant ownership by a wealthy individual or group of sympathisers. Lady Bathurst, for instance, inherited the diehard Conservative *Morning Post* from her father, Lord Glenesk, in 1908. Tired of losses, she sold it to a syndicate of Conservative sympathisers in 1924. Eventually it amalgamated in 1937 with Lord Camrose's *Daily Telegraph*.

Northcliffe's initiative in detaching the financial control of the daily press from the party system, while simultaneously extending readership among the mass of voters, reverberated down the century. The consequences varied. Between the two world wars, the press and party system became dislocated. Popular support for an unsettled party system was not reflected proportionately in the number and distribution of partisan papers, nor in the consistency of their loyalty. For thirty years after the Second World War, in a revived two-party system, proportionality and party loyalty also revived. There was always a disproportionately large number of Conservative titles – though not always of aggregate circulation, but from 1974 onwards the Conservative press increasingly dominated. During election campaigns, its loyalty was solid (until the dramatic changes of the 1997 election); between elections, less so. Commitment to the Conservative party in office was always likely to clash with a contradictory and equally historic professional reluctance to get too close to the government.[11]

In principle, then, the detachment of the press involved a range of possible changes, observable in varying degrees across the decades. There was a general depoliticisation of contents, as newspapers covered 'life as a whole'. Within that, there might be a variable or declining loyalty either to official party policy, or to the established leadership. Beaverbrook and Rothermere, for example, famously fell out with Stanley Baldwin when the latter was Leader of the Conservative party in the late 1920s and 1930s. To the extent that papers remained reliably partisan, there could be variations in the party balance of titles and circulation.

Taken together, these possibilities constituted a destabilising force in the organisation of British politics. Except for the *Daily Herald* in its heyday (about twenty years from the mid-1930s), the daily press played a smaller part than it might have done in sustaining mass-based political parties. Equally, major shifts in party support could not be reflected and promoted by the establishment of new papers. Most obviously, neither the Liberal party from its revival in the 1960s, nor the Social Democratic Party during its rapid growth in the early 1980s, had the advantage of its own daily paper. The SDP enjoyed enormous media support. But this was volunteered: it was not the same as support in publications which the party actually controlled, or which were owned by party sympathisers, and it drained away fairly quickly.

The very depoliticisation of the popular press had important implications. Papers still had political opinions: explicitly, in the leader columns, and implicitly in the values determining the choice and presentation of news and features. The latter could well seem the more sinister. The fact that press barons might be winning people's minds without people realising what was happening, simply made the barons' unaccountability worse. An extreme example, at least in specific circumstances, was the annoyance aroused in Labour supporters by the pro-Conservative *Sun* during the Thatcher era (more especially near its end). Here was a tabloid, preaching Thatcherite values of uncaring materialist individualism; trivialising and deriding politics and Labour politicians; yet reaching into the heart of Labour's historic natural constituency of the working class – and claiming after Labour's narrow 1992 election defeat that 'IT'S THE SUN WOT WON IT'.[12]

The overt politics of the mass circulation press necessarily tends towards populism. A paper cannot afford to move too far away from the attitudes of its readers without risk to its circulation. Even if the risk is only imagined, the fierceness of competition means it must be taken seriously. The reactions of Northcliffe's contemporary, J.A. Spender, are interesting to observe. Spender edited the Liberal *Westminster Gazette*, one of the old political papers, which did not adapt to the Northcliffe era and duly disappeared. Papers such as the *Daily Mail*, Spender argued, concentrated 'in the hands of a few individuals who are responsible to nobody but themselves a power which is a serious rival to Parliament, and upon which in the last resort Parliament depends'. Even the editor of the annual *Labour Year Book* in 1925 would have agreed. At least in the old days, the

Year Book grumbled, 'the falsehoods and misrepresentations of one party were promptly exposed and refuted in the national organs of the other' but now, the right-wing press was under 'purely capitalistic control'.[13]

So by what star did Northcliffe steer? Spender cheerfully admitted that Northcliffe was 'the only completely convinced democrat that I ever knew. He did really believe that things ought to be decided by the mass opinion about them, and to find out what that was or what it was going to be, and to express it powerfully, seemed to him not only profitable but right and wise'. To Spender himself, of course, this was the grossest folly: 'Long meditation on the probable opinions of large numbers of inarticulate people' – there is an almost nasal quality to the prose – 'produces this singular detachment from what is called the merits of an argument'.[14]

Such populism is discernible in the late 1990s in many of the editorial attitudes of the *Sun* (not least about Europe) and of the other tabloids. But it has always co-existed with the opportunity to exercise active, rather than reactive, editorial leadership. Northcliffe's enduring legacy in this particular form is the media baron who may promote his own agenda – and without even having to live with the consequences, if, like several barons, he chooses to be domiciled abroad. Governments fear to curb such individualists, partly at least because they know (and rightly) that if they did so, they would interefere with an instrument of their own public accountability.

Their detachment from political parties did nothing to discourage the press barons from seeking office. If anything, the independent power with which they were credited gave them more leverage. Lloyd George offered Northcliffe the non-cabinet post of Secretary of State for Air in 1917. Northcliffe did not want his hands so firmly tied, and Lloyd George gave the job to his brother Rothermere instead. Northcliffe went off to be Director of Propaganda in Enemy Countries. Earlier, he led an official war mission to the United States. Waldorf Astor (the *Observer*) held two Parliamentary Secretaryships between 1918 and 1921. Lord Beaverbrook was a cabinet minister in 1918 (strictly, of cabinet rank but not in the war cabinet) – and again, much more centrally, in the Second World War (1940–42, in the war cabinet, and 1943–45 outside it). He seems to have believed he might even have become Prime Minister if Churchill failed. Brendan (Lord) Bracken (*Financial News*, later *Financial Times*) was in

Churchill's caretaker government in 1945 and had been Minister of Information, outside the cabinet, from 1941. Sir John (later Lord) Reith, the Director-General of the BBC (1926–37) may be included in the list. He was in Chamberlain's last cabinet in 1940 and had two non-cabinet ministerial posts under Churchill until early 1942.

Since 1945, by contrast, no press baron has been either an MP or a minister. Cecil King (*Mirror* group) was said to be keen for office in the 1960s and to have been snubbed by Harold Wilson. Robert Maxwell's brief period as MP for Buckingham (1964–70) was before he became a media baron. Lord Hollick (Meridian TV and the *Express* group) was a donor to the Labour party and a Kinnock nomination to the House of Lords. In the Blair administration he had a part-time role as 'adviser' at the Department of Trade and Industry, but it appeared shadowy and insubstantial. The media barons in the Lords, certainly in the postwar era, have not even used the chamber as a forum for their views. Much was made of Lord Rothermere's announcement that he would sit on the Labour benches after the 1997 general election, but he gave no indication how often he would actually go there, and he died in August 1998. Some of the former journalist peers (i.e. not proprietors) have been, by comparison, quite voluble.

With the proliferation of media, concentration of ownership, and the opportunity, especially, to combine press and broadcasting properties, it is understandable that the barons no longer tie themselves to formal office in ministry or legislature. Even when they did, much of their influence continued to come from informal politicking. Moreover, a Conrad Black or Rupert Murdoch is too much a citizen of the world to work the pump in one parish only.

The end-of-century heir to Northcliffe fits into politics rather differently. Three ways can be singled out. The first, which remains close to the political system of Northcliffe's own time, is the possible deliberate use of his papers as a kind of embryo political party in themselves. This was exactly what Beaverbrook and Rothermere did in the early 1930s. They used their papers as an alternative to geographical constituencies, in order to conduct a campaign against the Conservative party leadership on the issue of Empire free trade. Beaverbrook ran the Empire Crusade, Rothermere the United Empire party. Until the economic crisis of 1931 intervened, they put up candidates in by-elections – although without much success. This was no arcane argument between party leadership factions: in an age of mass circulations, such a campaign had the potential to topple the Leader.

Between 1992 and 1997, most of the Conservative press was similarly hostile to the official party line on Europe. They did not go quite so far as those predecessors. But in the 1997 general election *The Times* urged its readers to vote for Eurosceptic candidates, regardless of party, and highlighted them sharply in its columns. There was the germ of political organisation in such behaviour; certainly something more than comment and evaluation. Sir James Goldsmith, Leader of the Referendum party, founded specifically to fight the election, owned no newspaper, but he delivered an amazing five million party videos through the nation's letter boxes.[15] This was the electronic equivalent at least of a campaign newsletter. In an earlier age, he would surely have founded a party paper.

Much the best contemporary example of the media organisation as substitute for a political party was the successful campaign of Silvio Berlusconi's Forza Italia movement in the Italian general election of March 1994. Berlusconi owned Italy's largest advertising agency, a huge supermarket chain, insurance and property interests, the AC Milan football team, and a major slice of broadcast and print media. All this gave him a grasp of 'life as a whole' that Northcliffe would have envied. In just three months he sold the Italian people a political party which won more votes than any other and propelled him, as head of the Freedom Alliance coalition, into the premiership. Then he showed how governing is not the same as campaigning, for by the end of the year his administration collapsed. Britain has had no Berlusconi yet. Maxwell showed a few of the signs: he was involved in football club ownership long before other media entrepreneurs, for instance. But the significant point, surely, is that the institutional and legal barriers preventing a media baron erupting into British electoral politics are weak. Chief among them are the statutory restraints against partisanship in the broadcast media. In practice these are weakening yearly, as the number and diversity of channels grow.

In the late Victorian heyday of the party press, there co-existed with it the idea of newspapers as a disinterested forum of political argument – part of a wider public sphere. This idea survives generally in the broadsheet papers. But with the depoliticisation of the popular press, it has progressively shifted to broadcasting. From almost total non-involvement in politics in the first half of the century, broadcasting moved through several stages – first as unobtrusive observer (the microphone as vase of flowers) – to its present position of dominance. Now, in everything from soundbites to hair styles, politics and politicians adapt to television, where formerly television adapted to them. The Prime Minister's press secretary can even peremptorily instruct the Foreign Secretary to choose between his mistress and his wife.[16] There is nowhere the broadcast media cannot pry, indirectly if not directly. Everywhere, potentially, is a place of – and therefore for – political communication. Beginning with Bernard Ingham in 1979, the hitherto unexceptionable job of Downing Street press secretary has thus turned twenty years later into one of the three or four key jobs in the Prime Minister's entourage.

In Northcliffe's time, then, a press baron controlled the major media forum of political reporting – the link between electorate and elite. In addition, he could participate as a partisan. Seventy-five years later, Northcliffe's successors still control the major forum – because now they own electronic media (the BBC apart) as well as the press. The difference is that, precariously, they are restrained from using their broadcast properties explicitly and deliberately in pursuit of political goals.

The third and last point about Northcliffe's end of century heirs adds a rider to the other two. For most of the twentieth century the engine of organised behaviour in parliamentary politics has been the political party. In, say, the last quarter century it has lost ground. Mass membership has gone: humiliatingly, groups like the Royal Society for the Protection of Birds outnumber either party. The two major parties' share of the vote at general elections slumped from 96.8 per cent in 1951 to 75.8 per cent in 1997. Popular support is volatile. The permanent party machines are smaller and chronically in debt. Fundraising is rarely easy and is an ethical mess. Parties' capacity to generate solidly researched programmes has declined. (Contrast the preparations of the Heath government before entering office in 1970 and Blair in 1997). The main functions of party are the generational renewal of a pool of parliamentarians and ministers-in-waiting, and the organisation of election campaigns.

As parties have lost ground, interest groups have gained. Most of the things parties used to do, interest groups do as well or better.

Active members; assured resources; policy expertise; Whitehall knowhow; media skills, public relations and education: these are all features of a wide range of groups within social, educational, commercial, cultural, environmental, consumer and industrial fields. From the start of its cautious coverage of 'current affairs', the organisation of broadcasting stressed the balanced expression of a variety of voices. This has suited the politics of plurality. In the same way, the broadsheet newspapers have increasingly spoken with a diversity of voices, within each paper, as columnists and sectionalisation have proliferated.

The modern press baron thus controls publications and broadcast channels which to a great extent comprise the political arena. In some, he can freely fight a partisan battle. He can use his papers as an interest group – not least, to protect his own commercial interest, as it routinely alleged against Rupert Murdoch. In broadcast media, he shapes (within statutory limits) the format and agenda of political discourse. The result is an awesome potential influence over the popular mind, none the less for being difficult to define and measure, and all the more for being open to unpredictable and eccentric use.

The political importance of the press at the end of the century is entwined with that of electronic media. That part which may most plausibly be considered Northcliffe's legacy is limited to the two big changes he pushed along: the citizen's expectation that mass media firstly will be entertaining and cheap, and secondly will not be laying down a line dictated by party bosses. Northcliffe's sin, in the eyes of progressives (let alone socialists) was that he aimed low. Accounts by contemporaries, such as an editor of *The Times*, Wickham Steed, and near contemporaries, such as an editor of the *Daily Herald*, Francis Williams, are fraught with the imagery of debasement and corruption.[17] Such critics want to believe it could have been otherwise: mass circulation – but 'quality' content. Incontrovertibly, Northcliffe bolstered capitalism by encouraging acquisitive, materialist and individualist values. But could he on any other basis have succeeded in reaching unprecedented numbers of readers for his magazines and papers, or would they simply have ignored him? The same question runs through arguments about the introduction and consequences of 'commercial television' (as ITV was routinely called when first introduced in 1955), and even, at the century's end, about the coming digital revolution. Northcliffe's two changes gave the press baron financial independence, political leverage – and precious little popular accountability beyond a general responsiveness to the market. At the millennium, that is how things remain.

Notes

1 For an example of the signature, see the frontispiece of Tom Clarke, *My Northcliffe Diary*, (London: Gollancz, 1931).

2 The *Guardian* has remained in the same ownership, but it cannot be counted as a fully 'national newspaper' until well after 1945.

3 I thought I could trace the first comment but have failed. The second is from *The History of The Times*, Vol. 3 1884–1912, (London: Times Publishing Co, 1947), p. 106.

4 Quoted in Harold Herd, *The March of Journalism*, (London: George Allen and Unwin, 1952), p. 241. The source, unspecified, is almost certainly Northcliffe's pamphlet *Newspapers and their Millionaires*, published in 1922, of which I have not seen a copy.

5 Quoted in Tom Clarke, p. 34.

6 Apart from its tragic Dickensian theme, the whole episode makes a hilarious read, involving bishops, brothel-keepers, the Salvation Army and Victorian do-gooders such as Josephine Butler. Stead served two months and seven days in a comfortable cell, from which he continued to edit the paper. His meals were brought in, and he had a stream of visitors. His wife said she saw more of him than in the entire previous six months. The tale is succinctly told in J.W. Robertson Scott, *'We' and Me*, (London: W.H. Allen, 1956), pp. 231–5. The prison photograph is reproduced in J.W. Robertson Scott, *The Life and Death of a Newspaper*, (London: Methuen, 1952), at p. 82.

7 A.G. Gardiner, 'C.P. Scott and Lord Northcliffe', *19th Century and After*, Vol. CXI, 1932, p. 250.

8 Jean K. Chalaby, *The Invention of Journalism*, (London: Macmillan, 1998), p. 184.

9 Stephen E. Koss, *Fleet Street Radical: A.G. Gardiner and the Daily News*, (London: Allen Lane, 1973), p. 38.

10 David Lloyd George, *The Truth about the Peace Treaties*, 2 vols. (London: Gollancz, 1938), vol. 1 p. 266.

11 On the press and the party system between the wars, see Colin Seymour-Ure, chapter 10 in Gillian Peele and Chris Cook (eds), *The Politics of Reappraisal 1918–1939*, (London: Macmillan, 1975). On the post-1945 period, see Colin Seymour-Ure, *The British Press and Broadcasting since 1945*, (Oxford: Blackwell, 2nd edn, 1996), ch. 8.

12 *Sun* headline, 11 April 1992. The claim was hastily withdrawn.

13 J.A. Spender, *The Public Life*, 2 vols, (London: Cassell, 1925), vol. 1, p. 114. *The Labour Year Book 1925*, (London: Labour Publications Dept), p. 352.

14 The first Spender quotation is from J.A. Spender, *Life, Journalism and Politics*, (London: Cassell, 2 vols, 1927), vol. 2, p. 170. The second is from J.A. Spender, *The Public Life*, vol. 1, p. 108.

15 This figure is quoted in David Butler and Dennis Kavanagh, *The British General Election of 1997*, (London: Macmillan, 1997), p. 219. The pollster MORI found 22 per cent of households claiming to have received the video.

16 This is the claim made about the circumstances in which Foreign Secretary Robin Cook told his wife he was leaving her, shortly after the election of the Blair government in 1997. Margaret Cook, *A Slight and Delicate Creature: the Memoirs of Margaret Cook*, (London: Weidenfeld, 1998).

17 H. Wickham Steed, *The Press*, (Harmondsworth: Penguin Books, 1938); Francis Williams, *Dangerous Estate*, (London: Longman, 1957).

2
Northcliffe: Proprietor as Journalist

*Jean Chalaby**

This chapter is part of a broader argument about press barons which states that these particular press proprietors were successful because of their ability to combine managerial and editorial skills. These press proprietors stood out in the field of the press as investors, profit-makers and empire builders. They were also conspicuous for their exceptional degree of commitment to the newspapers they owned and because they distinguished themselves as editors of great experience and skill.[1]

The chapter develops the latter argument about the editorial side of press barons' talent for newspaper ownership by giving an account of Northcliffe's capabilities in journalism. It argues that Northcliffe was a newspaper proprietor of great journalistic skills – which is slightly different from saying that he was a great journalist. His place in history is due to his understanding of journalism as a press proprietor. It is his use and adaptation of journalism to the requirements of a modern newspaper that are so striking. This claim posits that Northcliffe may be the founder of the modern newspaper, but certainly not the 'founder of modern journalism', as David English put it, and before him a long list of hagiographers.[2] Northcliffe applied, improved and developed journalistic techniques rather than devised new ones.

* Research for this article was supported by the Swiss National Science Foundation. The author is grateful to the editors and anonymous reviewers for their constructive comments.

When Northcliffe first forayed into the daily press of the 1890s, British journalism had been developing for several decades. The repeal of the stamp duty in 1855 opened up the possibility of selling newspapers for a penny. This enlarged the market of readers, but set circulations soaring and attracted newcomers to the field of the press.[3] Facing increased pressure under renewed competition, newspapers began to adapt their content to the changing economic circumstances. The new *Daily Telegraph*, for example, downplayed politics well before the *Daily Mail* reduced its parliamentary column to a couple of short paragraphs (see below).[4] Years before the *Daily Mail* indulged its readers in more sensationalism than any previous daily newspaper with claims to at least a modicum of respectability, the *Daily Telegraph* sensationalized the writing of crime reports and scattered them around the paper.[5]

In the 1880s, the London evening gazettes were the breeding ground of 'New Journalism'.[6] In these gazettes, journalists began to experiment with reportorial techniques, notably a lighter writing style, a vivid way of picturing reality, and the occasional sensational overtone, that were picked up later by the editorial team of the *Daily Mail*. As will be discussed later, Northcliffe was an insatiable press campaigner. This route, too, was first opened by New Journalism's most forceful exponent, W.T. Stead. Editor of the *Pall Mall Gazette* between 1883 and 1890, he indulged in many crusades during his editorship and developed a campaigning style that presaged that of the *Daily Mail*.[7]

Most professional values and discursive norms specific to modern journalism developed prior to Northcliffe's arrival in the daily press. By the end of the nineteenth century, the distinction between truth and fiction was established, journalists were duly concerned about the 'accurate reporting of facts', and the claims to objectivity in reporting had gathered pace.[8] Newspapers had also begun to depart from party politics. By the 1880s, most newly established papers claimed to be apolitical, and one third of all papers declared themselves to be free from political ties.[9]

Northcliffe's contribution to the history of the press is not as a journalist but as a press owner who had an extraordinary understanding of the implications of journalism for the daily press. He applied and developed journalistic practices more than he invented them. He brought the daily newspaper into the twentieth century and modernized journalism in the process. Northcliffe had an impact on the history of journalism, first because he stretched journalism to new limits, and also because newspaper ownership had become a crucial element in the development of journalism.

This chapter discusses Northcliffe's concept of journalism and reviews the key journalistic techniques he and his editorial teams employed. It is divided into three sections. Section 1 examines Northcliffe's philosophy of news. Section 2 explores two of the press baron's most oft-used discursive strategies, sensationalism and 'crusading'. Section 3 proposes an explanation of his commercial success and suggests that it could be attributed to his journalistic skill combined with his constant effort to discern and respond to readers' tastes.

Northcliffe's philosophy of news

Early in his career, and more acutely than most of his contemporaries, Northcliffe became aware of the importance of news in journalism and realized that news was one of the main selling points of newspapers. He expressed this view on countless occasions; in 1921, for example, he told his staff that the only way to bring up the *Daily Mail*'s circulation to two million was 'by getting plenty of exclusive news, plenty of good pictures, good serial stories, and by intensive publishing'.[10] Northcliffe's journalism was news-based and information-oriented, which he blended in his newspapers with entertainment material and magazine features. He is on record for saying that 'It is hard news which captures readers [...] and it is features which hold them'.[11] In accordance with that principle, one of his most consistent strategies was to ensure that his papers provided readers with a great quantity and a great variety of news.

With regard to the quantity of news, Northcliffe opted for the strategy of offering more news to readers than his competitors. To that effect he developed the news-gathering forces of the *Daily Mail*, and later of *The Times*, and ensured that his papers offered the best overall news coverage amongst London dailies. For instance, he expanded at great expense the coverage from the United States and the British Empire and, in the process, forced his closest rivals to raise their standards in foreign coverage.[12] Northcliffe also improved the collating of information. Lucy Brown illustrates the press's casual way in handling information as late as 1895 with reports on gales throughout Europe in the winter of this year. She mentions that national newspapers did not collate reports on storms that resulted in over 400 lives lost on ships, and notices that 'it needed the imagination of a Northcliffe or a Stead to see the possibilities of such information'.[13] Finally, Northcliffe invested heavily in war reporting. The *Daily Mail* coverage of the Boer War was extensive and he plunged greater sums than any of his competitors into the reporting of this conflict.[14] One of the early *Daily Mail's* greatest coups was its scoop on the peace talks held at Vereeninging in 1902.[15]

Northcliffe had a singular aversion to being beaten by competitors in the field of news. First thing in the morning, the newspaper proprietor read the press and rang his editors to 'cross-examine [them] about the contents of the rival morning papers'.[16] Clarke, the editor of the *Daily Mail*, could learn over the phone 'whether [he] had won or lost the previous day in the incessant quest for "scoops"'.[17] But to reduce the risk of being scooped Northcliffe always gave his newspapers both the human and technical means to beat competitors in the daily news-hunt.

Regarding the variety of news, Northcliffe pursued a strategy that consisted of providing readers with information on a great range of topics. His *policy of diversity*, as this strategy may be called, was implemented in three different ways. The first was to reduce the amount of political reporting in his newspapers. Particularly conspicuous in this process of depoliticization was the reduction of the parliamentary column, following the trend the *Daily Telegraph* had already clearly established towards shorter accounts of parliamentary proceedings. Under the dynamic ownership of Edward Lawson, the *Daily Telegraph* was a commercially successful newspaper and could lay claim to the largest circulation in the country. To this end, it had published for some time considerably shorter parliamentary reports than those of *The Times*, by approximately two-thirds in 1865.[18]

Northcliffe applied the same technique to the *Daily Mail* but went much further. At its inception, the *Daily Mail* was conceived with the aim of containing less politics than any other general daily newspaper on the market. One of the first advertisements for the *Daily Mail* enticed readers to buy the paper promising that '[f]our leading articles, a page of Parliament, and columns of speeches will *not* be found in the *Daily Mail* on 4 May [1896], a halfpenny'.[19]

Indeed, the *Daily Mail* kept parliamentary debates to a strict minimum, and the reports from Westminster rarely exceeded two short paragraphs. During its first month of existence, the average size of the *Daily Mail's* parliamentary column was seven lines for the Lords, and eight for the Commons. These proportions remained the same until the beginning of the century, when the *Daily Mail* ceased to report the debates on a daily basis. Henceforth, summaries appeared sporadically.

Northcliffe avoided politics in the paper he launched, and depoliticized those he acquired. To the editorial staff of *The Times*, he asked for more topicality, more 'readability', lighter contents, and 'fewer and shorter articles on politics'.[20] A telegram read: 'Humbly beg for a light leading article daily until I return – Chief'.[21] Similarly, when Northcliffe bought the *Observer*, in 1908, he was aiming for a circulation of 40000. Thus he exhorted James Garvin, its editor, to 'interest more people' and to avoid 'heavy politics', since politics, as Northcliffe put it, 'will prevent your getting circulation'.[22] With him, politics lost its privileged position and became a topic competing for space among many others. 'We must not let politics dominate the paper', he said to an editor of the *Daily Mail* ; '[t]reat politics as you treat all other news – on its merits. It has no "divine right" on newspaper space'.[23]

Alongside the reduction of the amount of politics in his papers, Northcliffe expanded the range of newspaper topics. He developed specialized news and improved the coverage of topics such as agriculture, transport, new technologies, sports, fashion, leisure activities and entertainment. Society news and an interest in the rich and famous had been popularized by O'Connor's *Star* in the late 1880s, and the *Daily Mail* took the genre a bit further by publishing the diaries of famous people (e.g. *Daily Mail*, 2 February 1900). The *Daily Mail* was also filled with snippets on an incalculable number of events of little importance, but which Northcliffe and his editors deemed of interest to *Daily Mail* readers. In the 1890s, few dailies would have published stories on the illness of three bishops or the health of the Indian army, as the *Daily Mail* did on 8 February 1898. Northcliffe's aim, as the repeatedly explained to his staff, was that his newspapers should 'touch life at as many points as possible'.[24] As a result, the press magnate's newspapers explored new territories and reported aspects of personal and social life previously unrecorded in the daily press.

The policy of diversity is clearly reflected in two representative pages of the *Daily Mirror* on 13 October 1908, which contained no less than 33 news items. Readers were entertained with the divorce of the Earl of Yarmouth; the opening of a school of orators by an anti-socialist union; the charge of cruelty to a cat brought against a lieutenant-colonel by the Humanitarian League; the story of a woman killed to save her dog from a motor-car; a romance between an Italian duke and an American lady; the death of Ireland's allegedly oldest inhabitant; a taxicab dispute; a balloon race accident; the journey of the King to Newmarket; and a British warship's movements off the coast of Spain. With this policy, Northcliffe was applying to the daily press one of the techniques he had learnt with his magazine publishing business. *Answers*, an imitation of Newnes's *Tit-Bits* launched in 1888, was entirely made of snippets of information on a great variety of topics deemed to be of interest to readers.

Finally, Northcliffe's philosophy of news was embedded in his resolutely modern approach to newspaper publishing. He adopted the reader's point of view to his papers and thought that, above all, papers should captivate the readers. To him, a newspaper should not merely inform but also amuse and entertain. This implied a significant broadening of the traditional understanding of the role of the newspaper. By the time Northcliffe was publishing daily newspapers, the notion of newspapers as organs of opinion had been receding for several decades.[25] However, it was still common understanding that a daily newspaper should primarily be an organ of information centred on public affairs. Northcliffe was among those who contributed to a change of attitude in this matter, and, by the Edwardian decade, most proprietors and editors of popular and mid-market newspapers, such as the *Evening News*, *Star*, *Daily Express* and *Daily Dispatch*, were anxious to strike a balance between entertainment and information.[26]

Northcliffe's definition of news clearly conveyed his concept of the ideal newspaper. He was not the author, as often implied, of the legendary 'when a dog bites a man, that's not news; but when a man bites a dog, that's news'.[27] However, he entirely subscribed to this adage, which he himself attributed to Charles Dana, and he insisted that '[i]n the *Daily Mail* we paid little or no attention to the dogs which bit men – and the dogs didn't like it – I mean the politicians, the bigwigs, the people who laid foundation-stones and presided at banquets and opened Church bazaars'.[28] In line with the

American adage, Northcliffe defined news as 'anything out of the ordinary', adding that this is 'the only thing that will sell a newspaper'.[29] The same concept of news prevailed in his request to the editor of the *Daily Mail* to '[m]ake the paper a happy one, fresh and free from dullness'.[30] He was more specific concerning the main news page, which he called the 'surprise page'.[31] There, editors had to 'get more news and more varieties of news', to create 'contrast' (the 'salt of journalism'), and to 'catch the reader's eye' with short articles and distinctive headings.[32]

The success of the *Daily Mail* forced other proprietors to adapt the content of their newspapers and follow suit, even though they owned newspapers for purposes that were other than purely commercial. This was notably the case of the *Daily News*. In 1919, although the Cadbury family was anxious to propagate their Liberal creed through this newspaper, George Cadbury had to ask the editor, A.G. Gardiner, to drastically reduce the parliamentary report and the religious column. In subsequent letters, Cadbury suggested to Gardiner the introduction of features which proved popular in the *Daily Mail*, such as pictures, arguing that they had allowed Northcliffe's flagship paper to 'capture it [the *Daily News*'s circulation] by having pictures every day on the back'.[33] Neither of the two wanted these changes (Gardiner finally resigned in 1921), but pressure from rival newspapers, most notably the *Daily Mail*, had deemed them long overdue.

Sensational news and press campaigns

Northcliffe resorted to at least two methods to add elements of surprise and excitement to his newspapers: sensational news and the newspaper crusade. His biographers often report that he despised vulgarity and the use of sex-related news items in his newspapers.[34] Indeed, Northcliffe, unlike William Randolph Hearst, was not a natural sensationalist. However, evidence suggests that many of Northcliffe's daily newspapers, notably the *Evening News*, the *Daily Mirror* and the *Daily Mail* published a fair amount of sensational material in their columns.

This essay argues that sensational material, as a news category, cannot be confined to sex-related items and the report of crimes and murders. It suggests an encompassing definition of sensational material that includes the news selection and coverage of two sorts of events. The first are those which present an extraordinary character. They comprise happenings which are unusual, rare and infrequent; those which are bizarre and uncanny – this includes the coverage of unexplained phenomena;[35] events which are atypical and abnormal; and events of a violent nature. Examples of such events include natural disasters such as floods and earthquakes; accidents, such as steamship explosions, railways tragedies and fires; novelties such as technological innovations and weather records; unusual forms of behaviour such as acts of heroism; alleged supernatural phenomena, miraculous healings and tales of exorcism and spiritualism. The second type of sensational material is crime news; it being understood that all crime coverage is not necessarily sensationalized.

Northcliffe's editors in the *Evening News*, *Daily Mail* and *Daily Mirror* kept an eye out for these events and printed a considerable amount of news about such occurrences. In the early copies of the *Daily Mail*, the least sensational and most up-market of all three papers, the police and law court reports occupied a half-page to a page. Moreover, much space in the main news pages was devoted to news that was sensational. Page two of the issue of 11 May 1896, for example, included the following articles: 'A Spanish Lady's Death in Pimlico'; 'Death From Excitement'; 'Murder near Matlock: An Unaccountable Crime'; 'Extraordinary Scare at Forest Hill'; 'Corpse in a Burning House'; 'Ghastly Scene in Camberwell'.

Sensational news pervaded most sections of the paper, including the foreign news page. On 18 May 1896, page five of the *Daily Mail* read, *in extenso*: 'Texas Tornado: Two Hundred Lives Lost: Enormous Damage'; at Bida: 'Terrible Explosion: Two Hundred People Killed'; 'Fire in Glasgow: Exciting Scenes'; 'Rioting in Paris'; 'Zola on the Jews'; 'Brigandage in Italy'; 'Distress in Italy'; 'The Cholera in Egypt'; 'Tribal Fighting at Berbier'; 'Germans in Africa: Sensational Story'; 'The Transvaal: Suicide of a Prisoner'. Once the paper had established its position in the market, it did indeed become more respectable, although Northcliffe himself once underlined the danger for the *Daily Mail* of becoming 'too respectable'.[36]

Although these news items were not necessarily sensationalized in their treatment, the news selection of the *Daily Mail* reveals a clear liking for the exceptional and the uncanny. But the writing style of many stories testified to the intention of stirring readers' emotions. When 21 miners remained trapped down a mine for several days, their experience was 'terrible', their 'fight for life' 'desperate', their narrative 'thrilling', their meeting with the rescue team 'dramatic', their escape 'miraculous', their emotions 'indescribable', and the suspense 'dreadful' (*Daily Mail*, 31 March 1906). The sensationalism of the *Daily Mirror* probably surpassed that of its sister paper. Many news stories were given a sensational spin, and in many cases the selected angle deliberately emphasized the most dramatic elements. When a young woman was found mutilated on a railway line, the *Daily Mirror* ran a series of articles on the 'murder or suicide' theme (22 February 1904). The police news section was entitled 'Law, Police, and Mystery'.

In both journals, the pathos that many news stories tried to convey was also blatant. Stories such as 'Heroic Mother's Futile Battle with the Flames' or 'Child's Pathetic Story of her Mother's Suicide' were balanced with happy-ending tales (*Daily Mail*, 1 September 1904, 1 October 1904). The *Daily Mirror* applauded the 'act of splendid hero-ism' of a boy who rescued a lifeboat crew and the 'heroic midship-man' who saved ten lives (4 October 1910, 15 October 1910).

The sensationalist policy of Northcliffe's papers was also apparent in the prominence they gave to sensational events. The *Daily Mirror*'s front page was progressively given over to dramatic happen-ings and was regularly devoted to full-page illustrations of murders, crimes, suicides and society scandals. Events selected for their dra-matic qualities over more mundane news items were given much newspaper space and became media events. During the trial of Dr Crippen, condemned to death for the murder of his wife, the *Daily Mirror* published some 12 pages of news and comments within three days (18–20 October 1910). The trial was lavishly illustrated with 35 pictures splashed on the front and centre pages. All three issues were suffused with the sombre atmosphere of the hearings.

The crusade was another means by which Northcliffe made his papers more vivacious. A crusade may be defined as *a campaign launched by a newspaper to call for action or reform*. Campaigns differ in style and purpose. Between the 1880s and 1920s, three archetypal crusades may be identified in the British press. First came the *social crusade*, or press campaigns that called for reforms on issues such as poverty and child abuse. The second type, the *jingo crusade*, was also developed in the closing decades of the nineteenth century. These campaigns had nationalistic and imperial overtones and many called for action about deficiencies and problems related to national security and British army operations overseas. Northcliffe was chiefly responsible for the development of the third type of campaign, the *stunt*. These crusades were the most entertaining type and included calls for action on issues of minor importance. They also possessed an unmistakable journalistic element.

W.T. Stead was among the first to develop a campaigning journalistic style. He made a consistent use of the crusade, particularly those of the first two kinds. Soon after he became editor of the *Pall Mall Gazette* in 1883 he wrote a series of indignant articles protesting against the living conditions of the deprived in the slums of London's poorest boroughs. The next year he launched campaigns for General Gordon to be sent to the Sudan and in support of a bigger and better Navy. In 1885 he demanded closer imperial ties. That year, he also launched his most famous campaign, the 'Maiden Tribute of Modern Babylon'. In this series of articles, Stead described the evils of juvenile prostitution in London brothels and called for legislation protecting girls below the age of 16 (see Chapter 1).

Northcliffe's use of the crusade was more frequent and on several occasions more blatantly commercial than Stead's. The style was aggressive, abrupt, and most of his campaigns were short-lived. None the less, several of his campaigns had a social dimension, notably his calls for purer milk, better housing and wholemeal bread, which was also a crusade for a healthier nutrition for children. Others were pure stunts, such as his calls for a new hat shape (the *Daily Mail* Hat), better roses, and bigger sweet peas.

Northcliffe's most prominent crusades were those he conducted along nationalistic and imperialist lines. From its launch in May 1896, the *Daily Mail* embraced the imperialist cause and called itself the 'Voice of the Empire'. This stance was aptly epitomized by Kennedy Jones, Northcliffe's associate: 'It was the policy on which we worked through the whole of my journalistic career – One Flag, One Empire, One Home'.[37] From the early days of Anglo-German antagonism until the 1919 Versailles peace conference, Northcliffe ceaselessly crusaded on jingoistic themes. For many years before the outbreak of the First World War he warned against Germany, demanded a greater defence budget (already substantial), called for rearmament and for the reorganization of the armed forces. Many contemporaries found Northcliffe's papers too jingoistic and bellicose, to the point that some journalists, such as J.A. Spender, editor of the Liberal *Westminster Gazette*, claimed that the press magnate bore some of the responsibility for the outbreak of hostilities.[38] This argument, presumptuous of journalistic power, reflected the contrast between the frenzy of the Northcliffe press and the pre-war hesitations of the Asquith cabinet.[39]

During the war, the *Daily Mail*'s crusades had a different purpose. They targeted the government's mismanagement of the conflict and were akin to calls for social reforms, but translated to war-related issues. In May 1915, Northcliffe heavily criticized Lord Kitchener, the Secretary for War, whom he blamed for the shortage of high-explosive shells. However, Northcliffe had himself previously called for Kitchener's appointment, a paradox he acknowledged.[40] He also campaigned for compulsory conscription, the creation of a ministry of munitions and the Allied War Council.

Why crusade? Was it commercial motivation or strength of conviction that urged Northcliffe to embark on these numerous campaigns? Biographers generally point out that Northcliffe was not a cynical character and felt quite strongly about the campaigns he conducted. On the other hand, personal convictions and commercial interest are not necessarily incompatible, and evidence shows that circulation can tremendously benefit from crusading.

As to stunt campaigns, at least they had no other purpose but to attract the attention of the reading public to the paper and induce them to talk about it. Even before his first foray into the daily press, Northcliffe had long held the conviction that, to sell successfully, a publication needs to attract attention. While still in the magazine business, he quickly realized that competitions and publicity schemes were about the only way to beat rivals and boost the circulations of his magazines.[41] Once involved in the daily press, crusades were one of the editorial means he used to achieve this objective.[42]

As a general rule, campaigns gave him the opportunity to make newspapers more exciting reading material. Much of his thinking on journalism revolved around the necessity to produce vivacious copy.[43] Concentrating on selected popular topics allowed him to add thrills to the day's issue. For example, he launched the 'sweet peas stunt' in 1911 with the explicit intention of diverting the public from a tense domestic political situation, which had lasted too long for his taste and which 'made today's paper look too much like yesterday's'.[44] He had complained to Marlowe, the *Daily Mail* editor, that they had got 'into a groove' and that the 'leading articles are like gramophone records'.[45]

In the case of jingoism, it can be observed that this was one of the most commercially viable stances the press lord could adopt. An inherent problem for mass circulation newspapers is that, as the relationship multiplies, it becomes increasingly difficult for the editorial board to avoid a divisive editorial line. Northcliffe knew that partisan politics was a hindrance to the commercial prosperity of his newspapers and that a too partisan position in politics would alienate a large number of readers. Jingoism offered to the newspaper proprietor the possibility of voicing a relatively safe political opinion and to transcend, as far as possible, the political divisions of the vast market of readers. Cynical as this argument may sound, Kennedy Jones showed in 1919 a line of reasoning not far different:

> It has been overlooked in Fleet Street how largely the British Empire is a family affair; that there is hardly a household or a family circle of any size which does not have one or more of its members earning a livelihood somewhere in the outer wards. Letters come here, perhaps irregularly, but telling just enough to awaken curiosity in the regions they refer to. The instant we lifted the Jameson raid out of the miasmal fog of party politics and put it in the clear light of reason and honourable motive the heartiest support was accorded to our paper by all classes. [46]

Northcliffe may have never articulated these thoughts and may not have been fully aware of the commercial viability of jingoism in journalism. There is no doubt that he was a genuine patriot and imperialist, and that his newspapers' policy reflected his most sincere beliefs and opinions in that manner. But whether they were instinct, calculation or sheer good fortune, these beliefs were commercially sound. The above quotation shows that this coincidence had not been lost sight of by everybody in Northcliffe's editorial team.

Although Northcliffe's jingoism proved excessive for many of his Liberal contemporaries, nationalism allowed him to be vehement and uncompromising on some political issues, without directly hurting the group or class interests of an important section of readers. Jingoism, in other words, brought the profits of resolute and determined political opinions without the commercial risks that such positions often imply.

Finally, it is significant that three out of the four greatest crusaders of the time were press magnates who were supremely successful in raising circulations. Northcliffe, and, in the United States, Pulitzer and Hearst, were at the same time the most ardent crusaders and the most gifted and enterprising press owners.[47] The fourth, who never achieved great circulation, was Stead. In the 1890s, Pulitzer's *World* carried on frequent campaigns, which were as ephemeral as they were emotional, calling for action to alleviate the plight of the poor and oppressed in New York.[48] Similar to Northcliffe's stance on imperialism, the New York *World* and Hearst's *Journal* adopted such a jingoistic stance during the Cuban crisis in 1898 that they remained for long one of the most oft-quoted causes for the intervention of the United States in the conflict with Spain in April of that year.[49]

Northcliffe and the reader's mind

Are these journalistic abilities enough to explain Northcliffe's success as a newspaper proprietor? His accomplishment is best explained by the combination of his profound understanding of the fundamentals of journalism and his extraordinary capacity for perceiving the needs of each reading market. There are many references in biographies to Northcliffe's life-long quest to satisfy the public's tastes. Widely regarded as a master of crowd psychology, he delivered lectures on many occasions to his fellow journalists on how to please the masses:

> The things [Northcliffe says] people talk about are news – and what do they mostly talk about? Other people, their failures and successes, their joys and sorrows, their money and their food and their peccadilloes. Get more names in the paper – the more aristocratic the better, if there is a news story round them. You know the public is more interested in duchesses than servant-girls. [...] Ask the Amalgamated Press [Northcliffe's periodicals

concern] whether they do better in Lancashire with serial or periodical stories of factory life, or stories of high life. Everyone likes reading about people in better circumstances than his or her own.[50]

One of the many significant elements this abstract reveals is Northcliffe's striving to design a newspaper *around* readers' tastes. The same feature is clear in his correspondence with staff. Many of his communications with his managers dealt with the problem of identifying the needs of various publics and the ways to satisfy them.

J.H. Lingard was *Daily Mail* circulation manager from 1904 until 1919. At Northcliffe's request, he detailed in a memo the reasons why the *Weekly Dispatch* 'still does not satisfy the Sunday reader'. One of his recommendations concerned the editorial department, which Lingard asked 'to take care that the contents of the paper satisfy the requirements of the reader'.[51]

Lingard's successor showed the same enthusiasm. In a memo to Northcliffe, Valentine Smith explained:

> I know Leernock will also get up special stunts for me, but what I want to impress upon you is that it is no use our competing with the *Mirror* or *Sketch* with small pictures when they are given whole pages – we are wasting our money and doing ourselves no good by advertising. [...] I know the difficulties of space, but what I do not think the Editorial yet realize is the importance of these big local features, such as pageants, shows, regattas, etc.
>
> I am confident that our sole chance of getting more sale of the *Mail* is by producing several slip editions every night with good pictures and large ones, therefore certain news will have to be sacrificed. I know it is a sad thing when the general public want paltry pictures, but they do – evidenced by sale of the picture papers – and unless we give them what they want we shall not progress as we ought.[52]

Countless letters discussed this topic and related technicalities (such as train schedules and printing problems) and they show that reading the public mind was one of Northcliffe's major preoccupations. His quote in Clarke's diaries shows Northcliffe identifying a need for escapism among the popular audience and his willingness to respond to this desire with more society news and celebrity gossip.

The care and professionalism Northcliffe brought to his marketing strategy is further illustrated in the successful pricing of the *Daily Mail*. When Northcliffe launched the paper in May 1896, he deliberately presented it as a traditional penny paper, but sold it for half that price. One of the ears of the paper read 'A Penny Newspaper for One Halfpenny'. This pricing strategy was one of the key factors in its success. Had Northcliffe designed the *Daily Mail* as a halfpenny paper, and sold it for that price, its fate might not have been the same.[53]

Finally, Northcliffe proved his grasp of a market's needs by his ability to deal with different types of readership. With the *Daily Mail*, the *Daily Mirror* and, eventually, *The Times*, he provided reading matter for every social class in Great Britain. He was not the only press proprietor to control different types of newspapers, of course, but he was the most successful in creating and maintaining newspapers for every branch of the reading public.

Conclusion

What Northcliffe succeeded in doing was to bring together on a new scale the production and the consumption sides of journalism. He had the ability to tailor each of his journalistic products to the specific needs of the different markets in which he was operating. When editing a paper, designing a stunt or writing a leading article, he was able to anticipate the reaction of the public to his material. He also correctly guessed the acceptable price of a modern daily newspaper, and he delivered the right amount of news, features and gossip readers expected for a halfpenny. Northcliffe was good at delivering the content and packaging it right.

It takes both qualities to become a press magnate. Northcliffe's brother Harold, Lord Rothermere, lacked comparable skill and interest in journalism. He is thus precluded from belonging to this exclusively defined club, despite his peerage, his inheritance of Northcliffe's empire and his alleged business acumen. When Rothermere picked up the reins, the verdict was ruthless: the *Daily Mail* surrendered its supremacy to Beaverbrook's *Daily Express*. Rothermere's third son, Esmond, who inherited the remains of the business on his father's death in Bermuda during the Second World War, was no more successful. In 1971, three decades of mismanagement and strategic mistakes finally took their toll. Just before retiring, Esmond Rothermere was negotiating the take-over of his conglomerate by Sir Max Aitken, heir of the Beaverbrook empire.[54] The fate of the two Rothermeres (and of Max Aitken, indeed) shows that newspapers are not as easily inherited as land or peerages. Their conduct requires a strong commitment to content and journalistic talent, and nothing illustrates this better than Northcliffe's career.

Northcliffe's insight into journalism may not have been shared throughout his family, but its benefits were felt further afield. In 1920, he was advising a friend whom he had met during the First World War and who edited the Melbourne *Herald*. His letters included the following tips:

> The first editorial should be the second thing read every day, the first being the main news... Smiling pictures make people smile... I, personally, prefer short leading articles... People like to read about profiteering. Most of them would like to be profiteers themselves, and would if they had the chance... Every woman in the world would read about artificial pearls... columns of items a day give the reader a great feeling of satisfaction with his three-penny worth... My young men say you don't have enough stockings in the paper. I am afraid that I am no longer judge of that.[55]

The subsequent gratitude of Keith Murdoch, the recipient of this letter and of many others, points to us that Northcliffe's guidance was instrumental in helping him establish his newspaper business. However, there is one word of advice which later generations may feel he did not pass on to his son, Rupert: 'Sport can be overdone, I believe, even in Australia'.[56]

Notes

1 See J. Chalaby, 'No Ordinary Press Owners: Press Barons as a Weberian Ideal Type', *Media, Culture & Society*, **19** (4), (1997), pp. 621–41.
2 D. English, 'Legend of "The Chief"', *British Journalism Review*, **7**(2), (1996), p. 6.
3 See C.D. Collet, *History of the Taxes on Knowledge* (London: Watts, 1933); A.J. Lee, *The Origins of the Popular Press in England, 1855–1914* (London: Croom Helm, 1976).

4 L. Brown, *Victorian News and Newspapers* (Oxford: Clarendon Press, 1985), pp. 246–8.

5 J. Chalaby, *The Invention of Journalism* (London: Macmillan, 1998), pp. 155–9.

6 See J.O. Baylen, 'The "New Journalism" in Late Victorian Britain', *Australian Journal of Politics and History*, 18, December (1972), pp. 376–85; B.I. Diamond, 'A Precursor of the New Journalism: Frederick Greenwood of the *Pall Mall Gazette*', in J.H. Wiener (ed.), *Papers for the Millions* (New York: Greenwood Press, 1988), pp. 25–45.

7 R.L. Schults, *Crusader in Babylon: W.T. Stead and the* Pall Mall Gazette (Lincoln: University of Nebraska Press, 1972).

8 A. Smith, 'The Long Road to Objectivity and Back Again: the Kinds of Truth We Get in Journalism', in G. Boyce, J. Curran and P. Wingate (eds) *Newspaper History* (London: Constable, 1978), pp. 157, 165.

9 A.J. Lee, *The Origins of the Popular Press in England, 1855–1914*, op. cit., p. 229.

10 In H. Fyfe, *Northcliffe: an Intimate Biography* (London: Allen & Unwin, 1930), p. 270.

11 In D. English, 'Legend of "The Chief"', op. cit., 7.

12 M. Engel, *Tickle the Public* (London: Hutchinson, 1996), pp. 63, 75.

13 L. Brown, *Victorian News and Newspapers*, op. cit., p. 254.

14 S.J. Taylor, *The Great Outsiders: Northcliffe, Rothermere and the Daily Mail* (London: Weidenfeld & Nicholson, 1996), pp. 55–72.

15 M. Engel, *Tickle the Public*, op. cit., pp. 76–8.

16 T. Clarke, *My Northcliffe Diary* (London: Victor Gollancz, 1931), p. 127.

17 Ibid., p. 126.

18 L. Brown, *Victorian News and Newspapers*, op. cit., p. 246.

19 In S.J. Taylor, *The Great Outsiders: Northcliffe, Rothermere and the Daily Mail*, op. cit., p. 32.

20 In The Office of *The Times*, *The History of* The Times, *The 150th Anniversary and Beyond, 1912–1948, Part I, 1912–1920* (London, The Office of *The Times*, 1952), pp. 140–1.

21 Ibid., pp. 140–1.

22 In S. Koss, *The Rise and Fall of the Political Press in Britain* (London: Fontana Press, 1990), p. 531.

23 In T. Clarke, *My Northcliffe Diary*, op. cit., p. 197.

24 In H. Fyfe, *Northcliffe: An Intimate Biography*, op. cit., p. 286.

25 See A.J. Lee, *The Origins of the Popular Press in England, 1855–1914*, op. cit., pp. 131–80; A. Smith, 'The Long Road to Objectivity and Back Again: the Kinds of Truth We Get in Journalism', op. cit., pp. 153–71.

26 J. Chalaby, *The Invention of Journalism*, op. cit., pp. 168–9.

27 Attributed to Amos Cummings, one of Charles Dana's editors, W. Breed, *The Newspaperman, News and Society* (New York: Arno Press, 1980), p. 254.

28 In H. Fyfe, *Northcliffe: An Intimate Biography*, op. cit., pp. 86–7.

29 Ibid., p. 86; see also F. Williams, *Dangerous Estate: The Anatomy of Newspapers* (Cambridge: Patrick Stephens, 1957), p. 144.

30 In T. Clarke, *My Northcliffe Diary*, op. cit., p. 197.

31   In T. Clarke, *Northcliffe in History* (London: Hutchinson, 1950), p. 181.
32   Ibid., p. 81.
33   G. Cadbury to Gardiner, 1 April 1919, A.G. Gardiner Papers (London: British Library of Political and Economic Science).
34   See H. Fyfe, *Northcliffe: An Intimate Biography*, op. cit., p. 64; R. Pound and G. Harmsworth, *Northcliffe* (London: Cassell, 1959), p. 416.
35   J.W. Carey, 'The Dark Continent of American Journalism' in R.K. Manoff and M. Schudson (eds), *Reading the News* (New York: Pantheon, 1986), p. 168.
36   In R. Pound and G. Harmsworth, *Northcliffe*, op. cit., p. 46.
37   K. Jones, *Fleet Street and Downing Street* (London: Hutchinson, 1919), p. 150.
38   J.A. Spender, *The Public Life, vol. 2* (London: Cassell, 1925), p. 140.
39   P. Kennedy, *The Rise of the Anglo-American Antagonism* (London: Ashfield Press, 1980), p. 384. See also N. Angell, *The Press and the Organization of Society* (London: Labour Publishing Company, 1922).
40   R. Pound and G. Harmsworth, *Northcliffe*, op. cit., p. 477. This crusade against a national idol he himself contributed to manufacturing is the only one that cost Northcliffe readers, ibid., p. 479.
41   Ibid., pp. 65–190.
42   See H. Fyfe, *Northcliffe: An Intimate Biography*, op. cit., pp. 44–7.
43   See, for example, T. Clarke, *My Northcliffe Diary*, op. cit., pp. 181–213.
44   R. Pound and G. Harmsworth, *Northcliffe*, op. cit., p. 404.
45   Ibid., p. 404.
46   K. Jones, *Fleet Street and Downing Street*, op. cit., p. 146.
47   On Pulitzer see G. Juergens, *Joseph Pulitzer and the New York World* (Princeton: Princeton University Press, 1966); on Hearst see W.A. Swanberg, *Citizen Hearst* (London: Longman, 1962).
48   G. Juergens, *Joseph Pulitzer and the New York* World, op. cit., pp. 263–330.
49   J.E. Wisan, *The Cuban Crisis as Reflected in the New York Press* (New York: Columbia University Press, 1934); W.A. Swanberg, *Citizen Hearst*, op. cit., pp. 101–69.
50   In T. Clarke, *My Northcliffe Diary*, op. cit., pp. 200–1.
51   J.H. Lingard to A. Harmsworth, 16 November 1905, Northcliffe Papers, Add. MSS 62 211 (London: British Library).
52   V. Smith to Northcliffe, 6 August 1913, Northcliffe Papers, Add. MSS 62 211 (London: British Library).
53   Not to mention the failed attempt of Sir George Newnes to sell a half-penny newspaper for a penny. A month before the launch of the *Daily Mail*, Newnes started the *Daily Courier*. Although Newnes's paper suffered from some notable editorial weaknesses, it would have undoubtedly survived longer than five months provided its owner had realized that the penny charge was too high for the lower middle class market the paper was aiming at.
54   S.J. Taylor, *The Reluctant Press Lord* (London: Weidenfeld & Nicholson, 1998), pp. 201–5.
55   In S.J. Taylor, *The Great Outsiders: Northcliffe, Rothermere and the* Daily Mail, op. cit., pp. 204–5.
56   Ibid., p. 205.

3
Popular Press and Empire: Northcliffe, India and the *Daily Mail*, 1896–1922

Chandrika Kaul

The appearance of Alfred Harmsworth's *Daily Mail* in 1896 coincided with the high point of nineteenth-century imperialism.[1] In the last thirty years of the century the British empire increased enormously in size, covering by 1900 one fifth of the world's land surface. Queen Victoria's Diamond Jubilee celebrations provoked Beatrice Webb to note in her diary in June 1897: 'Imperialism in the air – all classes drunk with sight-seeing and hysterical loyalty.'[2] That questions relating to the empire were in the forefront of public discussion can be partly attributed to increased press coverage. The growth of the empire 'was watched with pride by a largely sympathetic press.'[3] Imperial issues were a continuing preoccupation with editors of the quality press, while proprietors of the popular papers learned, says Messinger, 'the value of imperial drama as a way to sell their product' to the masses.[4] The *Mail's* coverage of the Jubilee was lavish, spectacular and unparalleled in 'orchestrating the enthusiasm of the nation'.[5] A glance at contemporary press directories such as *Sell's* or *Mitchell's* reveals the existence, often short lived, of a plethora of titles with imperial connections. Fleet Street ran imperial campaigns and exerted pressure on Government to varying degrees throughout the second half of Victoria's reign. A vivid example was Lord Esher's use of the *Pall Mall Gazette* to press Gladstone into sending Gordon to the Sudan in 1883, a cry taken up by other papers.[6]

Many editors were personally motivated to use their papers to publicise imperial issues. Geoffrey Dawson, H.A. Gwynne, C.P. Scott, J.A. Spender, J. St. Loe Strachey, H.W. Massingham, J.L. Garvin, and the journalists associated with the *Round Table*, were men of strong imperial views. Strachey wrote in 1922:

> To me the alliance of the self-governing Dominions, which con-
> stitute the British Empire, has a sacred character ... I feel further
> that throughout Africa, as throughout India, we have done an
> incomparable service to humanity by our maintenance of just
> and stable government.[7]

Gwynne, who had been Reuter's chief correspondent in South Africa
during the Boer War, reflected in 1911, when assuming the editorship of the *Morning Post*: 'I have given of the best part of my life and
intend to devote the rest of it to promote the objects I hold dear –
a united Empire, England secure on land as on sea'.[8] Such sentiments found a wider resonance in Fleet Street. Successive editors of
The Times, for instance, held strong opinions upon the importance
of Britain's imperial involvement.

Similar sentiments were expressed by many pioneers of the new
popular journalism, yet it is clear, also, that the commercial potential of imperial news stories was recognised. Colonial conflicts were
especially profitable. Reuters flourished on this diet during the late
Victorian and Edwardian period.[9]

> The popular press exploited this spectatorial fascination with
> colonial warfare, and its power was such that not only the jingo-
> ist *Daily Mail* but also labour papers like *Reynold's News* were
> swept up into it. In 1898 the Labour *Leader* complained that the
> working class were more interested in celebrating Omdurman
> than in supporting the Welsh coal strike.[10]

The Boer War saw the circulation of the pro-war *Mail* soar,
whereas W.T. Stead's tenure at the *Review of Reviews* was associated
with declining revenue and sales – at least in part because of his
'unrelenting opposition' to the conflict.[11] The first Imperial Press
conference, convened in London in 1909 on the initiative of metropolitan proprietors and journalists, was a landmark in press history.
Leading journalists from across the empire assembled together for
the first time, its proceedings being conceived as 'a replica in a freer
style' of the Imperial Conference taking place in the same year.[12]

Some of the relationships between empire and the Edwardian
quality press have been traced by James Startt, with a focus upon

'the imperial debate' conducted in the writings of Strachey, Spender, Garvin, and *The Times* journalists in the decade before 1914. Startt's work reveals the depth of interest in, and coverage of, imperial affairs in the press and the role of influential editors and proprietors in creating and sustaining a climate of opinion in Britain. Problems of empire were part of a set of 'core' issues permeating the entire era and any understanding of contemporary 'public debate' would be incomplete without an understanding of the contribution of the press. Accordingly Startt suggests that it was the quality, rather than the popular, papers that were 'central' to Edwardian politics. 'By their ongoing commentary on imperial issues from the beginning to the end of the era, they helped to make Empire one of the two or three commanding subjects of the time and extended the parameters of discussion about it.'[13]

However, although Startt acknowledges that imperial journalists generally took 'pride' in the *Raj* and believed that British rule there had 'a justifiable, even a moral foundation', he himself does not consider the place of India within Edwardian journalism. The Indian empire, he argues, 'never became a continuing controversial subject in the public debate'. It remained, like the dependencies, a 'special case' and 'largely in the domain of the experts'.[14] It was the evolution of the self-governing dominions, the prospect for imperial unity, and the implications for defence policy, which dominated the political vision of contemporary journalists. However, Startt's preoccupation with these issues causes him to overlook the fact that Indian affairs could generate significant press coverage, and the prominence of India in the press grew as the twentieth century unfolded.[15]

Empire and popular culture

The popularity or otherwise of empire has been a contested field amongst scholars, but, as Judith Brown has recently observed, in 'an ironic and productive shift, historians are again turning to the British scene to discuss not "what Britons did" abroad, but how the network of dependencies and connections affected Britain – if you like, "what empire did for Britain"'.[16] John Mackenzie and the *Manchester Studies in Imperialism* series have considered the impact on Britain's culture of her empire, examining it in the light of everything from hunting and sexuality to literature and art, showing how closely it was interwoven with social conditions and cultural institutions. The British imperial cult was made up of:

> a renewed militarism, a devotion to royalty, an identification and worship of national heroes, together with a contemporary cult of personality, and racial ideas associated with Social Darwinism.[17]

According to Mackenzie, the idea that empire was unimportant to the public arose from an excessive concentration by historians upon the effects of Britain on the empire. However the 'centripetal' effects of imperialism were as noteworthy as the 'centrifugal'. The empire was a fact of social history and gave British people 'a world view which was central to their perceptions of themselves'.[18] But how important was the empire to the British public in general? Mackenzie, Harcourt, Castle, MacDonald, and others, have argued that the literature and asscociations that empire generated did have significant impact and that this did not end in 1900 or 1918, but continued into the interwar period when empire was portrayed as a source of pride and as a means of arresting national decline.[19] A larger number of non-government agencies discovered that imperial patriotism was also profitable and imperial values were projected by such diverse means as music halls, missionary societies, churches, book publishers, magazines and juvenile literature, school texts, popular press, cinema, and organisations like the Boy Scouts and Girl Guides. Links between public and private propaganda were strengthened by the pressure groups which arose from the 1880s to lobby Parliament, working closely with political and military figures for 'larger military budgets and greater attention to the values of empire'.[20]

While Mackenzie and others successfully chronicle the volume of imperial propaganda, the moot point remains: how effective were such endeavours? Pelling contends that, with a few exceptions, no elections were won or lost on imperial issues, whilst Price's work on the Boer War suggests that the British working class was guided by its own 'frames of reference', was not uniformly 'jingo', and that the Conservative election victory in 1900 was due more to a weakened Liberal Party than to the popularity of the war.[21] Mackenzie acknowledges that there is need to have 'more precise evidence that such ideas struck home'. Given the difficulties of measurement the debate cannot be resolved and it is beyond the limits of this chapter to seek to do so. Rather, starting from the observation that the contemporary popular press took an active interest in imperial affairs, we consider the character of the *Mail*'s coverage of India and the factors which shaped the agenda of its reporting during the lifetime of Northcliffe.

Daily Mail and imperial coverage

According to Northcliffe's biographers, Pound and Harmsworth, the *Mail* was the 'most consistently efficient journalistic expression of his personality and purpose',[22] and from its inception the *Mail* announced that it stood for 'the power, the supremacy and the greatness' of the British empire, the paper being 'the embodiment and mouthpiece of the imperial idea'.[23] Besides being keen to exploit the potentialities for circulation that empire afforded, as well as tap latent home sympathies, Northcliffe's personal enthusiasm for the 'imperial idea', epitomized by the 'Empire first and parish after' policy, was responsible for bringing, in Wilson's words, 'the Empire, the world, to the cottage door'.[24] 'The spirit he sought to infuse into his newspapers was "living patriotism" '. He 'depised' the policy of the 'Little Englander', and wanted Britain to be 'strong and great, the loved and admired centre' of the empire.[25]

Ryan notes that the 'excitement' of home politics was 'never allowed to keep foreign and imperial affairs out of the headlines'. Northcliffe gave his readers 'frequent, lengthy and well-informed' accounts by a number of travelling correspondents. 'The initiative for arranging these visits were his own'.[26] He was forever seeking 'interesting' approaches to overseas news coverage. 'We have not', he declared, 'enough authoritative foreign or empire news in the paper ... We do not get sufficiently in touch with big men visiting London from our great overseas Dominions ... Dig them out. They have wonderful news stories to tell, and are most interesting and refreshing personalities'.[27] The basis for this coverage was provided by a massive investment in telegraphs and overseas correspondents. Within a few years of its establishment, the international news organisation of the *Mail* was second only to that the *The Times* and Reuters.[28] Northcliffe himself maintained that one of the sources of the journal's success was 'its free use of cable and private wire'. By the second anniversary of the *Mail*'s foundation, he could claim with satisfaction that the 'average cost of telegrams to any issue of the paper was greater than that expended by any rival in the U.K.'[29]

In November 1904 an *Overseas Daily Mail* edition was launched to meet the perceived need for 'a newspaper connection between the Old country and the scattered hundreds of thousands of Britons in the four corners of the world'.[30] This overseas edition would serve as a message from 'the home-stayers' to those who were 'bearing the White Man's burden across the seas'.[31] Issued at the uniform price of 5s per annum including postage worldwide, it would contain 'nearly one hundred columns of matter', being a concise summary of 'all the principal home and foreign news, leading articles, and essays', to have appeared in the *Mail* as well as a weekly review by a leading author. The interests of 'the ladies abroad' would not be overlooked and a special feature calculated to appeal to those living 'in far away Indian bungalows and Backwood settlements' was to be on 'What is Being Worn at Home'.

'I have given orders', noted Northcliffe, 'that although the newspaper cannot absolutely be non-political, it is to report each week equally speeches of ten leading men, and there will be a quotation from the 'Times'.[32] Writing to St. Loe Strachey, Northcliffe announced that 'the project has been an overwhelming success', and while he could not 'see the chance of making much money out of it, I do think it will effect some good from the Imperial standpoint'.[33] Its long-serving editor, John Evelyn Wrench, admitted that he had consistently tried to give the journal 'a definitely Imperial tone'.[34] According to Wilson, the wide circulation of the *Overseas Daily Mail* ensured that Northcliffe's name began 'to carry weight throughout the Empire'.[35] The formation of a popular image of empire had a great deal to do with its representation in the popular press, of which the *Mail* was a leading element. The mass circulation popular papers sought out the human interest in imperial stories, and in so doing made such news accessible to a much wider audience: the empire, their readers were reminded, was 'kith and kin'. Northcliffe spoke of the 'great responsibility' of pressmen towards their readership, for they were 'looking at life through a peephole for all those people'. Who were these readers to which the *Mail* directed its appeal? Northcliffe's targets were the 'small shopkeeper and the ambitious clerk', those who 'simply wished to improve their own position ... satisfied to feel themselves a cut above the labouring poor and happy to be governed by their betters'.[36] They were 'tomorrow's 1000 a year men' or so they hoped or thought.[37] For Ryan the *Mail*, from Conservative defeat in 1906 up to the First World War, was 'a perfect mirror of bourgeois, moderate Conservative England'.[38] Northcliffe was not unaware that 'there was more than one public. There were millions on whom he could play with ease and there were the thousands who read The Times'.[39]

Daily Mail and Indian reporting

The coverage accorded by the paper to Britain's largest imperial possession is a curiously under-explored subject. The *Mail* had a separate Imperial and Foreign news page, though such news could also be scattered across its pages. In the absence of surviving records, it is impossible to ascertain the exact number of *Mail* correspondents stationed in the sub-continent or the financial outlay of the paper on Indian news coverage. It utilised the services of the telegraphic news agencies, including Reuters, Central News, Dalziel, and the Indo-European. By 1900 the paper had correspondents in Calcutta, Bombay, Simla and Colombo, some of whom, like Everard Cotes, were permanent, while others were engaged on short term contracts and as 'stringers', or worked in conjunction with other newspapers. Old India hands and servicemen were encouraged to contribute. The prominent Anglo-Indian newspaper, the *Times of India* in Bombay, acted as a co-ordinating office for the *Mail*, and its news collection network was no doubt strengthened after Northcliffe's takeover of *The Times* which boasted the longest established and most extensive network of Indian correspondents. Special reporters like William Maxwell and Valentia Steer were sent out to cover the kind of ceremonial pageants associated with the visits of the Prince of Wales in 1905 and 1921–2, Curzon's Durbar in 1903, and the Imperial Durbar in 1911. Interviews and firsthand accounts were regular features. In London, the paper's chief leader writer, H.W. Wilson, contributed substantially to the opinion columns. The *Mail* even claimed to have inspired halfpenny journalism in the East in the shape of the *Indian Daily News* edited by the well known Anglo-Indian publicist Everard Digby, with Cotes serving on its board. Cotes later left the *Mail* to set up a private news wire service in competition with Indian news agencies and Reuters.

On average the *Mail* carried several Indian news items each day. Many concerned personal tragedies and crises, reflecting the general belief of the paper that *Mail* readers were 'more interested in people than principles'.[40] Northcliffe did not attach any sanctity to political coverage. 'We must not let politics dominate the paper, but we must get the *news* in politics ... Treat politics as you treat all other news – on its merits. It has no 'divine right' on newspaper space'.[41] Editorials and opinion pieces on India were predominantly on political issues, but their number was small. Between 1909 and 1922, the percentage of leaders devoted to India varied between none at all in 1915, 0.2 per cent in 1913, 1916, and 1920, and 1.9 per cent in 1909.[42] The human interest factor was ever present and the personal dimensions of empire were fully exploited. Always on the look out for a scoop, the *Mail* was quick to despatch a reporter to Southampton to meet General Dyer when he returned to Britain in May 1920. Dyer had ordered the shooting at unarmed civilians including women and children on 13 April 1919 at the Jallianwallah Bagh, an enclosed walled garden in Amritsar, Punjab, resulting in the massacre of 379 and injuries to over 1 500 people. With a photograph of the General, 'burnt-red by 35 years service' in India, the *Mail* informed its readers that he was 'thick-set and fairly tall, with greying hair and kindly blue eyes'. Dyer's 'first words' on landing were: 'It was my duty – my horrible, dirty duty'.[43]

Emphasis was laid as much upon the presentation of news in the *Mail* as upon its content, the 'note' of the paper being 'not so much economy of price as conciseness and compactness'.[44] The paper was always concerned to avoid that 'arid vastness of type' presented by the established papers, which were to be 'explored from a club armchair or in port-mellowed leisure after dinner'.[45] Being a 'busy man's' paper it presented 'all the news of the hour in the brightest and briefest fashion'.[46] Leading articles were usually three short paragraphs in length, and made use of pithy and often provocative headings, such as: 'Shall We Give Up India?', 'Montagu's Mistakes', 'Gandhi's Failure', 'Indian Situation – Cult of Treason'. In matters of presentation Northcliffe was greatly influenced by the techniques evolved by Joseph Pulitzer on the New York *World*.[47] Through its type-faces and layout the *Mail* created an impact on the reader and Northcliffe was a staunch advocate of 'extraleaded' headlines. As Wrench remarked, he 'saw life largely in headlines'.[48] Several tiers of headers with different typefaces and degrees of boldness characterised the main stories. For example, the report of 24 December 1912 on the assassination attempt upon the Viceroy employed 6 headers, each varying in size and boldness: ATTEMPT TO MURDER INDIAN VICEROY – BOMB FROM A ROOF – LORD HARDINGE'S 6 WOUNDS – OUTRAGE AT STATE PROCESSION – EXPLOSION ON BACK OF AN ELEPHANT – ATTENDANT KILLED. Even for less dramatic reports, several headers introduced the topic and summed up its main features.

As far as content was concerned, the *Mail* provided coverage of variety and depth. In the years leading up to The First World War, crimes and 'outrages' received regular treatment. This may be attributable to the increase in political extremism in India from the turn of the century, but it also reflected Northcliffe's near obsession with crime reporting. 'They are the sort of dramatic news that the public always affects to criticise but is always in the greatest hurry to read'.[49] From the official statistics for 1902 the *Mail* was able to inform its readers that more than 23 000 criminals were sentenced to be whipped and that there were 23 000 fatal snake bites per annum![50] The potential of the exotic East was also fully exploited in features recounting the peculiarities of the Amir of Afghanistan's 'Appearance, Amusements, Tastes and Wives', or his prowess on the cricket pitch where, 'it is not etiquette, certainly not good policy, to get the Amir out too quickly, nor to send him "tricky" balls difficult to hit to the boundary'.[51] The Indian caste system, the practice of sati, and the religious customs of the Brahmins were among the other topics that arrested the attention of the paper.[52]

In addition to this underlying continuum in its coverage, certain key issues were treated in greater detail. One such high point was associated with the security of the empire. War was the *Mail's* forte and imperial conflicts were covered with the same attention to individual heroism and military detail as other wars around the world. The North West Frontier campaigns in the 1890s, including the Chitral and Tirah expeditions, the march on Lhasa in 1903, and the third Afghan war in 1919, all provided ample opportunity for dramatic reporting.[53] The heroism of the British race was reflected in the gallantry displayed in these fighting fields where they earned the right to rule through superiority in arms. Referring to the expedition in Chitral in 1897 an editorial argued that the war 'must be

finished, and we must win. Eastern folk, like the Boers, have no delicate appreciation of a generous enemy, and unless we administer a
very severe punishment, and prove our superiority beyond doubt, we
shall be troubled by the tribes for all time with expeditions *ad lib'*.[54]
The 'Mutiny' of 1857–58 occupied a sacred position in this context
and the *Mail* made frequent references to British courage, proclaim-
ing on the occasion of its fiftieth anniversary: 'In the whole history
of Great Britain there is probably no record which has a deeper hold
upon our hearts than the stirring story of the Indian Mutiny.'[55]

Famine, plague and the *Daily Mail*

But social and humanitarian issues were not overlooked. Plague
broke out in Bombay in 1896 and India experienced a catastrophic
famine in 1896–97, the total population affected being well over 30
million. The *Mail* rose to the occasion and handled the tragedy with
sensitivity and in depth. The newspaper accorded due weight to the
economic and political implications of the famine, and in the scale
of coverage it may be ranked alongside such stalwarts of the quality
press as the *Manchester Guardian* and *The Times*. The *Mail* devoted
daily coverage to the calamity, covering a range of issues over a
period of several months. In hard-hitting editorials it expressed the
view that while there was rapidly increasing distress in India, England
was 'holding back from the task of giving help to the starving
natives'.[56] It accused the Secretary of State and the Indian Government of wilful procrastination in setting up relief, 'little concerned
with the probable death of a few hundreds or thousands of insignifi-
cant black men in remote country districts'.[57] In responding to the
distress in Western India the *Mail* urged its countrymen to contribute
generously to relief funds being belatedly set up in Britain.

> The fact is that English people do not yet realise the sufferings of
> the people of India. We are so lamentably unacquainted with the
> normal conditions under which the masses in India live from day
> to day that it is in a measure not surprising that we have hitherto
> remained inert and passive spectators of the dismal tragedy.[58]

In urging public action, the *Mail* stressed that 'it falls to us to defend
our Empire from the spectral armies of Famine...Our weapon is

good honest British money, and every Englishman who has at heart the greatness of our Empire ... can serve England right and well and loyally today by helping India in her hour of bitter need'.[59] In the Jubilee year of Queen Victoria's reign, the paper argued, the Famine Fund would be a fitting memorial: 'We want to make our Queen a present; let us present her with a garland of human lives.' This would also serve to further bind the empire together.[60] Such spirited fund raising undoubtedly contributed towards a massive public contribution of over £170000 by the end of January 1897 alone. The explicit emotionalism of such language was a new departure with important implications for the future, prefiguring newspaper coverage of subsequent humanitarian crises throughout the twentieth century.

By evocative descriptions the horrors of the famine were brought home to the British public.[61] Yet at the same time the opportunity was taken to counterpoise the religious mysticism and obscurantism of the East with the medical advances and rational methods of the West in tackling plague and disease. Thus, for instance, the coverage of 'Prayer and Plague' in Bombay noted how '50000 Mahommedans Petition Allah' for relief.[62] The 'fanaticism' of Muslims, the *Mail* claimed, was responsible in many instances for obstructing official sanitary and innoculation programmes. Similary Spenser Sarle, an Anglo-Indian contributor, noted how vaccination was resented by 'an intensely conservative and fatalistic race like the Hindoos, who regard as impious any attempt to check the ravages of smallpox which does not take the form of an offering to the goddess *Kali*, the tutelary deity of that disease'.[63]

Monarchy and the *Daily Mail*

Another preoccupation of the *Mail's* coverage was monarchy, which invested the East with glamour. Cannadine has identified the period beginning in the late 1870s and extending until the outbreak of the First World War as 'the heyday of "invented tradition", a time when old ceremonials were staged with an expertise and appeal which had been lacking before, and when new rituals were self-consciously invented to accentuate this development'.[64] The image of the British monarch became 'splendid, public and popular'. Developments in the media from the 1880s aided this process, with the advent of a sensationalist and increasingly conservative popular press, and new

techniques in photography and printing. By the end of the nineteenth century the great royal ceremonies were being described with
'unprecedented immediacy and vividness in a sentimental, emotional, admiring way, which appealed to a broader cross section of
the public than ever before'. Every great royal occasion 'was also an
imperial occasion', with the press as 'one major agent in exalting the
monarchy to venerated Olympus'.[65]

Successive visits of the royal family to India, as well as imperial
durbars, provided the *Mail* with the pomp and pageant well suited
to its conceptions of public interest. Monarchism was at the core of
imperial propaganda in the high noon of empire: 'imperialism made
spectacular theatre, with the monarchy its gorgeously opulent cen-
trepiece'.[66] On the occasion of the Prince of Wales's tour in 1905 the
Mail's special correspondent William Maxwell enthused about
India's great welcome to 'Our Rajah': 'No lustre of wealth and orna-
ment which the loyalty of India can furnish was wanting.'[67] When
he returned as King for the Delhi Durbar in 1911, Maxwell was
again at hand to cover the occasion and the royal 'boons' that the
Emperor bestowed. These included the shift in the capital from
Calcutta to Delhi, a city with significance for the British, as the editorial in the *Mail* noted with passion: 'it has a great sacredness; its
soil is holy ground, fragrant with the memories of the immortal
dead who served the Empire in the dark hours of the Mutiny.'[68]

When George V's son followed in his father's footsteps during the
winter of 1921–2, the *Mail* welcomed the continuation of the royal
precedent of establishing 'personal touch with the loyal millions' –
a duty given added significance by India's service during the First
World War. The popular press highlighted the personal exploits of
the royal visitor, to convey an image of a virile Prince representative
of a vibrant monarchy. The glamour of big game shooting, the British
world of trophies and *shikar*, had traditionally formed a background
to royal progresses through India, and the Prince himself sought to
emulate his father's exploits: 'with his skill at tiger-shooting, I was
keen to make my mark in the field of horsemanship.'[69] The Prince
was described by the *Mail* using a host of superlatives – 'Magnetic
Prince', 'Tireless Prince', 'Happy Prince'.[70] The grandeur of the Raj
was captured in widespread photographic coverage, often on the
back pages to guarantee wider impact. The *Mail* found it 'impossible
to exaggerate the magnificence of the reception and the lavishness

of the hospitality' in the princely states of Rajasthan, and noted in general the 'many scenes of picturesque pageantry and Oriental splendour'.[71]

The patriotism of the popular press was reflected in the glossing over of opposition to the Prince's tour during Gandhi's non-cooperation movement of 1920–22,[72] the first 'continental campaign' which marked 'a major change in the depth and dimensions of concerted political hostility' to the Raj.[73] In the words of the eminent *Times* journalist Valentine Chirol:

> It is assuredly no mere figure of speech to say that India is actually at the parting of the ways – either towards renewed and fortified faith in the British connection or towards a convulsive period of estrangement and revolt which, if it does not lead to the overthrow of British rule, will weaken and perhaps paralyse all its best and most fruitful energy.[74]

The Indian National Congress opposed the visit of the Prince, who was greeted with major nation-wide *hartals* or strikes and disruption which led to police clashes with demonstrators. However, the *Mail* correspondent strove to emphasise the positive dimension of events:

> One does not wish to minimise the present discontent in India and the difficulties of the problem which are serious enough, but it remains that the extremists are small in numbers, and the immense mass of the people are moderate and well inclined. That mass, when it is not terrified, has shown every desire to express its loyalty, and I have nowhere been able to hear stories of the Prince's visit and personality doing other than good, and I have heard from no source, whether European or Indian, any suggestion that the Government should do other than to continue to show its determination to govern.[75]

The governance of India and the *Daily Mail*

The *Mail* considered itself 'the voice of empire' in London journalism and favoured a strong and united empire.[76] Early in its lifetime it had earned a reputation as a jingoist organ from its bellicose coverage of the Boer War and conflicts in Sudan and China. Yet its coverage of India reflects a more thoughtful and considered position. On many occasions it was relatively liberal in its stance, and certainly far removed from others on the extreme Conservative wing of the political spectrum, such as the *Morning Post, National Review,* and *Saturday Review.* The Indian empire was undoubtedly the jewel in Britain's crown, a sacred and glorious trust that needed to be nurtured. The position of the Viceroy was crucial and required respect. On the occasion of the military controversy that led to the Viceroy Curzon's resignation in 1905, the *Mail* strongly supported Curzon against the Commander-in-Chief Kitchener and maintained the supremacy of civilian over military rule as the basis for governance in India. It advocated greater parliamentary interest in the affairs of the sub-continent, reflecting in 1897 what an 'insulting thing' it was that the House of Commons should postpone its annual discussion on the affairs 'of our great Indian empire to the extreme and lifeless end – to the very dregs of the session'.[77]

The paper insisted upon the necessity of suppressing Indian unrest,[78] which appeared particularly pressing as the Edwardian years saw an increase in political terrorism, the reality of which was brought closer to home in 1990 when Curzon Wylie of the India Office staff was assassinated while addressing a meeting of Indian students in London. This did not, however, imply tolerance of brutal measures, and the paper supported the Government's criticism of General Dyer, embodied in the Hunter Committee Report on the Jallianwallah Bagh massacre.[79] The loyalty of India during the First World War brought forth much praise, this support from members of a different race demonstrating the 'spiritual existence' of the British empire.[80] The arrival of Indian troops for the first time on European soil in October 1914 was welcomed by the *Mail,* and their fortunes were followed in its pages as the War progressed. Though always advocating the deployment of 'the strong hand' in India, the *Mail* realised that the First World War marked the dawn of 'a new age' which would embrace the Indian empire. The resulting alteration in the aspirations of Indians had to be dealt with in that spirit of sympathy and justice which were the hallmark of British, as opposed to German, government.[81] The paper favoured constitutional reform and saw the appeasement of moderate and loyal Indians as essential for the security of the Raj, but it eschewed any hasty measures towards the granting of complete self-government.

It supported the Secretary of State Edwin Montagu's declaration of intent in August 1917 (and the subsequent Government of India Act 1919), to increase association with Indians in the administration and to develop institutions to this effect, albeit gradually, whilst maintaining India as an integral part of the British empire.

Northcliffe and India

Exceptionally among newspaper proprietors of the time, Northcliffe travelled twice to India, and on each occasion displayed a keen interest in the sub-continent. On the first trip, undertaken as a recuperative tour only a few months after the launch of the *Mail*, he was accompanied by his wife and Reginald Nicolson, his private secretary (who had himself previously worked on the Indian railways). Travelling extensively, especially in the plague and famine areas of Western India, Northcliffe assumed the mantle of a roving special correspondent. In presenting his articles the *Mail* was at pains to stress that Northcliffe spoke 'with the authority of immediate personal knowledge', having spent the previous two months in that 'unhappy country'. What he had to say was 'uncoloured by local prejudices' and 'unaffected by the politic reticence' which the paper claimed deprived many official reports of their significance.[82]

His six articles, entitled 'Hard Truths from India', appeared in February 1897. Assisted by T.J. Bennett, proprietor of the *Times of India*, they show him to have been well read in recent literature, while his sketches of the plague and famine district testified to his zeal as a reporter. (These articles were later reprinted and sent post free to any subscriber for 1½d on application to the publisher.) India, he observed, was suffering an average of 1500 to 2000 weekly fatalities. This calamity was until very recently 'minimised to a ridiculous, nay criminal degree. The fact is that the commercial community in Bombay has been trying for months to persuade itself that the plague is no plague'.[83] Among the factors making it difficult to ascertain the truth about the famine was the belief that it was 'largely used as a political cry' by Indians; that many 'native merchants welcome the special fund, not because of its help to the poor, but for the sake of their own market manipulations'.[84] Another article provided a graphic portrayal of his visit to 'A Starvation Camp': 'The spectres, the gaunt, shrivelled old men and women, the babes, who seem all head and staring eyes, are in camps called poor houses. May

I never go through such experiences as I have encountered in these awful settlements'.[85] Northcliffe was outspoken in his criticism of the average Anglo-Indian, as well as of his countrymen who argued that everything was a gross exaggeration. The 'horrors' depicted in the illustrated journals were 'rare', Northcliffe observed, 'but not so rare as the average Anglo-Indian pent up in his office all day, and at his club and dinner-party in the evening might consider'.[86]

Northcliffe referred to Bombay as 'The City of Fear' and subjected to unrelenting criticism the city's municipal authorities and its 'conspiracy of silence'. He also criticised the Secretary of State, George Hamilton, for 'trying to minimise the real state of affairs in this fearfully afflicted community'.[87] Hamilton was quoted in the British press referring to 'sensational cable messages'. 'I have not seen any exaggerated plague reports', wrote Northcliffe. 'None such have yet reached India. But they must be monumentally mendacious if they exceed the truth about Bombay'. In quoting the Director General of the Indian Medical Service, who estimated that 300 000 people had fled Bombay, Northcliffe asked: 'Will Lord George Hamilton venture to deny that that is a sensational statement, or say that it is misleading? The "Times of India", which is a most accurate journal, yesterday gave the death figures as 12 157, adding that this is probably but half the truth.'[88]

Yet the famine relief measures that had been taken were praised and Northcliffe highlighted British strength in the face of adversity: 'The calm confidence of our people has been most gratifying'.[89] 'With more railways, canals, roads, with the steady progress of legislation for the masses, famine will continue to be less and less frequent.'[90] Thus for Northcliffe the empire worked and was beneficial. This was a heroism of a different magnitude from that displayed on the field of battle in defence of the empire; however, both served to confirm and consolidate the superiority of the British as empire builders.

Northcliffe revisited the sub-continent in 1921–22 on his world tour. He travelled the length of India, from Ceylon via Madras to New Delhi, where he stayed at the invitation of the Viceroy, Rufus Isaacs, Lord Reading, with whom he shared a warm friendship that went back to 1907 when the latter had defended Northcliffe in the 'Soap Trust Case'.[91] During the First World War Reading had succeeded Northcliffe as head of the British War Mission to America. Reading wrote to Montagu: 'I am glad he will be here for we may be able to get him interested in Indian affairs and I have always liked him.'[92] For the Government this was an important visit, and Northcliffe was in receipt of the best of official hospitality – in his own words 'motor cars, pleasant guides to show us about, a warm welcome and a good send-off'.[93] Reading was pleased to find Northcliffe:

> undoubtedly desirous of helping in the present trying state of affairs and [he] will give greater publicity to Indian news and situation. I never read our English newspapers out here without wishing that they were better informed ... But to the average Englishman India is a long way off and the picture of it to him is I fear antiquated.[94]

Montagu approved these initiatives, and he promised on Northcliffe's return to 'do everything in my power to meet him and to see if we cannot establish good relations'.[95] Northcliffe had 'much talk with many officials and newspaper men – many, many hours of it'.[96] The tour, according to Tom Clarke, did much to 'reinspire' Northcliffe as the 'apostle of a world order based on the fabric of a more closely integrated British Empire'.[97]

Pound and Harmsworth, Ferris, and recently Taylor, have ignored or minimised the significance of these tours. They refer to the expressions of distaste contained in Northcliffe's diary during 1921–22, and Pound and Harmsworth conclude that 'he did not like India'.[98] Covering vast distances and not in the best of health and spirits, he found travel not surprisingly to be 'tiring, and very dusty'.[99] 'Excepting the hills, it is a wearisome country', he remarked.[100] 'What do we want India for? Prestige? Perhaps. Cash? We certainly don't get any from it. The thousands of able men from home here could do far better almost anywhere else.'[101] Northcliffe disliked Congress extremists and the English educated *Babus*: 'These people have got swelled heads.'[102] Nevertheless, Northcliffe continued to admire the spirit of service that for him underlay the Raj. 'Lord!', he remarked, 'how much British blood we have lost in India, and how unselfishly'. Yet he saw that the British way of life was passing.

> Now we have the swaggering, boastful, whisky-and-soda drinking, horn-spectacled, and fountain-pen-wearing Babu, who likes to think that, because he has the imitative and blotting-paper

mind that enables him to pass examinations, he is the equal of the Anglo-Saxon, and, *knowing* his own inferiority, is bitter and dangerous.[103]

His punishing schedule and the rigours of Indian travel contributed, no doubt, towards his professed dislike of some aspects of his trip. Northcliffe's diary also reflects many prejudices and an overt anti-Congress bias. What concerns us here, however, is the extent of his involvement with Indian issues, and the consequences this had for their coverage in the *Mail*. Whereas plague and famine confronted Northcliffe on his first tour, the non-cooperation movement greeted him on his second. To both he responded actively by contributing lengthy articles and giving interviews, resulting in a heightened coverage of Indian issues in the London press. He highlighted the grave concern that existed in India about the economic upheavals of the War and its aftermath, the impact of hostilities upon Indian opinion, and the growing demands for political change articulated by Indian politicians. Critical was the need to silence rising nationalist clamour and reward India's War effort with a positive portrayal of British goodwill and the granting of reforms. Northcliffe was astute in pin-pointing the importance of the Muslim question and postwar settlement over the Khalifa as well as the changed nature of the general political climate and the fact that British rule would need to accommodate these forces of change.[104]

Conclusion

Thus the links between the *Mail* and India – symbolised by Northcliffe's two visits – were closer than many would anticipate. However, it remained the case that India itself was often viewed in superficial terms. The eye of the *Mail* was caught by the extremes of opulence and poverty, the fantastical religious beliefs, the crimes and incidents that provided reliably arresting copy. Although there was an awareness of deeper issues, as manifested in coverage of famine and plague, here, too, language and imagery were highly coloured.

Overall the conception of India was dominated by the imperial connection. The *Mail* was confident of the benefits of British rule and optimistic for the future. In Kiplingesque fashion, India was seen as the White Man's Burden – a sphere of duty, sacrifice, and the heroic shedding of blood. The inherent paternalism of this position was evident in its critical line during the famine, when the framework of Government duty appeared to have broken down. In general, however, the paper assumed British rule was a necessary condition for Indian progress; reflecting which, it welcomed the steady, but slow, moves to extending political rights to Indians while it criticised heavy-handed displays of military force. In this the 'new journalism' as represented by the *Mail* and the old journalism of the quality press were at one.

Many of these attitudes reflected those of Northcliffe. As we noted, he was a firm imperialist, for whom the Indian visits reinforced his sense of Britain's selfless service in the imperial cause. Yet by the time of his second visit in the immediate postwar years, tensions within this position were apparent. Northcliffe saw that the educated Indians were not content to wait patiently for responsible government to trickle down, and he resented their willingness to assert their entitlements – in contrast with the paternal approach to government favoured by the British. Northcliffe was shrewd to detect the dichotomy and where it might lead. Together with the heat and dust, this contributed to his gloomy verdict on India in 1921–22. His death a few months after his return to England meant that he escaped a painful process of readjustment.

For the India Office these were years of readjustment too, not simply in imperial politics but in its relationship to Fleet Street and British opinion. Imperial rule depended to an important extent on a monopoly of information and control over its interpretation, both factors which came under pressure due to the inroads of the London press and the communications revolution of the late nineteenth and early twentieth centuries.[105] By the end of the nineteenth century international communications had been transformed by the electric telegraph and the international news communications agencies like Reuters. These broke the government monopoly of information necessary for formulating policies at the time when decisions were taken. The rupture was particularly significant with the coming, from the 1890s, of mass-circulation newspapers directed towards a large class of people who had hitherto been effectively outside the reach of politics.

Spearheaded by the *Mail*, these papers took the discussion of Indian issues beyond the manageable world of the political elite into the emotive realm of general popular feeling. The new breed of pro-prietors, such as Northcliffe, Rothermere and Beaverbrook, were large scale capitalists who sought a mass readership through more populist presentation of the news. The arrival of a mass male elec-torate and the extension of the franchise to women would, it was commonly believed amongst the governing classes, open the door to demagogues and newspaper proprietors who would appeal to the poorly educated and excitable new electors. Significantly, Northcliffe's control both over *The Times*, the most influential quality daily on India, and over the *Mail*, the most successful popular one, along with his pretensions to political power amounting to megalomania, as evidenced during the First World War, appeared to confirm these fears and meant he could not be ignored by imperial politicians.

In seeking to shape and influence the reporting of papers like the *Mail*, the Government adapted techniques conventionally employed for the quality press.[106] Thus James Dunlop-Smith, private secretary to the Viceroy, Lord Minto, described a meeting with H.W. Wilson of the *Mail*, during a visit to England in 1910:

> He is just the sort of man to find in the Daily Mail office... frankly opportunist, and seems to care little for facts, so I had to tackle him on different lines from those I have usually adopted here. I am not altogether proud of my share in our interview, but one has to suit one's weapons to the work in hand.[107]

It was believed at the India Office that *The Times*'s coverage of Indian affairs during 1919 was distorted by the estrangement between Lloyd George and Northcliffe, who was bent on destabilising the Coalition. Sir Thomas Holderness, Chief Under Secretary of State at the India Office, wrote to the Viceroy, Lord Chelmsford, giving his version of events concerning the 'frequent attacks' made in *The Times*

> on the policy of the Government of India, especially in its con-duct of frontier affairs, but latterly also in response [to] the Amritsar shooting affair and other similar incidents in the Punjab. The India Office has also come in for censure...they are annoying and create a prejudice among people who know noth-ing about India...The *Times* has a general 'down' on Lloyd George's Government, due, people say, to Northcliffe's quarrel with the P.M.; and an attack on the Indian Government and the

Secretary of State for India is in accordance with this general policy ... I am also told that there is no central editorial authority at Printing House Square, and that the several leader writers can go their own ways and run their own hobbies, subject to edicts which from time to time Northcliffe sends down from the sick room.[108]

The popular press did not exert a direct influence upon elite opinion formation. Its influence, if it existed, was indirect, exerted *via* the massed numbers of its readers. Northcliffe, for instance, liked to believe that 'his financial and circulation success was balanced by an equal power to influence public and political opinion'.[109] Williams, however, doubts this claim, believing that he voiced rather than formed the political prejudices of his readers.[110] On the other hand, Spender was of the opinion that Northcliffe was 'immensely important, however much solemn people might try to blink or evade the fact. He and his imitators influenced the common mind more than all the Education Ministers put together; of all the influences that destroyed the old politics ... he was by far the most powerful'.[111] Here again perceptions helped to create reality. In Inwood's words, it was 'not the fact that Northcliffe controlled public opinion, but the fact that many politicians thought he did, that gave him his power'. The *Mail* 'did not persuade politicians, but it frightened them, and Northcliffe acquired an influence over those who feared him'.[112]

Notes

1 The title Northcliffe will be used throughout for the sake of consistency.
2 Cited in S. Koss, *The Pro-Boers* (Chicago: University of Chicago Press, 1973), p. xix.
3 R.H. MacDonald, *Language of Empire* (Manchester: Manchester University Press, 1994), p. 2.
4 G.S. Messinger, *British Propaganda and the State in the First World War* (Manchester: Manchester University Press, 1992), p. 13.
5 S.J. Taylor, *The Great Outsiders Northcliffe, Rothermere and the Daily Mail* (London: Victor Gollancz, 1996), p. 46.
6 J.O. Baylen, 'Politics and the New Journalism', in J. Wiener (ed.), *Papers for Millions* (Connecticut: Greenwood Press, 1988), pp. 110–11.
7 J. St. Loe Strachey, *Adventure of Living: a Subjective Biography* (London: Hodder and Stoughton, 1922), p. 298.

8   Gwynne to Lady Bathurst, 27 July 1911, 1990/1/2162, Glenesk Bathurst Collection, Brotherton Library, Leeds.
9   D. Read, 'War News from Reuters', *Despatches*, Autumn, No. 4 (1993); P. Knightely, *The First Casualty, War Correspondents from the Crimea to Vietnam* (London: Deutsch, 1975).
10 J.M. Mackenzie, *Propaganda and Empire* (Manchester: Manchester University Press, 1984), pp. 6–7.
11 J.O. Baylen, 'A Contemporary Estimate of the London Daily Press in the early Twentieth Century', in M. Bromley and T. O'Malley (eds) *A Journalism Reader* (London: Routledge, 1997), p. 93; similarly the *Manchester Guardian* continued to lose circulation till 1907.
12 J.A. Spender, *Life, Journalism and Politics* (London: Cassell and Company Ltd, 1927), Vol. I. p. 224; T.H. Hardman, *A Parliament of the Press* (London, Horace Marshall, 1909).
13 J.D. Startt, *Journalists for Empire* (Connecticut: Greenwood Press, 1991), p. 214.
14 Ibid., pp. 3–4, 207.
15 See Chandrika Kaul, 'Press and Empire: the London Press, Government News, Management and India, *circa* 1900–1922', Unpublished doctoral thesis, University of Oxford, 1999.
16 J.M. Brown, *Winds of Change* (Oxford: Clarendon Press, 1991), p. 12.
17 Mackenzie, *Propaganda and Empire* op. cit., p. 2.
18 Ibid.; also J.M. Mackenzie (ed.), *Imperialism and Popular Culture* (Manchester: Manchester University Press, 1986); H. John Field, *Toward a Programme of Imperial Life* (Oxford: Clio Press, 1982), p. 20. For a comparative perspective see T.G. August, *The Selling of the Empire: British and French Imperialist Propaganda 1890–1940* (Connecticut: Greenwood Press, 1985), which focuses upon direct and indirect official propaganda; W.H. Schenider, *An Empire for the Masses: the French Popular Image of Africa, 1870–1900* (Connecticut: Greenwood Press, 1988).
19 Mackenzie, *Imperialism*, pp. 10–11; K. Castle, *Britannia's Children* (Manchester: Manchester University Press, 1994).
20 Messinger, *British Propaganda*, p. 14.
21 H. Pelling, *Popular Politics and Society* (London: Macmillan, 1968); R. Price, *An Imperial War and the British Working Class* (London: Routledge and Kegan Paul, 1972), pp. 70–135.
22 R. Pound and G. Harmsworth, *Northcliffe* (London: Cassell, 1959), p. 837. The Editor between the years 1899 and 1926 was Thomas Marlowe.
23 Quoted in R. McNair Wilson, *Lord Northcliffe: a Study* (London: E. Benn Ltd, 1927), p. 120.
24 Ibid. p. 125.
25 Ibid. p. 3.
26 A.P. Ryan, *Lord Northcliffe* (London: Collins, 1953), p. 103.
27 Ibid. p. 202.
28 M. Palmer, 'The British Press and International News,' in G. Boyce, J. Curran, and P. Wingate (eds), *Newspaper History from the Seventeenth Century to the Present Day* (London: Constable, 1978), p. 217.

29 Cited in Ryan, pp. 77, 89.
30 *Daily Mail*, 9 November 1904.
31 Ibid.
32 Northcliffe to J. St. Loe Strachey, 22 November 1904, Strachey Papers, S/11/4/15, House of Lords Record Office, London.
33 Northcliffe to Strachey, 18 November 1904, Ibid.
34 J.E. Wrench, *Uphill* (London: 1934), p. 241.
35 Wilson, *Lord Northcliffe: A Study* p. 169.
36 F. Williams, *The Right to Know: the Rise of the World Press* (Harlow: Longmans, 1969), p. 75.
37 Ibid, p. 76
38 Ryan, *Lord Northcliffe*, p. 96.
39 Ryan, *Lord Northcliffe*, p. 113.
40 Williams, *The Right to Know*, p. 77.
41 Cited in T. Clarke, *My Northcliffe Diary* (London: Victor Gollancz Ltd, 1931), p. 197.
42 Chandrika Kaul, 'Press and Empire', p. 74.
43 *Daily Mail*, 4 May 1920.
44 *News in Our Time 1896–1946*, Golden Jubilee Book of the *Daily Mail* (London: Associated Newspapers Ltd, 1946), p. 8.
45 Ibid. p. 6.
46 *Daily Mail*, 1 Jan 1897, editorial.
47 R.W. Desmond, *Press and World Affairs* (New York: D. Appleton-Century Co., 1937), p. 182.
48 J.E. Wrench, *Struggle 1914–1920* (London: Nicholson & Watson, 1935), p. 311.
49 Clarke, *My Northcliffe Dairy*, p. 199.
50 *Daily Mail*, 10 November 1904.
51 *Daily Mail*, 5 May 1908.
52 *Sati* – the burning of widows on the funeral pyre of their husbands, see *Daily Mail*, 9 May 1905.
53 *Daily Mail*, 6 August, 20 and 22 November 1897; January and February 1898, September 7 1899; 11 and 18 May 1908, etc.
54 *Daily Mail*, 22 November 1897.
55 *Daily Mail*, 16 May 1908.
56 *Daily Mail*, 6 January 1897.
57 Ibid.
58 *Daily Mail*, 7 January 1897.
59 *Daily Mail*, 9 January 1897.
60 *Daily Mail*, 12 January 1897.
61 *See coverage in Daily Mail*, January–April 1897.
62 *Daily Mail*, 4 January 1897.
63 *Daily Mail*, 26 August 1897.
64 D. Cannadine, 'The Context, Performance and Meaning of Ritual: The British Monarchy and the "Invention of Tradition", c. 1820–1977', in E. Hobsbawm and T. Ranger (eds), *The Invention of Tradition* (Cambridge: Cambridge University Press, 1983), p. 108.

65 Ibid. pp. 120–4.
66 Mackenzie, *Propaganda and Empire*, p. 5.
67 *Daily Mail*, 8 November 1905.
68 *Daily Mail*, 13 December 1911.
69 Duke of Windsor, *A King's Story* (London: Reprint Society, 1953 edn), p. 167.
70 *Daily Mail*, 26 October 1921.
71 *Daily Mail*, 1 and 29 December 1921.
72 See case study on the tour in Chandrika Kaul, 'Press and Empire', pp. 193–214.
73 J.M. Brown, *Modern India: Origins of an Asian Democracy* (Oxford: Oxford University Press, 1985), p. 217.
74 Chirol to Viceroy, 15 March 1921, MSS Eur F118/10, Reading (Private) Collection, India Office Library, London.
75 *Daily Mail*, 15 December 1921.
76 Kennedy Jones quoted in Taylor, *The Great Outsiders*, p. 37.
77 *Daily Mail*, 6 August 1897.
78 *Daily Mail*, 10 September 1914, 31 January and 21 August 1919, etc.
79 *Daily Mail*, 9 July 1920.
80 *Daily Mail*, 10 September 1914.
81 *Daily Mail*, 21 August 1917.
82 *Daily Mail*, 8 February 1897.
83 *Daily Mail* 9 February 1897.
84 Ibid.
85 *Daily Mail*, 16 February 1897.
86 Ibid.
87 *Daily Mail*, 24 February 1897.
88 Ibid.
89 *Daily Mail*, 8 and 24 February 1897.
90 *Daily Mail*, 23 February 1897.
91 This refers to the libel action brought against the *Mail* and its associated papers by the soapmakers, Lever Brothers, after the former attacked the quality of their products as part of a wider attempt by Northcliffe to resist a proposed 'trust' in the industry.
92 Viceroy to Secretary of State, 12 Jan 1922, MSS Eur D 523/14, Montagu Collection, India Office Library, London.
93 Cecil and St. John Harmsworth (eds), Lord Northcliffe, *My Journey Round the World* (London: John Lane, 1923), p. 235.
94 Viceroy to Secretary of State, 26 January 1922, MSS Eur D 523/14, Montagu Collection, op. Cit.
95 Secretary of State to Viceroy, 1 February 1922, MSS Eur 523/13, Montagu Collection.
96 Northcliffe, *My Journey*, p. 241.
97 T. Clarke, *Northcliffe in History* (London: Hutchinson, 1950), cited in R. Jones, *A Life in Reuters* (London: Hodder & Stoughton, 1951), p. 245.
98 Pound and Harmsworth, *Northcliffe* p. 821; P. Ferris, *The House of Northcliffe* (London: Weidenfeld & Nicolson, 1971), p. 247; Taylor

devoted three lines to Northcliffe's first trip and none to the second, p. 46.
99 Northcliffe, *My Journey*, p. 232.
100 Ibid. p. 237.
101 Ibid.
102 Ibid. p. 250. *Babu* – Indian gentleman.
103 Ibid. pp. 235, 244.
104 *Daily Mail*, 25 January 9 March 1922.
105 See Chandrika Kaul, 'Press and Empire', and 'Imperial Communications, Fleet Street and the Indian Empire, c. 1850–1920s', in Bromley and O'Malley, pp. 58–86; Chandrika Kaul, 'Press and Empire', Chapter 2.
106 Chandrika Kaul, 'A New Angle of Vision: The London Press, Governmental Information Management and the Indian Empire, 1900–1922', *Contemporary Record*, **8**(2), (1994), 213–38; Chandrika Kaul, 'Press and Empire'.
107 Dunlop-Smith to Viceroy, 20 April 1910, MSS Eur F166/9, Dunlop-Smith Collection, India Office Library, London.
108 Holderness to Viceroy, 24 December 1919, MSS Eur E 264/16, Chelmsford Collection, India Office Library, London.
109 F. Williams, *Dangerous Estate* (London: Longmans, 1957), p. 158.
110 Ibid. pp. 129–63.
111 Spender, *Life, Journalism and Politics*, Vol. II, p. 170.
112 S. Inwood, 'The Role of the Press in English Politics during the First World War, with special reference to the period 1914–1916', Unpublished doctoral thesis, Oxford University, 1971, p. 25.

4
'Where there's a tip there's a tap': the Popular Press and the Investing Public, c1900–60

*Dilwyn Porter**

What sells newspapers? Kennedy Jones, the Kelvin MacKenzie of his day and an important editorial influence in the early years of both the *Daily Mail* and the *Daily Mirror*, thought he knew the answer. Wars and state funerals were good for circulation: and it was hard to beat 'a First-class murder'.[1] So it seems a little curious that the popular press, in its pursuit of novelty and human interest, should have paid any attention at all to news of finance. The 'money article', after all, was notoriously dull. Despite the efforts of 'new financial journalists' at the end of the nineteenth century, finance was a difficult subject to popularise. In most turn-of-the-century newspapers it remained the province of the specialist who, in supplying market intelligence, made few concessions to inexpert readers. Would-be small investors, as Ellis Powell of the *Financial News* observed, tended to be 'awfully puzzled' by the technical language of the money article, not to mention the City *argot*. 'As for the brokers and the jobbers, the "stags", "bulls", "bears", and other similar specimens of our animated City life – all these, you say, have completely "moithered" you'.[2]

Yet, although there were reasons to believe that financial journalism would sit uneasily in the popular press, it was there from the start. When the *Daily Mail* went on sale on 4 May 1896, four columns on page two were allocated to finance. An item headed

* The author wishes to acknowledge the support given by the Wincott Foundation which has enabled him to pursue research into the history of financial journalism.

'Advice to Investors' set out the *Mail's* commitment, promising that 'the wants of the small investor will receive particular notice'. Readers were encouraged to write to the City editor who undertook 'to explain technicalities to those who do not understand them'. 'We shall endeavour', the *Mail* continued, 'to interpose between the inexperienced and the loss of their money; but they must get into the way of asking our advice before they act'. Financial coverage in the *Daily Express*, when it first appeared four years later, was on similar lines and from 1903 readers of the *Daily Mirror*, in its first incarnation as a paper designed to appeal especially to women, were treated to a few paragraphs of Stock Exchange news. It would have been no surprise, however, if an item, albeit in bold type, headed 'THE STOCK EXCHANGE BUOYANT' had seemed less compelling than the adjacent 'JEALOUS WOMAN'S GIFT: SENDS HER RIVAL TWO VIPERS IN A JEWEL CASE'.[3]

If journalism, as Jones liked to observe, was merely 'a branch of commerce' then it followed that the money article had to pay its way. News from the City secured its niche in the popular press because it was profitable. In particular, it helped the *Mail* and other new titles to attract a share of the advertising revenue generated by Britain's expanding corporate sector. The benefits to be derived from this source had become apparent even before the advent of the *Mail*. The *Star*, a London evening paper, had surged into profit in 1889 on a wave of financial publicity generated by its City article. Advertising copy in the form of prospectuses for new share issues and 'paid-for' company meeting reports, 'poured into the office'.[4] The proliferation of joint stock companies, which continued in fits and starts through to 1914, underpinned the expansion of financial coverage in the press generally. Its scale should not be underestimated. As the new issue boom of 1910–13 ran its course the *Times* alone carried 2 897 advertisements inviting public subscriptions; the *Mail's* City coverage in the same period often stretched to two pages to accommodate prospectuses and other company publicity.[5] Although financial advertising was relatively less important in the popular press new titles, like the *Mail*, had to take the City seriously. They could not afford to turn their backs on a significant source of revenue.

Awareness that the number of small investors was growing was also important in securing the commitment of the popular dailies to some form of financial journalism. The *Mail*, as Salisbury claimed,

might have been run 'by office boys for office boys' but it was increasingly likely that clerks and other lower middle-class readers would
have some reason to scan the latest City prices. Low denomination
shares at a pound or even ten shillings fully-paid had been commonplace from the 1880s onwards as company promoters sought to
attract new investors. It no doubt remained true, as Charles Duguid
suggested in 1901, that 'for many thousands of newspaper readers
the money article and the City page on which it appears is so much
wasted space' but there was a significant and growing minority who
took an interest. 'These people are nowadays to be found', he wrote,
'not only among those who go down to the City in motor-cars, but
also among clergymen, country town shopkeepers and others of
almost every sort and occupation who have discovered that the science of money is really supremely interesting'. One estimate, in
1906, placed the number of individuals holding marketable securities at around 250 000. Each bull market thereafter tended to raise
the number of private investors and, it seems likely, the number of
readers with an interest in financial news and comment. There were
probably 2.0 to 2.5 million individual shareholders by the 1960s.[6]

The 'New Financial Journalism', imported from New York by Harry
Marks when he founded the *Financial News* in 1884, cemented the
link between the press and what Powell called 'the modern investing public'. Making use of short, cross-headed paragraphs, often sea-
soned with sardonic wit, the *News* indicated ways in which useful
information might be conveyed to readers who were relatively unfamiliar with the City and its business. There was also a mission,
somewhat imperfectly fulfilled by the *News* as it turned out, which
appeared to address the requirements of private investors. Marks
had aimed, he later recalled, to establish a journal 'conducted on
behalf of the many who buy investments rather than of the few
who manufacture them'.[7] The influence of New Financial Journalism
spread through the London press in the 1890s and 1900s, dovetail-
ing with the transformation initiated by Harmsworth. 'By reason of
its very nature', Duguid noted in 1903, 'the City page may always be
the dullest and most forbidding in the paper but it is rapidly becoming less so'.[8] Even before the advent of the *Mail* those who wrote
about stocks and shares had found a way of addressing a wider public.

Thus, by the 1890s, as Britain's popular press began to emerge, the
expansion of the corporate sector had generated a corresponding

increase in the number of individual shareholders. At the same time the New Financial Journalism made it possible for the press to reach out to an investing public which was much more broadly based than it had been in the mid-nineteenth century. The foundations of a lasting relationship between the popular press and the investing public were in place. This imposed special responsibilities on journalists who had to recognise that many readers were inclined to make investment decisions on the basis of what they saw in the papers. In 1959, asked to identify 'who or what' had persuaded them that it would be 'a good thing' to buy shares, 42 per cent of shareholders sampled pointed to the press.[9] Moreover, it was clear that readers came to trust financial journalists to an extent that was 'remarkable'. This ran 'across the board – from the widow in Bournemouth to the institutional fund manager in the City'.[10] The intention here is to survey the financial coverage offered by popular daily newspapers in the first half of the twentieth century. What kind of financial news service did they provide for their readers? How well did they serve the investing public, especially those of limited experience and relatively modest means?

Financial journalists in the early years of the century, even those who worked for specialist papers, were aware that they were addressing an expanding audience, 'its personnel numbered by hundreds of thousands and representing every class of society except the absolutely destitute'.[11] They were also very conscious of the risks attached to investment at a time when 'the amount of investor protection on offer was nugatory, with the underlying assumption of the market remaining the bracing, *caveat emptor*, "let the buyer beware"'.[12] Banks and building societies were often not what they seemed and those who sought a secure home for their capital in stocks and shares often learned the hard way that London's largely self-regulated financial sector was 'the company-monger's elysium'. In the 1890s and early 1900s, as markets rode the switchback of boom and slump, there were ample opportunities for those with inside information to profit at the expense of outsiders. 'The fact is', wrote two stock market insiders, 'that the company-promoting clique is small, rich and unscrupulous, while the investor is completely lacking in any sort of organisation in his own defence'.[13] It did not help that small investors were inclined to be gullible, especially when they cast caution aside on a rising market. In these circumstances those who compiled the City pages in popular newspapers were obliged to do rather more than simply report what was happening. They were also required to guide and protect their readers, supplying them with information and advice which might place them on a more equal footing with City insiders.

By the mid-1890s exploitation of outsiders was causing significant concern. Too many companies were being created simply for the purpose of fleecing the unsophisticated investor, 'the struggling parson, the widow or spinster of slender means, and that large number of persons who, having appearances to keep up on inadequate incomes, are obliged to hide their losses and their sufferings'.[14] Public concern peaked in November 1898 when Lord Chief Justice Russell, on an official visit to the City, seized the opportunity to protest against declining standards of commercial morality.[15] Financial journalism, as Duguid and other contemporaries argued, might help stem this tide but there was a major difficulty in that the press was perceived to be part of the problem. It was not just that a debased form of journalism flourished in 'bucket shop' papers published by rogue financiers seeking to create markets for worthless shares. There was also the unfortunate publicity generated by high-profile bankruptcy cases, like that of the company promoter Edward Hooley, which suggested that the favourable opinions of financial journalists at all levels were a purchasable commodity. The *Financial News*, for example, was attracting a good deal of criticism in this respect.[16] If the City pages of the popular papers were to satisfy 'the wants of the small investor', it would be necessary to establish standards of conduct which few of their specialist contemporaries adhered to systematically.

This may help to explain the somewhat conservative aspect of City coverage in popular dailies before 1914. The *Mail*'s first money article, headed simply 'THE CITY', was not unlike that to be found in the *Times*, essentially a record of the previous day's price movements in paragraph form with minimal concessions to readers unfamiliar with market shorthand. 'Grand Trunks felt the full force of the bad March statement, and lost severely in price; but there was little selling and the decline was in the nature of marking down'. A rather half-hearted attempt was made to dramatise the day's dealings in 'Chartereds' (British South Africa Company) but, 'as neither buyers nor sellers of moment put in an appearance', this did not make for lively copy. The most innovative feature was the column headed 'CHAT ON 'CHANGE' which ran alongside the money article. Here market intelligence was relayed in such a way as to convince readers that information was being passed on by an insider. Thus, though the March statement which had depressed Grand Trunks had been 'as bad as it could be...let it be remembered that the new manager only got to work in April'.[17] This format, balancing the formalities of the conventional money article with market gossip, was also favoured by the *Express* after 1900. By 1914 *Express* reports from the money market and the stock market were appearing as 'IN LOMBARD STREET' and 'IN THE HOUSE' respectively, reinforcing the impression that inside information was being conveyed.

The first City article published by the *Express* was indicative of the difficulties facing the reporter who sought to flavour his copy with human interest. Share prices had fallen on the previous day's trading; 'in the case of American rails the fall amounted to a semi-panic'. The *Express*, however, could find 'no particular reason' to explain these events beyond 'realisations before the account'.[18] Readers on the Clapham omnibus could have been forgiven if this left them unenlightened and unmoved. Financial coverage in the *Daily Mirror*, though less extensive, was more successful in finding a human angle. A Stock Exchange 'hammering', for example, was reported sympathetically:

> Sometimes, of course, these Stock Exchange failures cause a good deal of trouble, for the stocks held speculatively by the unfortunate member who finds himself in difficulties have to be sold... Happily, Saturday's failure was a mere trifle...the unfortunate member concerned being a dealer in quite an unimportant way in American rails.[19]

The *Mirror*, as originally conceived, was Harmsworth's big mistake, prospering only after it was relaunched as an illustrated daily in 1904. Its new format permitted only minimal coverage of finance. For the restyled *Mirror* the annual Stock Exchange walk from London to Brighton was both more photogenic and more newsworthy than the everyday business of the City.[20] Its main rival as an illustrated daily, Edward Hulton's *Daily Sketch*, started in 1909, showed more interest. Though its 'MONEY MATTERS' article, supplied by 'Contango', consisted of no more than a few paragraphs insignificantly placed, it took the trouble to provide a formal summary of price movements before passing on to insider gossip. 'West African are a very good market, and the fact that Consolidated Goldfields... and other well-to-do African houses are interesting themselves in this field, makes it advisable to follow their lead'.[21] The *Sketch*, from the very start, was not shy when it came to a tip.

Financial journalists, as Powell observed, were primarily concerned with 'writing contemporary financial history'. But, by the start of the twentieth century, they had come to realise that more was required. 'Since not all the interested parties will possess the knowledge or the capacity rightly to appreciate the significance of what is going on there arises the necessity for guidance in the shape of comment, criticism and forecast'.[22] Though there were problems connected with advising the public in this fashion – not least the greater possibilities it afforded for corruption – it was a function which journalists in the popular press performed from the start, mainly in relation to company news. There was, noted the *Express* in its first number, 'an agreeable air of bona-fides about the prospectus of the Johnson-Lundell Electric Traction Company which is not always present in new issues'; the views of Lord Kelvin 'and other experts in the electrical world' added strength to its claims. This type of recommendation was commonplace. Replies to queries, published daily in the advice columns of both the *Mail* and the *Express*, were another important source of advice for small investors. This feature expanded and became an important item on the *Mail*'s City page within weeks of its debut, sometimes containing thirty or more gobbets of wisdom.

AFRICAN ESTATES (M.A.W., Stafford):- We do not recommend these shares, and we cannot undertake to quote them...
URUGUAY NEW LOAN (Small Investor, Norwood):- You may apply for a moderate number of this stock in safety.[23]

Though invented 'answers' to hypothetical 'queries' were not unknown, the cautious tone suggests a serious attempt to provide a useful service for individual readers. Replies in the *Express* were especially circumspect, often conveying a message that could have been fully understood only by the correspondent concerned.[24] In this way the City editor personalised the service while simultaneously circumventing any possible impropriety.

Contact with readers, either directly by letter or through the advice column, was part and parcel of financial journalism at all levels. 'Reader's queries' were 'frequent', noted Wynnard Hooper of the *Times* in 1910.[25] They tended to enhance awareness of the unique burden of responsibility falling on those journalists who took it upon themselves to offer advice to investors. The knowledge that 'replies' were sometimes devised to stimulate demand for a particular security added point to routine protestations of integrity.[26] Harmsworth, ennobled in 1905, was especially anxious that the *Mail* should be beyond reproach and signalled this clearly by recruiting Duguid as City editor in 1906, ordering him to 'make a page that is independent and interesting'.[27] Among all the practitioners of the new financial journalism Duguid had been foremost in articulating ethical guidelines, declaring unequivocally that 'the first qualification of the City editor is integrity'.[28] Under Duguid, who was given his own byline, those who looked to the *Mail* for advice were on relatively safe ground. Northcliffe, hovering anxiously, supplied a further guarantee. This was, perhaps, most evident in 1913 when he took steps to persuade Reuters to abandon its City advertising agency, fearing that a major source of financial news was about to be compromised by disguised advertisements and puffery.[29] It was important, Duguid explained on behalf of his employer 'to avoid any misconception as to the entire independence of the editorial columns'.[30]

Although the extent of corruption in the financial press probably declined in the years before the First World War it remained wise to be cautious. One handbook for the small investor, published in 1913, went so far as to suggest that he was best advised to make decisions regarding the purchase of stocks and shares 'without permitting himself to be influenced by what he reads about them in the press'.[31] The success of the '*Daily Mail* Stock Exchange', a regular feature from June 1912 until the early days of the war, indicated, nevertheless, that Duguid's efforts to secure the confidence of the small investor had not been wasted. It was a brilliant piece of opportunism that cashed in on the reluctance of small investors to pay broker's commission at the rates then prevailing and their general dissatisfaction with the Stock Exchange and its 'cumbersome machinery'. For a nominal 'announcement fee' and a modest commission (only five shillings for transactions under £100) small investors were able to use the *Mail's* columns to trade directly with each other.[32] There were some difficulties regarding non-completion of transactions and, more seriously, announcements by sharepushers masquerading as private investors, an intrusion which caused Northcliffe to impose more stringent conditions than Duguid thought necessary. It seems clear, however, that the venture prospered. According to Duguid in October 1913, it was 'bringing in a clear hundred a week'.[33] The flood of small investor advertising continued; an estimated 80 000 announcements had been published by August 1914 when the *Mail's* Stock Exchange had its finest hour. With the London markets temporarily closed at the outbreak of war there was 'no Stock Exchange to chat on'. In these difficult times, as Duguid reminded his readers, the *Mail* was 'the only organisation for the exchange of securities which is left open'.[34]

The First World War almost silenced the financial press. With the stock market closed until January 1915 and subject to strict Treasury regulation thereafter there was little to report. It seems likely, nevertheless, that the total number of investors grew between 1914 and 1918 as patriotic savers bought government securities. 'War loans', noted the first *Sunday Express* within weeks of the armistice, 'have proved the finest advertisement the Stock Exchange has ever had'. 'Many hundreds of thousands of people with capital', it continued, 'have for the first time in their lives interested themselves in investment'.[35] The hope was that this new type of small investor would develop a more general interest in securities. In the meantime cross-headings such as 'WAR LOAN STOCK ADVANCE' reflected the changed priorities of the investing public. When restrictions on new issues were lifted in March 1919 the popular press reflected the City's delight. 'Another shackle gone!' boomed the *Daily Express*, which was in the forefront of the campaign to roll back the state. Investors could now support home industries 'without the irritating and inexplicable interference of a modern Star Chamber'.[36]

The floodgates opened to a wave of company promotion, much of it speculative, with new issue advertisements in the *Times* totalling 548 in 1919 and 556 in 1920. Although this receded, a second wave in the late 1920s helped to draw in more investors while underpinning further expansion of financial coverage in the press generally.[37] 'We have certainly got a new class of savers and investors', observed Hartley Withers at the end of the decade. 'We have also got a new class of speculators', he added, 'fed on financial tips furnished by an enterprising press'.[38]

In addressing their readers the City pages of the popular dailies tended to follow the pattern established before 1914 in an expanded form. Finance featured in the *Sunday Express* from 1918 and had been restored to the *Daily Mirror* by the end of the 1920s with two half-columns offering advice on 'HOW TO INVEST YOUR MONEY'. The approach was a little more relaxed than before the war. Sometimes the *Mail*'s 'Chat on 'Change' ran a light-hearted paragraph which would not have been out of place elsewhere in the paper. As, for example, on 1 February 1919 when it reported that 'for the first time in the history of the Stock Exchange, as far as anyone seems to recall, its portals were entered yesterday by a dog'. The interloper was black '(which they say means luck) and he had a look at the Chartered, the Rubber and the Miscellaneous markets'. This informality owed something to the bond which had developed between financial journalists and their readers over the previous twenty years or so. When Duguid left journalism for a post in the City in 1920 the *Financial News* observed that 'the great financial public' was now 'almost on personal terms with the men who, as editors of financial dailies and as City editors of political newspapers, cater for their needs day by day'. Duguid and his colleagues were not only liked but also trusted.[39]

The 'great financial public' remained in need of reliable guides, friends they could trust. It was not just that investment conditions became more difficult after 1929; there was also the continuing problem of fraudulent finance and, in particular, the traps set for the unwary by unscrupulous 'bucketeers'. The years spanning the slump and before the Prevention of Fraud (Investments) Act of 1939, as one City sage later recalled, were 'the heyday of the bucket-shop keeper'.[40] Small investors were especially vulnerable. 'As a rule', observed Hargreaves Parkinson of the *Economist*, 'the customers of bucket-shops are found among people of limited means, in humble walks of life, who have patiently saved for the proverbial "rainy day", and are attracted by the prospect of extremely high returns'.[41]

Financial journalists continued to warn against such perils and the popular press played its part, often prompted by intelligence from readers. 'Judging by numerous letters we receive', observed the *Mail* in 1919, 'the fraternity that issues circulars inviting subscriptions for "operating trusts" and other such blind pools and get-rich-quick schemes is pursuing its trade with advanced vigour'. Readers were advised 'to consign all such literature to the waste-paper basket or send it to the police'.[42] It seems probable that blanket warnings of this kind were less likely to influence the behaviour of small investors than cautionary tales, of which there were many. 'ANGRY WOMEN AT CITY COMPANY MEETING DEMAND THEIR PIGS' headlined a report on a meeting of the creditors of Little Wadhurst Farms Limited which went into liquidation in 1929. The company had issued 50 000 certificates at £3 each entitling the shareholder to the ownership of a pig that would later be sold at a profit. When only 2 400 pigs could be found the company crashed, '... there being a deficiency of nearly 48 000 pigs'. It was, observed the *Mail*, 'the end of a dream of vast profits in pork, and hundreds of men and women, who thought they owned pigs, came to the meeting to try and save their bacon'. Such stories had obvious human interest, they were instructive and they often gave the newspaper a chance to say 'We told you so'. *Mail* readers had been warned months before that it would all end in tears and that the company's 'Redeemable First Mortgage Debentures in Piggeries (No 1) Limited' were to be avoided.[43]

Investors in stocks and shares in the 1920s, provided that they bought wisely, had the advantage of a rising market. London prices almost trebled between 1922 and 1929 and the prevailing outlook was optimistic. 'Now everybody is a potential investor or speculator, with the balance in favour of a speculative tinge', commented the *Financial Times* as late as January 1929.[44] Those who looked to the financial pages of the popular press for advice on what to buy would not have been disappointed. In the *Mail* and the *Express*, though the essential structure of the prewar page remained, the content was gradually modified to accommodate the ubiquitous tip. Paragraphs of City gossip in the *Mail* were, by the late 1920s, increasingly likely to appear under the heading 'WHAT INVESTORS ARE BUYING' and to conclude with an unambiguous recommendation. Similarly, in the *Express*, 'WHAT THE MARKET SAYS' was supplemented by notes for investors supplied by 'Ellessdee'. Oscar Hobson, then at the *Financial News* and a stickler for propriety, viewed this development with alarm, regarding it as one of the 'less creditable' developments of postwar journalism. What he objected to was not 'the carefully considered and properly qualified recommendation by a writer of judgement and experience'; he was more concerned with the blatant 'market tip' which might generate a short-lived speculative bubble. 'The large circulation papers in particular', he added pointedly, 'sometimes found the temptation to ill-considered tipping hard to resist, because with their countless readers almost any tip is assured of a Pyrrhic success'.[45] Hobson probably had more reason to worry about the *Sketch* in this respect than the *Mail* or *Express*. Moreover, financial news in the *Sketch* often appeared to relate almost exclusively to the companies that advertised in its columns. Its 'HINTS TO INVESTORS' feature on 5 March 1929, for example, largely comprised complimentary puffs for Watney's debentures and the ordinary shares of Trowbridge Tyre and Rubber. It was bracketed by the relevant prospectus advertisements and helpfully drew the attention of the reader to the application forms printed on the same page. This was not so much financial journalism as undiluted public relations.

Debentures were almost certainly a better buy for most investors in 1929, the year that Wall Street crashed and ordinary share prices in London lurched into a three-year slide. The crash itself, a series of dramatic falls towards the end of October was widely reported in Britain's popular press in terms that could only have made readers rather nervous, especially as the initial collapse was attributed to 'scare-selling by small investors throughout the States'. It could not have helped that the word 'panic' was so freely deployed or that the tragic circumstances of ruined investors caught in the fall-out supplied the principal element of human interest. 'Panic conditions prevailed in the brokerage offices', ran a typical *Mail* report from Montreal, 'where red-faced men and sobbing women struggled to save something from the wreckage'.[46] The London Stock Exchange was badly shaken by the collapse but serious damage was confined to traders who specialised in 'Americans'. There was a tendency, reflected in the financial press generally, to take a rather superior view of what an *Express* leader called 'frenzied finance', the over-speculation which had undermined Wall Street. The crash, it seemed, was a severe but necessary adjustment from which it was possible to derive some hope for the future. A front-page article by the City editor, entitled 'WHAT THE SLUMP MEANS TO BRITAIN', developed this point in a reassuring fashion.

> Apart from the speculative losses the slump in America will be beneficial ... The immediate result of the slump will be a further improvement in the value of the pound sterling as measured in dollars, a demand for fixed interest securities and bonds both here and in America, and eventually cheaper money and a reduction in the Bank rate.

A few days later, while reports of further disasters were still arriving from New York, the *Express*, in its City notes, was drawing attention to 'an increasing disposition on the part of British investors to buy back some of the more popular issues after their heavy falls'.[47]

In the circumstances of October 1929 this was bold speculation rather than prudent investment. It was some time before prices recovered sufficiently to show any prospect of capital gain. The fall was less precipitous in London than in New York but there was no significant upturn until late in 1932. Gone, at least temporarily, were the days when everybody had been a potential investor. One sign of the times was the BBC's decision in mid-1932 to suspend its stock market closing report which now interested only 'an extremely small proportion of listeners'.[48] As companies slashed their publicity budgets the advertising revenue on which newspapers relied was significantly reduced. Trade journals were inclined to ask if the financial press would survive.[49] The money pages of the popular newspapers were probably under less pressure than the specialist titles in this respect as they could be cross-subsidised from general advertising revenue attracted by other sections of the paper. They tended to be a little more conservative in their recommendations than previously as those small investors left in the market were now more inclined towards debentures and preference shares. But there was still room for the inspired tip, arguably a more valuable commodity when markets were depressed. The *Sketch* did not disappoint readers who sought the light of opportunity amidst the encircling gloom. Market intelligence indicated that local government boundaries on the south coast were to be readjusted.

'You won't be disappointed if you are a holder of Bournemouth and Poole Electricity Supply shares ... At the current price, 61s 6d, a purchase ought to prove a profitable investment'.[50] After 1932, as prices recovered and confidence revived, the popular press responded to the changed mood. Coverage tended to expand and City insiders with the knack of turning a pithy paragraph were much in demand. Donald Cobbett, who began his career as a clerk with a firm of jobbers in 1933, soon learned how to supplement his income by 'fragmentary scribbling plus a weekly City column in the *Catholic Herald*'.[51] As in the period before 1914, growth of advertising revenue underpinned the development of financial journalism in general. The unit trust movement, initiated by Municipal and General Securities (M&G) in 1931, was especially important here. By the mid-1930s around seventy trusts had been launched and 12 per cent of all expenditure on financial advertising in the press was from this source.[52] It was natural, given the experience of 1929–32, that investors should look for ways to spread their risk. The City pages helped to promote unit trusts as a means to this end, especially after 1935 when it became possible for fund managers to shake off the constraints imposed on the original 'fixed' trusts. In 1939, for example, the *Mirror* adopted a very positive tone when reporting that unit holders in the Universal Fixed Trust had accepted a conversion offer which would permit the fund to be managed more actively. Its City editor used the story to draw attention 'to the popularity of this form of investment with the public'. [53]

Competition amongst newspapers for middle-class readers intensified. The *Daily Telegraph* moved downmarket in 1930, cutting its price to 1d; almost simultaneously the *News Chronicle* emerged from the union of the *Daily News* and the *Daily Chronicle* with a coherent appeal to readers of a centre-left political persuasion. The *Mail*, although it lost ground, mainly to the *Express*, retained its attraction for a significant group of middle-class readers, especially outside London.[54] Financial news, in these circumstances, had its role in the struggle to gain or secure market share. It was important to provide something every morning for readers like the schoolmaster, an early client of M&G, and his staff-room colleagues who liked 'to look up the companies these trusts were invested in'. 'It gave you an interest', he explained.[55] Interested readers saw the last traces of the nineteenth-century money article disappear as rival newspapers fought for their attention in an overcrowded market. It became fashionable, in the popular papers, to address them more directly. City editors abandoned their anonymity and, in the *Express*, closing prices were now listed under the headline 'HOW YOUR SHARES START TODAY'. In the *Mail* the daily state-of-the-market report was reduced to a few lines and boxed in for those who wanted to take in 'The Stock Exchange at a Glance'.

> Weak at first, but sharp rebound in 'street' dealings. Some stocks higher on the day.

Here, for 'the busy man', was a snapshot of the market on a day which had been transformed, late in the afternoon, by the news that Chamberlain was to fly to Munich. Having glanced at this summary it was more than likely that he would have wanted to read on; indeed it would have been hard to ignore the main story by L.D. Williams, the *Mail's* City editor, headlined 'STREET MARKETS ABLAZE ON MUNICH NEWS: BIG RISES'.[56] The remodelled City page in the *Express*, edited by Stewart Gillies, was, perhaps, the most successful version of the new look. It included a bold, boxed summary with an arresting heading, such as 'MARKETS SPURT', followed by a short paragraph and a simple table indicating how popular shares had moved. The layout of closing prices was probably easier for the uninitiated reader than the list of the day's runners and riders to be found on the racing page.

'Peace in our time' did not cut ice for long in the City or amongst those who reported its affairs in the popular press. Although there were great hopes of 'further political appeasement in Europe', noted Williams in the *Mail*, 'there is still no expectation that it will be possible to take more than a comparatively short view'. While the cheers still echoed, Bernard Harris in the *Sunday Express* was recommending Mather and Platt £1 Ordinary, 'a sound investment' at 43s, on the basis of 'increased activity in the fire engineering section following the speed-up of A.R.P. plans'.[57] A year later, in September 1939, the main concern of City editors was to spread reassurance as the crisis deepened. The news that Prudential Assurance, had deferred an interim dividend payment would, it was acknowledged, 'come as a shock to both shareholders and investors'. It was possible,

Mirror readers were informed, that evacuation plans provided a simple explanation; whatever the reason, there could be 'no doubt concerning the financial strength of the company'. The temporary closure of the Stock Exchange was reported in a similar fashion; it was an inconvenience but it would pass. Brokers and jobbers had made emergency arrangements, noted the *Mirror*, in what was to be its last City article for many years. 'There should, therefore, be some form of a market in securities, but naturally it will be a narrow one for a time'.[58] This was not quite 'business as usual' but it addressed the immediate anxieties of those who had money tied up in stocks and shares. In 1939–40, as the war news worsened, it became more difficult to find a positive angle although the *Sketch*, which continued to supply financial notes in an abbreviated form, was inclined to look for the silver lining. While its news pages reported the horrors that the *Luftwaffe* had brought to the Netherlands ('WOMEN DIE AS BOMBS LEVEL HOMES'), readers were advised to hold on:

> the start of the Blitzkreig supports the view that this will be a shorter war than has hitherto been expected, and as there is complete confidence in the final outcome, investors are likely to refrain from heavy selling.[59]

By the end of the 1930s financial coverage in the popular daily press had been modernised. In appearance, the City pages of the *Mail* and the *Express* more closely resembled what was to come than what had gone before. The war put a temporary brake on further development; 'the financial press died a death, metaphorically if not literally'.[60] With the markets subject to close regulation and new issues severely restricted there was often little to report and little in the way of advertising revenue. A restricted supply of newsprint added to this catalogue of woe. This may not have been entirely disadvantageous. Oscar Hobson, City editor at the *News Chronicle* from 1935, always 'aimed to write simply on every subject however complex'. According to Richard Fry of the *Manchester Guardian*, who admired Hobson greatly, 'war-time paper rationing at the *News Chronicle* further compressed and clarified his style'.[61] Hobson's daily 700-word piece was, indeed, a model of lucidity although he was allowed more scope than City editors in other popular newspapers. A typical week's contributions might focus on topics ranging from the shares of Austin Motors to trade with Belgium, with an essay 'On Economic Freedom' thrown in for good measure. In the *Mail* Williams was usually limited to three or four paragraphs of City news, about 500 words in total, and a short list of shares which had moved significantly.

Though the press welcomed the swift implementation of emergency controls at the start of the war City editors soon began to reflect the underlying sentiment of a financial sector accustomed to free markets and self-regulation. 'Complaints about controls of one sort or another are pouring in', the *Express* reported on 20 October 1939; 'the situation becomes serious'. The context in which financial journalists worked had certainly changed. Contacts with City insiders, valued before the war as sources of market intelligence, were now less important than briefings by ministers and their public relations specialists. There was a danger in wartime, as Fry observed in February 1945, 'that the press, in its efforts to explain the nature of the war effort, might become a mouthpiece of the authorities'. He was confident, however, that this had not happened; 'independent criticism has not disappeared'. The attachment of most financial journalists to the City and its robust market culture tended to insulate them from uncritical adherence to the official line. At best, the wartime state and the high levels of taxation that came with it were seen as unfortunate necessities; at worst, they were the thin end of a socialist wedge and the first step on the road to public ownership. The financial press sought to address the needs of investors by reporting such market activity as there was while keeping a critical eye on the implementation of controls. In this respect 'the watch of the press', according to Fry, was 'almost as helpful as the system of parliamentary questions in preventing mistaken policies from becoming permanent'.[62]

The Labour landslide of 1945 shocked the City. 'SHARE PRICES SLUMP: CLOSE AT LOWEST' was the headline with which the *Mail*'s City page greeted the New Jerusalem. 'Obviously', it explained, 'the election results are acutely disappointing from a Stock Exchange point of view'; almost the first response was to mark down 'shares liable to be affected by nationalisation proposals'. At the same time investors were nudged towards the idea that they could learn to live with a majority Labour government:

> But in a short time investment business is likely to revive and even expand again. The new Government will require 'cheap' money as much as the old, and a maintenance of high gilt-edged prices will help to keep equities up, while the economic trend will be inflationary for the time being, and that favours the equity holder.[63]

Though it was not always easy to take an upbeat view of market prospects this tone prevailed in the City pages of the popular press in the late 1940s despite nationalisation and all that it entailed for the private investor. The opposition to Labour's plans, at least before 1948, was generally somewhat muted; Morgan argues that 'the champions of private enterprise had only limited zest for the fight'.[64] This probably underestimates the role of the *Financial Times* but, as far as City editors in the popular press were concerned, there was little space, with newsprint still rationed, for a general assault on Labour and all its works. They concentrated instead on their core business – reporting on the financial sector and making use of informed judgement to advise readers on investment.

'And if Labour after all comes back?' Hobson, writing on the eve of the 1951 general election, 'could find no-one in the City willing to visualise so unpleasant a contingency'.[65] This time they were not to be disappointed though, even under the Conservatives, it was several years before markets were free of the constraints imposed during the 1940s. By the late 1950s, however, the climate for investment had been transformed and the demand for equities was booming. 'Full employment and high wage levels', it was noted in the *Accountant*, 'have helped to open the gates of the Stock Exchange to a vast number of small investors'. At the same time unit trusts, free again to raise new capital, were offering a range of financial products designed for 'a wider target market than in pre-war days – from the comfortable middle class to the new investor of the 1950s who was characterised by smaller holdings and who had previously shown no desire to go into Stock Exchange securities'. [66] As advertising revenue soared the preconditions for a great leap forward in popular financial journalism fell into place.

The demand for investment information increased rapidly, both in the popular form suitable for small individual investors and in the sophisticated form required by specialist investment managers. At the same time more advertising revenue became available, and this in turn justified publishers in employing more and better financial writers.[67]

The popular press, with the exception of the *Sketch*, responded to the new situation. Those who aspired to write for the City pages learned 'to go for "stories" rather than essays, and to write fast'.[68]

What was striking about popular financial journalism at this time was the excitement and urgency that it brought to topics once considered dull and obscure. There was also a proselytising tone as it sought to convince readers of the benefits of popular capitalism. 'This is the age of the small investor', declared the *News Chronicle* on 25 January 1960. 'More people are investing than ever before, and the movement is going to grow'. The money page in the *Sunday Express*, now headed 'EDWARD WESTROPP IN THE CITY', embodied the key characteristics of the new approach. Westropp's article on 7 February 1960 ('HOW I'D MAKE THAT £5000 G-R-O-W') was centre page, hemmed in, on both sides by financial advertising. It recounted, for the benefit of all readers, the advice given to Mrs Rudd, winner of the paper's recent 'Road to Fortune' competition, 'as we celebrated her success with a champagne lunch in the Gloster Hotel at Cowes'. He then picked five shares likely to appreciate substantially over eighteen months 'although they may wobble about in the meantime'. These included 'my old favourite P&O – a very suitable choice, I might remark for a sailor's wife'. There were a few paragraphs of City news with an emphasis on personalities and an item headed '£100 TO INVEST' aimed at the very small saver. Curiously, space was found at the foot of the page for 'THE STARS AND YOU'. Geminis were advised to 'play for safety in money matters'.

Adjustment to the new condition of affluence was easier for newspapers that leaned to the political right. For the *Mirror* it was more difficult.[69] It had abandoned its City article in 1939 and made little effort thereafter to discourage readers from believing that high finance was not for them. 'IF I HAD A FORTUNE', a feature based on readers' letters in 1950, was indicative.

Thirty thousand pounds! I should be scared stiff if I had half that. I don't think I could sleep or eat. What a worry! No, just give me Father's fiver on Fridays as always and I'll be satisfied.[70]

By 1960, however, there were a number of indications that the *Mirror* was coming to terms with working-class affluence. The clearest signal was the appointment of a City editor, Derek Dale, recruited from the *Evening Standard* to supply a major weekly feature on finance. There had been, it was noted, 'a revolution in the savings habits of Britain'; the City was no longer 'the exclusive domain of Big Money'. The people's paper underlined its interest in popular capitalism with a strip cartoon, 'Keeping Up With The Joneses', described as 'a daring new idea in financial journalism', in which 'Uncle Forsyte' explained the mysteries of investment to 'Joe and Prudence Hope'. Dale, who had edited a breezy and personality-packed page at the *Standard*, reached out and grabbed *Mirror* readers by the metaphorical lapel, demanding the attention of 'the cloth-cap investor'.

All right. All right. So many of you have had a lot of fun and made a lot of money playing the market.
But pay heed. I warn you bluntly.
THE HONEYMOON IN STOCK MARKETS IS MOST CERTAINLY OVER FOR THE TIME BEING.[71]

The style was conversational, knowing and direct, not unlike Patrick Sergeant in the *Mail* who wrote, according to Fry, 'like a Dutch uncle, giving good advice to men and women concerned with improving their savings by intelligent investment'.[72] Contemporary observers were in no doubt that the *Mirror's* 'leap into the City' was an important development. For Paul Bareau, the editorial decision to drop 'Jane' in favour of 'the Joneses' indicated that 'a memorable and highly significant milestone [had been] passed – highly significant given the faithful reflection of popular taste which that newspaper provides'. [73] It supplies a convenient point from which to assess the development of popular financial journalism over the previous sixty years.

There was a significant difference between the role of financial journalists writing for popular newspapers in 1960 and that of their counterparts at the turn of the century. Both undertook to report on the financial sector in accessible language and to advise their readers but, in addition, mid-twentieth-century journalists were concerned with promoting the idea of investment, especially amongst people who previously, if they had any savings at all, would have ventured no further than the Post Office Savings Bank. This is why financial journalism became so ubiquitous in the early 1960s, resurfacing in the *Mirror* and popping up in the most unlikely places. It was to be found, for example, in *Honey*, a magazine aimed at young women in their teens, alongside 'I'M ASHAMED OF MY MOTHER', 'HOT DOG, IT'S A SAUSAGE PARTY' and other delights. Readers were reminded that it was possible to invest as little as £3 a month in a unit trust and encouraged to join *Honey* Investment Clubs.[74] The point was that teenagers who brought *Honey*, like many of their parents, were for the first time sufficiently affluent to consider investing their savings in stocks and shares, unit trusts and other financial products. Given the importance of financial advertising revenue to the newspapers that employed them it was only natural that City editors, like Dale in the *Mirror* or Sergeant in the *Mail*, took it upon themselves to open the gate and point the way towards a property-owning democracy where 'everyman' could be a small-scale capitalist.[75]

They were in a position to undertake this role by 1960 because of the way in which their relationship with the investing public had developed since the advent of New Financial Journalism at the end of the nineteenth century. The communication skills of popular financial journalists had certainly improved over the years, especially their ability 'to translate the jargon of the City into a language that all will understand'.[76] Dale's City article for the *Mirror* was, in this respect, far more intelligible to the uninitiated than the in-house gossip of 'Chat on 'Change' in the first *Daily Mail*. Their recommendations may not have made millionaires out of small investors but they were likely to be derived from reliable market intelligence and provided a relatively firm basis on which to make decisions. In any case, as Harold Wincott of the *Investor's Chronicle* noted, there was little future of the City editor who failed investors in this way. Readers were inclined to overlook a few mistakes but were inclined to look elsewhere if too many recommendations 'came unstuck'. [77] The sheer volume of personal inquiries addressed to City editors by the 1960s suggests that this was not a problem and that readers had confidence in them.[78]

It seems probable, however, that the most important achievement of popular financial journalism in the first half of the twentieth century was to steer readers safely around the pitfalls of finance. Before the Prevention of Fraud Act, when 'bucketeers' abounded, the financial press, 'more than any other agency', had exposed their activities. This tradition continued into the postwar era and was reinforced as new investors, vulnerable through inexperience, came to the market. 'BEWARE OF THESE POSTAL SHARE SHARKS', warned Sergeant in the *Mail*, concerned that readers were 'being circularised by tipping sheets suggesting investments that one can only say are on the dangerous side of dubious'. Addressing readers very directly he shared with them the wisdom of the City insider: 'Do remember that where there's a tip there's a tap, and the greedy small investor usually pays for the tap'.[79] This kind of advice carried weight because financial journalists generally had gained the trust of their readers over the course of the first half of the twentieth century. From time to time an instance of corrupt practice might surface; a journalist, for example, might buy shares in advance of a tip calculated to move the market in his favour. But they had succeeded in distancing themselves from the corrupt practice that had once generated so much hostile criticism.[80] Whereas, at the start of the century, it had been commonplace to warn the public of the dangers lurking in the financial pages this was no longer necessary. Those thinking of buying shares for the first time were now steered towards the press. 'You will find that, as in so many circumstances, the City columns of newspapers can be a most valuable guide'.[81] With his house more or less in order it was possible for the City editor to undertake a crucial role in the promotion of popular capitalism.

Notes

1 Kennedy Jones, *Fleet Street and Downing Street* (London: Hutchinson, 1919), pp. 198–201.
2 Ellis Powell, *Letters to a Small Investor: a Non-Technical Introduction to the Science of Investment* (London: Financial News Ltd., 1916), p. 11.
3 *Daily Mirror*, 3 December 1903.
4 T.P. O'Connor, *Memoirs of an Old Parliamentarian* (London: Ernest Benn, 1929), ii, 259–60.

5 For the growth of advertising revenue see Karin Newman, *Financial Marketing and Communications* (Eastbourne: Holt, Rinehart and Winston, 1984), pp. 56–60.

6 Charles Duguid, *How to Read the Money Article* (London: Pitman & Sons, 1901), pp. 1–2; 'How the British Public Invests', *Financial Review of Reviews*, February 1906, p. 79. For the number of individual shareholders in the 1960s see John Moyle, *The Pattern of Ordinary Share Ownership 1957–70* (Cambridge: Cambridge University Press, 1971), p. 8.

7 Harry H. Marks, 'A Retrospect', *Financial News*, Twentieth Anniversary Supplement, 23 January 1904.

8 Charles Duguid, 'City Editing', *Sell's Dictionary of the World's Press and Advertiser's Reference Book* (London: Henry Sell & Co., 1903), p. 132.

9 *Wider Shareholding* (London: The Acton Society Trust, 1959), tables IV and IVd, pp. 27, 29.

10 Kenneth Fleet, *The Influence of the Financial Press* (London: The Worshipful Company of Stationers and Newspaper Makers, 1977), p. 7.

11 Ellis Powell, *The Evolution of the Money Market 1385–1916* (London: Financial News Ltd., 1916), p. 466.

12 David Kynaston, *The 'Financial Times': a Centenary History* (London: Viking Books, 1988), pp. 2–3.

13 Godefroi Ingall and George Withers, *The Stock Exchange* (London: Edward Arnold, 1904), p. 101.

14 Hugh Stutfield, 'The Company-Monger's Elysium', *National Review*, February 1896, pp. 838–9.

15 See Geoffrey Searle, *Corruption in British Politics, 1895–1930* (Oxford: Oxford University Press, 1987), pp. 33–40.

16 See Dilwyn Porter, 'A Trusted Guide of the Investing Public: Harry Marks and the *Financial News* 1884–1916', *Business History*, **28**(1) (1986), 1–17.

17 *Daily Mail*, 4 May 1896.

18 *Daily Express*, 24 April 1900.

19 *Daily Mirror*, 2 November 1903.

20 See *Daily Mirror*, 2 May 1914 for illustrated coverage of the walk. By 1914 *Mirror* coverage of City news was gestural although the current share prices of Northcliffe companies were assiduously recorded.

21 *Daily Sketch*, 3 March 1909. 'Contango' was nicely suggestive of insider knowledge. It was a Stock Exchange term referring to an agreement to carry over the settlement of a bargain into the next account.

22 Ellis Powell, *The Mechanism of the City: An Analytical Survey of the Business Activities of the City of London* (London: P.S. King & Son, 1910), p. 75.

23 *Daily Mail*, 27 June 1897.

24 See, for example, *Daily Express*, 4 May 1914.

25 News International Record Office, London: The Times Newspaper Limited Archive, Wynnard Hooper Managerial File 1906–35, Memorandum on the rearrangement of the Financial and Commercial Department, n.d., (probably 1910).

26   See Henry Hess, 'The Critic' Black Book (London: The Critic, 1901–02), pp. 164–5, 176–7 and 182–4 for examples of bogus replies used for this purpose.

27   Reginald Pound and Geoffrey Harmsworth, Northcliffe (London: Cassell, 1959), p. 202.

28   Charles Duguid, 'The City Editor', Journal of Finance, June 1897, p. 161. See also Dilwyn Porter, 'City Editors and the Modern Investing Public: establishing the integrity of the new financial journalism in late nineteenth-century London', Media History, 4(1) (1998), 49–60.

29   For a succinct account of this dispute see the Newspaper Society's Monthly Circular, December 1913, pp. 5–8.

30   British Library (henceforward BL): Northcliffe Papers, Add. MSS 62202, ff. 93–4, Duguid to Northcliffe, 3 November 1913.

31   Alfred Mayhew, Mayhew's What's What in the City (London: Mayhew's Financial Publications, 1913), p. 30.

32   For details of the scheme see Daily Mail, 12, 13, 14 June 1912.

33   BL: Northcliffe Papers, Add. MSS 62202, f. 84, Duguid to Northcliffe, 25 October 1913.

34   Daily Mail, 3, 8 August 1914.

35   Sunday Express, 29 December 1918.

36   Daily Express, 25 March 1919.

37   See Newman, Financial Marketing and Communications, pp. 58–61.

38   Hartley Withers, The Quicksands of the City and a Way Through for Investors (London: Jonathan Cape, 1930), p. 18.

39   Financial News, 12 February 1920.

40   See Donald Cobbett, Before the Big Bang (Portsmouth: Milestone Publications, 1986), pp. 100–1; see also Newman, Financial Marketing, pp. 62–5.

41   Hargreaves Parkinson, The ABC of Stocks and Shares, (London: Longmans, 1925), p. 46.

42   Daily Mail, 3 February 1919.

43   Daily Mail, 26 October 1929.

44   Financial Times, 2 January 1929, cited in Newman, Financial Marketing, p. 59.

45   Oscar Hobson, 'The Financial Press', Lloyds Bank Limited Monthly Review, January 1934, pp. 6–7.

46   Daily Mail, 25 October 1929.

47   Daily Express, 25, 30 October 1929.

48   See Adrienne Gleeson, People and their Money: 50 Years of Private Investment (London: M&G Group, 1981), p. 23.

49   See Kynaston, p. 113.

50   Daily Sketch, 14 April 1931.

51   Cobbett, Before the Big Bang p. 39. The Catholic Herald's 'Trade and Finance' article began on 13 January 1934.

52   Newman, Financial Marketing, pp. 144–6; for the origins of the unit trust movement see Gleeson, People and their Money, pp. 23–5.

53   Daily Mirror, 6 January 1939.

54 See Tom Jeffrey and Keith McClelland, 'A world fit to live in: the *Daily Mail* and the middle classes 1918–39', in James Curran, Anthony Smith and Pauline Wingate (eds), *Impacts and Influences: Essays on Media Power in the Twentieth Century* (London: Macmillan, 1987), pp. 27–40. For the market positioning of the *News Chronicle* see David Hubback, *No Ordinary Press Baron: A Life of Walter Layton* (London: Weidenfeld and Nicolson, 1985), pp. 132–3.

55 Cited in Gleeson, *People and their Money*, p. 37.

56 *Daily Mail*, 29 September 1938.

57 *Daily Mail*, 3 October 1938; *Sunday Express* 2 October 1938. Harris also observed that Compton Sons and Webb, manufacturers of Army uniforms, was 'one of the firmest shares in the industrial market'.

58 For the Prudential story see *Daily Mirror* and *Daily Mail*, 1 September 1939; see also *Daily Mirror*, 2 September 1939 for the closure of the Stock Exchange.

59 *Daily Sketch*, 13 May 1940.

60 For the impact of the war on the financial press generally see Kynaston, *The 'Financial Times'*, pp. 135–9.

61 Wincott Foundation, London (henceforward WF): Richard Fry, 'Financial Journalism in Britain: Notes on the proposed history', f.18B.

62 Richard Fry, *The Work of a Financial Journalist* (Manchester: Manchester Statistical Society, 1945), pp. 15–19.

63 *Daily Mail*, 27, 28 July 1945.

64 See Kenneth Morgan, *Labour in Power 1945–51* (Oxford: Oxford University Press, 1984), p. 109.

65 *News Chronicle*, 25 October 1951.

66 Gordon Cummings, 'The Changing Ownership of Industry', *The Accountant*, 20 September 1958; Newman, *Financial Marketing*, pp. 146–63, 185–93.

67 WF: Fry, 'Notes', ff. 78–9.

68 WF: Fry, 'Notes', f. 60 commenting on what young financial journalists learned under Fred Ellis at the *Daily Express*.

69 See Anthony Smith, *Paper Voices: the Popular Press and Social Change, 1935–1965* (London: Chatto and Windus, 1975), pp. 158–64.

70 *Daily Mirror*, 10 January 1950.

71 *Daily Mirror*, 4, 9 March 1960.

72 WF: Fry, 'Notes', ff. 48–9.

73 Paul Bareau, 'Financial Journalism', in Rodney Bennett-England (ed.), *Inside Journalism* (London: Peter Owen, 1967), p. 153. See also the *Daily Mirror*, 11 March 1960, for the reaction of Granada's *What the Papers Say*.

74 *Honey*, April, July 1960.

75 This was certainly on the political agenda by 1960. The Conservative Political Centre had published an influential pamphlet, *Everyman a Capitalist*, in time for the general election of 1959.

76 *Daily Mirror*, 4 March 1960.

77 Harold Wincott, *The Stock Exchange*, (London: Sampson, Low, Marston, 1946), p. 99.

78 By 1968 the *Mirror* was receiving around 25 000 inquiries annually. See Jeremy Tunstall, *Newspaper Power: the New National Press in Britain* (Oxford: Oxford University Press, 1996), p. 359.

79 See Wincott, *The Stock Exchange* pp. 96–7; *Daily Mail*, 17 March 1960.

80 For the probity of the financial press see Bareau, '*Financial Journalism*', p. 160; also Fleet, *The Influence of the Financial Press* pp. 12–13.

81 Charlotte Square, *The Investor's Vade Mecum* (Edinburgh: William Blackwood and Sons, 1962), p. 42.

5
Circles of Confusion[1] and Sharp Vision: British News Photography 1919–39

Peter Twaites

The activities of press photographers in the interwar years probably had more of a 'sting' than those of their predecessors or present day counterparts who have been branded 'paparazzi'[2]. The pursuit of royalty is nothing new. The camera's invasions of personal and institutional privacy are not a present day phenomenon. Earlier practices of faking, and inventive distortions of the representations of subjects and objects, of the 'truth' of events, are still matched. The prurient, fixing, gaze of the press camera has changed little since the days when photography was set free from the studio.

The practice of photography for the newspaper and magazine press has been described in many ways. It is essentially concerned with the production of a photograph that is valued, because it captures, and communicates a sense of meaning that is labelled 'news'. There is a dual value in a news photograph. The photograph gains an inherent value in the fact of the camera 'being there', having recorded a news incident, by 'freezing' a moment in time, and the 'evidential force' of its image. These values are combined with the value of the configurations of the image's content, the sense-making communication of representative meaning, of the news event itself. It is this combination of values, that have helped to establish the strongly held belief in the 'reality' of the images of news photography; resulting from the privileged position of the camera, as the eyewitness to news events.

There are also characteristics that determine the 'news' values of press photographs, to which must be added categories of 'value' which determine their ideological contents. These factors are based upon the cultural practice of journalism, of which press photography is an integral part. In this sense, press photographers are not free agents, simply 'being there' at news events, to record by a neutral mechanical device, the natural occurrences of human experiences. Press photographers are tied to the cultural characteristics, and ideological categories, of values to be found in the practice of journalism. Their images offer a feigned naturalness of the 'news', wherein lies their myth. It is these factors that this essay is principally concerned with, set in the context of the role that news photography has played, as representing the social and political interests of the majority of the people.

In the mythology of press photography[3], the practice has been described as the recording of news events, through the 'unforgetting eye of the camera', as 'a witness of the times', which 'cannot lie; but...can be an accessory to untruth'.[4] Much of this mythology rings true, but only to a limited extent. Indeed, such implied 'authenticity' as is granted to the news photograph is tainted. It is vitiated by the traditions of the news value culture of journalism, and the competitive commercial demands of the newspaper industry. It was upon such a collaborative framework that the practice of photography for the popular press[5] was built at the turn of this century.

The purpose of this chapter is to examine the practice of news photography, and the characteristics and categories of the news value culture of journalism. An interpretation of the discourse of news photography will be made; and developments of visual news communication practices will be evaluated. The survey will not follow a strict chronological account of developments. Newsgathering practices will be highlighted, in relation to particular news value considerations. A comparison will be made between the popular daily press and the weekly pictorial magazine press.

The chapter will begin with a review of the institutional origins of photography for the press, at the beginning of the twentieth century. It was during this period that taking photographs, with a 'news' interest, was fully admitted to the world of professional journalism, and became an essential arm of the 'picture paper' popular press. This will be followed by an examination of the news characteristics, and value categories, that determined the cultural and ideological news values of press photography.

There were other factors that influenced the changes in the form, and content, of news photographs in the late 1920s and 1930s. They were the techniques of photographers, pre-press decision makers, and the technology of photography. These combined to challenge the orthodoxy of news photography, and led to the emergence of 'modern photojournalism', in the mid to late-1920s, arising from a distinct change in practitioners' attitudes to news photography. These factors will be addressed in the third section. To conclude, it will be argued that until the emergence of the practice of 'modern photojournalism', which led to the creation of popular weekly picture magazines, press photography represented only a narrow field of view of British society.

Institutionalised visions of the 'popular'

The arrival of photography in the pages of the daily popular press was seen as a revolution in production methods and readership appeal.[6] At the turn of the century much of British journalism was stagnant in its production techniques and content styles. Proprietors sought new ways to attract readers to their newspapers and magazines. To meet the potential for economic exploitation, changes in the culture of professional journalism were introduced. Newspapers reduced the dominance of traditional 'grey', verbatim, reports of politics, the Stock Exchange, and sport. No longer could there be an assumption, by proprietors and editors, that their only readers were the wealthy and leisured classes; attracted by 'tutorial' and 'intellectual' topics of interest.[7] The daily newspaper was considered to be 'as necessary to...daily life as bread itself'. Readers demanded that their news be presented briefly, to be more easily read and quickly absorbed.[8] The news photograph was part of the answer to such a demand.

With great astuteness, proprietor Alfred Harmsworth recognised the shift in readers' expectations. He adopted a marketing policy of 'giving the public what they want', and used the fishing analogy of baiting the hook with 'what the fish wants – not what you want him to want'.[9] In order to do this Harmsworth embellished with photographs the dramatised and individualised the focus of the news stories of the day. In the view of 'the Chief' the 'fish' he angled after were women, middle- and working-class readers.[10] The bait for this potential market was news that Harmsworth claimed would extend to 'life as a whole'. News was presented as facts, and without minimising its importance was presented in new ways typographically and editorially, and 'played upon the feelings of millions'. Other popular press newspapers, such as the *Daily Express* (launched in 1900), *Daily Sketch* (1909), and *Daily Herald* (1912), also adopted 'ballyhoo' headlines to attract readers.[11]

The *Daily Mirror* 'picture paper', launched on 7 January 1904, was the first all-photographically illustrated newspaper in the world. After Arkas Sapt, the Hungarian technical manager of Harmsworth's weekly *Illustrated Mail*, had perfected his 'crazy notion' of reproducing news photographs on rotary presses turning out 200 000 papers an hour, there were dramatic changes to the contents of the popular daily press. The use of photographs supplemented the letterpress content in the *Mirror*; they became 'as newsy as the reports'.[12] News photography became a regular feature in the *Mirror*, the paper's rotary presses being able 'to print so many so quickly' that same-day news photographs became possible. The paper became the first on the popular press dailies to reproduce quantities of up-to-the-minute news photographs.[13]

Harmsworth became dissatisfied with the lack of a sense of immediacy and news value, of tripod-bound freelance commercial photographers who supplied his newspapers. He employed staff photographers and armed them with hand-held cameras, for mobility and speed of operation, packing them off around the world to cover news events at first hand.[14] For the first time in Britain a vast range of readers became vicarious onlookers of local, national, and world-wide, day-to-day news events; through the institutionalised popular press visions of society, which were recorded in the main by staff press photographers. Bernard Grant was despatched to cover the arrest of the murderer Crippen and his accomplice Ethel Le Neve in Canada in 1910, the Sidney Street siege in London in 1911, the war in the Balkans in 1912, and a royal visit to Paris in 1914. Others were sent on perilous expeditions: they photographed the inside of Mount Vesuvius; climbed Mont Blanc; took dramatic aerial shots as they crossed over the Alps in the basket of a hot-air balloon; and journeyed to Antarctica in 1913, to photograph the burial place of Captain Scott and his colleagues.[15]

However, news photographs were dominated by the categories of 'Society' events, novelty, spectacles of major sporting events, criminal law cases and royal and civic ceremonial. The speed of operations was such that an hour after photographers arrived in the office with undeveloped images of news events, their pictures were printed, half-tone blocks processed, run off the newspaper presses, and on the streets.[16] Other daily papers and major news agencies, based in London, also employed photographers as specialists in the gathering of visual news. The popular daily press embraced news photographs in their pages, recognising that they had journalistic and commercial values, and that these 'had risen a thousandfold in sixty years'.[17]

In this sense, newspapers were said to have portrayed the age to which they belonged, and reflected the 'spirit of their age', presenting readers with the 'feel and smell of life about them'.[18] News photographs were part of the essential dynamics of the new journalism of the popular press in the first decade of the twentieth century, and met the wider demands of a growing market of readers. This helped popular press proprietors to prise pennies from jangling pockets of potential readers, and pounds from wallets of likely advertisers. It was in this period that photography for the press was fully incorporated into journalistic practice, as part of the decisive restructuring of the newspaper press, and the shaping of reader demands.[19] In 1914 one observer was able to comment that 'the 'all picture' paper has come to stay'.[20] What also arrived to stay were the limited social representational values of news photographs.

News photography gave readers visual confirmation of written accounts of events reported in the popular press. No longer were readers presented with mediated and contrived illustrations by 'black and white artists' who provided interpretations of news events.[21] The institutionalisation of the practice of news photography was consolidated within the world of the popular press, bringing with it an identifiable change in the practice of photographic illustration of the news. There was a transition from the haphazard 'taking of photographs with a news interest' to the practice of photography specifically intended for newspapers.[22] A new breed of photographers was born with a specific purpose in life.

Press photographers are hunters – they are hunters of visual news. They hunt alone, or in a pack. Their stalking grounds cover the world, but are not selected at random. Their prey is anything and anyone that is caught in their sights, and the net of news. The success or failure of predatory expeditions, is determined by the range of the individual's ingenuity. Their success in the hunt depends also on their camera-shooting skills. Their objective is to 'hang' their captured images, as if trophies, in the galleries of the pages of news-papers or magazines. Their purpose is to visually inform the public of the 'news' event they are reporting about. For this they have been pilloried and praised. In 1933 one observer remarked that prejudice against the press photographer was justified, particularly when ' ... he invades the privacy of life...' or lies in wait for 'the unguarded moment at a public banquet...' and '...snapshots his victims...' who are anxious to avoid publicity.[23] The period under review was arguably a 'golden age' for those following the calling of press photography.

Characteristics and categories of news values

Press photography during the interwar period was regarded as the all-seeing eye of journalism. Practitioners, in the main, saw their work from a perspective that was deeply riddled with myth and ideology. From its origins the practice of news photography, for the popular press, was believed to be the honest reflection of represen-tations of 'life as a whole', of British society and the wider world. However, photographers only focused upon the lives of certain people, those who conformed to the formula of news values of the popular newspaper press.

The practice of press photography was myopic; what the camera witnessed, what readers saw, was limited in its vision. The practice was far removed from focusing upon the wider view of ordinary peoples' daily lived experiences, although not entirely. Rare expedi-tions were made, beyond the boundaries of the 'detached' news val-ues of journalism, into a wider field of socially concerned press photography. In 1920 Alfred Barratt, who specialised in photograph-ing scenes in law courts, was commissioned by the *Daily Telegraph* to take a series of pictures of the homeless who slept out on the Embankment. The political effect (reminiscent of the late 1980s and early 1990s in British cities and towns) was that a 'bureau' was set up to provide overnight shelter for the homeless and work for those who were unemployed.[24]

The characteristics of photographic news values were recognised in the early days of photography.[25] These characteristics rested upon the authenticity, the 'realism' and 'truth', of the news signification of photographic images. This was combined with a sense of immediacy, which acted upon the minds and emotions of readers in providing an understanding of 'news visibility'. In essence, this visibility depends upon the formal news value culture of professional journalism. They are journalism's formal news value characteristics. These require the fulfilment of a set of criteria: the 'action' of a news event, its happening, the event's 'temporal recency', its immediacy.[26] These values demanded that the photographer, and newspaper production technology overcome barriers of time and space to meet the criteria. The breaking down of these barriers was essential in order to meet competing daily newspapers' deadlines.

There are other values that are associated with the news photograph. These give a description of forms, a cluster of common sense values of content configurations, identified as 'frozen moments in time' of the image. They are the news, decisive, visual, symbolic, and historic moments in time.[27] These values may well offer a basis upon which to judge whether the configurations of a picture are 'good' or 'not good'; but they offer no basis from which to determine social and ideological choices of representational news values. They are values of raw meaning. It is only by interrogating the news value categories of the culture of journalism that social representations can be revealed.

In the development of press photography there is evidence of uncertainty in critically determining the values of news photographs. In 1905 the advice given to photographers was to supply the newspaper press with pictures of the 'Homes and Haunts of Celebrities', 'Scoops or Unexpected Events'. These types of pictures, it was suggested, would find favour with editors.[28] Twenty-five years later there was an attempt to give a more concise 'tabulation' of categories of news value, and were described as either 'something happening' or the 'effect of something that has happened'. They were described as 'the news picture proper' – it conveyed *news*.[29] Types of photographs were listed as the 'purely novel', and the 'purely picturesque'.

Categories now are more clearly prioritised as: hard news, the news photographs of the day, which are identified in advance; unscheduled, natural and human catastrophic events that are referred to as 'spot news'; soft news, feature pictures of general interest, that have no sense of immediacy; special topics, such as sporting events and crime.[30] The categories of hard news and spot news pictures, are the principal distinguishing terms that can be given to the products of press photography. Much of the work of popular press photography was (and still is) concerned with these categories, as and when they occur daily. Many of the social representational values of photographs were those identified above; each of these types of photographs was based on journalists' prioritising judgements, of the combination of characteristics and categories of news values.

Feature photographs have no requirement of temporal recency, or immediacy of the event, in the sense that hard news and spot news photographs do. They can stand on their own as a journalistic type, with a brief caption, or serve to illustrate feature story topics. Photographs having aesthetic interest also made the pages of the popular press. James Jarché's photographs of an idyllic 'golden age' English country village, or of the quaintness of a gypsy encampment at Epsom Downs, were given half pages of space in the *Daily Herald*.[31]

In terms of the news value characteristics identified, experiments were carried out in the transmission of photographs over a cable system in 1907. There was a successful 'wiring' transmission of photographs, over a telegraphy circuit of 1 500 kilometres, between Paris and Lyon, from the offices of *L'Illustration* with the largest size of photograph, 18×24 cm, being transmitted in a period of time of one minute, per square centimetre. Transmission facilities were installed in the *Daily Mirror* offices in London in the same year, connecting with Paris.[32] This system was not a total success for the *Mirror*. When the King and Queen visited Paris in 1914, the paper hired a special train from Paris to Calais, and a ship to Dover. The train and ship were fitted out for photographic and process block making, which was carried out by staff during the journey. At Dover a special train carried the prepared photo-mechanically engraved photographic 'block' to London for immediate printing on arrival and the meeting of the deadline for the next morning's paper.[33]

After the First World War there was improved efficiency in the technical and reproduction quality of photographs in the daily newspaper press. Air transport was to replace trains and ships in the 1920s and early 1930s. When working for the *Daily Sketch*, James Jarché was 'scooped' by a *Daily Mirror* photographer when covering a royal wedding in Belgrade. The *Mirror* had arranged to fly the photographic plates back to London. The *Sketch* was beaten 'hands down', and as Jarché acknowledged, 'Planes had come to stay' in beating time and distance deadlines.[34] As a photographer had noted some years earlier, '... In press photography hustling is the order of the day ...'[35]

By 1926 'scores' of photographs were being transmitted by cable across the Atlantic on a daily basis, and portable transmission systems were being operated.[36] The weekly press could not compete in terms of 'hard' news event photographs, published within hours of being taken. Such images were stale after a day, and the weekly press finally succumbed to the picture age revolution in newspaper design and content, and started to compete with the dailies for readers. Even if they could not meet the criterion of immediacy, they could compete on aesthetic and feature category terms.

Although technological improvements to transport, cameras and newspaper production undermined the ability of the weekly illustrated press to compete against the immediacy of hard news photographs, this did not prompt any immediate changes to their approach to the news value contents of pictures, even though journalism had by the interwar years fully entered into an age of pictures rather than words.[37] As a result, there were complaints that the press were merely repeating already published photographs. An extreme example of this practice was the use of photographs by several papers of skating photographs during the 'big freeze' in February 1933, which had in fact been taken twenty years earlier,[38] a recycling of material that also occurred in the contemporary newsreels. The weekly press had little alternative than to repeat the use of pictures seen in earlier publications of their rival dailies. In the early 1930s the popular press resorted to holiday snaps competitions to boost sales. These images were considered inferior to normal press work, and a 'blight upon the industry'.[39] This practice, nevertheless, provided the opportunity for publication of pictures that directly addressed readers' interests and representation.

The practice of publishing 'faked' photographs of news events was not new. One reader described as photographic 'outrages', the use of faked photographs 'day after day' in the popular press in 1905. He complained of photographs of supposed Japanese troops, returning from a far off battle, in '... battle trucks marked G.E.R....'; and described as an '...insult to Royalty...' the fake wedding pictures of two young people '...belonging evidently to the lower-middle class...', who were dressed up as a prince and princess, and captioned as newly-weds.[40] Photographs were published simply because they had the intrinsic value of being images of 'reality', in the eyes of the majority of readers. Such was the power of photographic images as a journalistic representation of the 'truth' of a news event. This practice continued into the 1920s and 1930s. These types of photographs were disingenuously referred to as 'novelty' pictures, and frequently appeared both in the pages of the popular daily newspapers and in the weekly illustrated press that was attempting to compete with the 'realism' of hard news photographs. Bert Hardy, who worked for the General Picture Agency in London, was a practitioner who flouted the idea of authenticity. His was a different kind of work to that of the established press photographers working for the popular dailies. His work involved '*making* pictures'. There is some justification to his claim that hard news press photographs 'make themselves', and in the competitive fury of press photography of the times 'silly ideas' were turned into pictures.[41]

Hardy's photographic inventiveness was extraordinary. Yet, the results were popular with readers, and snapped up and published by the popular press daily and weekly publications in the 1930s. Some of the topics and subjects that he created 'news' photographs from were: 'a singing mouse'; 'a shepherdess called Mary Lamp'; 'a wart charmer'; and 'the man who hypnotized alligators'. Each Christmas he photographed an out-of-work actor, dressed as Santa Claus, lying on a bench; captioned 'Found Late Last Night in London'! Other ideas included pictures of 'Britain's Only Bird Surgeon', which showed a budgerigar held with elastic bands to a piece of wood, supposedly about to undergo surgery.[42]

Notwithstanding such aberrations in the 'news' values characteristics of such photographs, the urgency of press photographers' work was a crucial part of the culture of professional journalism, to which they had become grafted. It was this sense of the immediacy and urgency of the news photograph that clearly had an effect on the readership market. Hardy's 'Fleet Street education' came with just such coverage; for instance, the stabbing of a newspaper seller in the Strand, London, in August 1937. He was on the spot to capture photographs of the attack, and the arrest of the attacker. These 'spot news' photographs were given a back page spread the following day.[43] Photographers, such as Hardy, may have had the characteristic of '... The man with a genius for getting something out of nothing ...';

but the speed and ingenuity of photographers were essential characteristics of their practice.[44]

The demands of competition for hard news photographs led to many excesses of behaviour, and downright guile, by press photographers. In a 1922 incident (a precursor to a similar press intrusion sixty-eight years later) two photographers took pictures of an unconscious doctor, who had been poisoned, lying in his hospital bed at the Royal Free Hospital, London. The photographers had gained admission to the hospital by claiming they had permission from Scotland Yard to take the photographs. This claim was challenged by the hospital authorities. Before being allowed to depart, the photographers handed over photographic plates which, they said, held the pictures of the unconscious patient. However, the plates had not been exposed, and they held on to those used to photograph the unconscious doctor. The popular press published the photographs the next day. The hospital issued a press statement, condemning the 'disgraceful act' of the photographers, and assured the public of the hospital's commitment to securing the privacy of patients.[45]

Pursuit of royalty figured largely in the hunting expeditions of the popular press photographers. The objective was to capture 'close-up' images of royal personages, rather than general shots of regal processions. It was in pursuit of such hard news photographs that the ingenuity of the photographer was tested to the full. On one occasion in 1922 James Jarché pretended to be a Swedish Court photographer. He gained access to Kensington Palace to photograph the Crown Prince of Sweden and Lady Mountbatten, soon after after her marriage to Louis Mountbatten, the great-grandson of Queen Victoria. Jarché got his 'scoop' pictures, and they appeared on the front page of the *Daily Graphic* the next morning. Other papers had to be content with somewhat boring pictures of the ceremonial procession through the streets. Such photographs could hardly be described as representative of 'life as a whole', or to be representing the life experience interests of the majority of readers. If anything the formal, posed connotations of class and power reinforced the perceptions of the social structure. On another occasion Jarché dressed as a monk to capture photographs of a pageant of celebrities.[46]

A hard news royal scoop was perpetrated by an unnamed press photographer, '...a delightful man with grey hair...', who evaded the tight security surrounding the venue of '...the greatest human interest story of the age ...' on the eve of the wedding of Wallis Simpson and the Duke of Windsor, near Paris on 2 June 1937. The photographer, known to the Duke, gatecrashed Court photographer Cecil Beaton's photographic session while the couple were being pictured in their wedding clothes. The photographer scooped the world's press. Photographs appeared the next day in the London *Evening Standard* hours before the wedding took place, and were wired to America.[47] The hunting instinct is sharpest when the predator is hungry and the prey has 'gone to earth'.

'Modern photojournalism' and sharper vision

From the First World War onwards, press photography was, in the main, firmly grafted to the culture of daily popular press journalism which had its own tradition of formal, institutionalised, news values. These values were predominantly the characteristics of immediacy, and the categories of hard or spot newsworthiness, and novelty feature news. This tried and tested formula continued to dominate the pages of the popular press throughout the 1920s and 1930s. The mainstay of types of news photographs were: human and natural catastrophes; 'Society' weddings; 'dated news events'; members of the Royal family; and 'football and cricket incidents'.[48]

In the early 1930s the popularity of the established daily picture papers began to wane, with their pictures becoming 'twee' rather than dramatic.[49] One observer made the point that readers were fed up with seeing 'silly stunt pictures' in their newspapers, when there was '... so much of real interest ... to be photographed ...'.[50] They were facing competition from the broadsheet papers that had increasingly embraced the use of news pictures in their pages. Industry watchers of the time advised the picture papers to change their tabloid format, to that of the broadsheet press, in order to maintain their popular appeal.[51]

The magazines increased their gathering, and publishing, of 'news' photographs of the week that appeared with the traditional drawn illustrations. However, they remained conservative in the choice of feature topics; pictures of flowers, and paintings exhibited at the Royal Academy, are examples of the limited social representation in many publications. In 1929 the German photojournalist,

Walter Bosshard, had pictures of an expedition to Central Asia published in the *Illustrated London News*, but similarly they had little direct social interest for readers; they were unique only in the sense that they were taken in the new style photography, 'naturalness'.[52] Nevertheless, there were signs that the approach to news value content was shifting. Jarché, who began work for the *Weekly Illustrated* in 1934, gives an account of expeditions to Scotland and Wales to illustrate feature stories about the working lives of trawler men and coal miners.[53] In 1937 the magazine claimed that it was much more than 'just a paper', and that photographs were its lifeblood. Its descriptive rhetoric of its press photography content could have been that of the daily popular press. It announced to its readers a 'New Journalism', based upon

> scoops from every part of the world – exclusive, first-hand news-picture records of things you might never see – some even beyond belief ... What few words it uses are vital and to the point, and it covers the talk of the land.[54]

The illustrated weekly magazines had not, in the earlier part of the decade, catered for the interests of the wider British reading public; they were competing with the daily press by using similar types of photographs, and followed a similar formula of news categories, but with more emphasis on novel and feature photography. In the main, the weekly illustrated magazines devoted most of their pages to serialised fiction stories. Nevertheless, with the emerging practice of 'modern photojournalism', which based its approach to news on the 'ideology of objectivity', a wider set of journalistic news values and a sharper vision of society – largely neglected by the popular press – were eventually brought to bear on the picture contents of magazines in Britain.

The 'new photography' movement began in Germany in 1924. Its philosophy had spread into photoreportage by 1928. It was a decade before it was to fully influence the firmly embedded, early twentieth-century culture of journalism that prevailed in Britain. The new style of photography began to reflect a more egalitarian and democratic representation of peoples' interests, more relevant to a wider class of readership that was both reported about and to. The new technique used the camera as a mechanical resource for the production of 'new visionary perspectives' which were concerned with the much wider social experiences of people.[55]

Importantly, modern photojournalism reflected an age of challenge to the social and economic status quo of the postwar years. The 'one-shot' press photographers' approach was still a common practice of daily newspaper press photography. However, this was challenged by a more encompassing style on two counts: the sharper vision, that was found in photographers' innovative approaches to news values, and corresponding pre-press selection decisions of editors. These changes gave rise to a new kind of press photography – photojournalism. Part of the new approach was the production of the picture-story, a series of associated photographs of a single topic of news.

There was resistance, from the established daily popular press photographers in Britain, to the new techniques of photojournalism. They were reluctant to take on the challenges of new equipment and techniques. One press photographer echoed the views of his colleagues in 1929, when he argued that their old, bulky, 5 × 4 inches and 9 × 12 cm plate cameras were speedier, easier to handle, and more reliable than the new cameras used by photojournalists. The quality of reproduction of larger glass plate formats, he asserted, was superior to the miniature, 35 mm film, camera film stock favoured by the new photo-reporters. As far as he was concerned 'For press photography the plate has it'.[56] It was almost five years later when he relented, suggesting that miniature cameras would soon replace the larger format cameras for press photography work.[57] However, the daily popular press photographers in Britain remained loyal to their trusty, large format, cameras until around the mid-1950s.

From the end of the 1920s, through to the mid-1930s, the old techniques and approach to press photography were said to have been in an intellectual blind alley. Practitioners were restricted to the traditional news value's formula of popular press journalism, and outdated equipment. They knew of no other than the culture of the practices they had been following since the early part of the century. Editors were also continuing along the same dead-end route.[58] In a sense they had no need of change. They had no reason to change from the culture of immediacy value and categories of types of press photography that had a limited vision of the news; these were, after all, the badge of identity of the popular daily press.

Commenting on the changes in approaches and techniques of modern photojournalism, one observer noted in 1939 that art editors of the popular press had been immersed in a tradition of sensational news pictures and daily 'scoops'. They had forgotten that people had interests other than '…battle, murder and shipwrecks…', resulting in many other pictures being dull.[59] Dullness was the complaint about the coverage of a soccer cup-tie match at Manchester in 1934. Seven out of eight pictures published were of distant shots of the spectators, and the other one was a photograph of the game itself.[60] What the new approach offered was an opportunity for the development of the modern, popular weekly, illustrated magazines, enabling them to compete with the popular dailies by providing an entirely different perspective on 'news'. What news photography had done for the daily popular press at the beginning of the century, modern photojournalism could also do for the illustrated weekly magazine in the 1930s.[61]

The pioneers of modern photojournalism are said to be Erich Salomon, Felix Mann, Wolfgang Weber, Martin Munkacsi, and Alfred Eisenstadt.[62] By the end of the 1920s they were leaders in their field of photojournalism. However, they practised mainly in Germany for illustrated magazines published in the major cities. Their approaches were those of the 'behind the scenes', candid camera photographer-producing picture stories, instead of the traditional single shot images, of hard news or spot news events, that were commonplace in the daily popular press. Their camera techniques included the use of the natural light that was available. This was part of the power of the sense of 'actuality' in their photographs. They scorned the use of artificial light sources such as magnesium flash powder and the flashbulb. The latter was marketed for the first time in 1930 and synchronised, with shutter speeds, in 1935. Their film stock cameras were those marketed for the first time in 1925, notably the 6×9 cm Ermanox, and the 35 mm Leica.[63]

These cameras enabled the photojournalists to take surreptitious photographs, with few overt incursions upon their subjects, and when necessary without their knowledge. The posed posturing of their news subjects was frowned upon. Subjects were captured on camera, in unguarded moments, with natural facial expressions and gestures, that were serious or light-hearted. This surreptitious photography was practised by press photographers in Britain from the turn of the century, particularly in the coverage of major criminal trials. The noisy operation of cameras, hidden in bowler hats or disguised as books, was covered up by loud coughing to avoid detection. Photographers were also assigned to take pictures of queues of people, hoping for gallery seats at the trials. Jarché records the hypocrisy of one hopeful member of the public, waiting to gain entrance to the 'Brides in the Bath' murder trial, who chased him down the street wielding her handbag, after he had photographed her in the queue.[64] Although it was frowned upon by judges, taking photographs in courts of law, and their 'precincts' was not illegal in Britain until the enactment of the Criminal Justice Act 1925, which came into force in 1926, which made it a criminal offence.[65] Erich Salomon fell foul of this law in 1929 after a photograph, taken with an Ermanox camera, of a judge in the High Court was published. His punishment included being banished from Britain.[66]

There was no hiding the bulky cameras of the popular press photographers, their presence was obvious, and news subjects responded accordingly. After all, they might appear on the front page next day. The introduction of the flashbulb added to the visibility of the daily newspaper press photographers, their staccato firing of bulbs being the sure sign of a newsworthy incident. Thus the press photographer was placed centre stage with their news subjects.[67] However, although the flashbulb gave the old-time press photographers more freedom to range in search of their prey, they were still tied to earlier news value traditions that determined the types of photograph they sought out. For the modern photojournalists, their quarry was far from the orthodoxy of the popular daily press news subjects.

By 1929 photojournalism was an established practice in Germany, and motivated the launchings of many popular weekly magazines devoted to the new style of journalism until the coming to power of the Nazi Party in 1933, which brought with it the suppression of press freedom. Salomon's expertise was in taking photographs of affluent and powerful social figures in the government and diplomatic circles of Europe. André Kertesz produced a picture story about Trappist monks, whilst Weber produced a series of photographs of American workers, life in a small town, and a pawnshop. Other topics and subjects covered by Germany's photojournalists included the circus; a theatre reportage on George Bernard Shaw; a juggler; car racing; a Paris ghetto; poverty in Hamburg; single women; drought in France; unemployment in a village; and a school for the deaf and dumb.[68] This wide variety of photographic story topics heralded a sharper focus of social representation in the pages of weekly magazines. Yet, they remained located within the soft news feature category of journalistic cultural practices.

If photojournalism encouraged a new style of popular weekly magazine, its motivating force was Stefan Lorant, who was appointed editor of the *Münchner Illustrierte Press* in August 1928. It was Lorant's sheer enthusiasm for the photograph as a primary journalistic way of communicating with readers which helped to drive forward the revolutionary new style of reporting. He built up stories out of photographs in a gripping and straightforward way. Lorant's philosophy of photojournalism was based on the following criteria: photographs should not be posed; photographers should use their cameras as a trained reporter uses a notebook to record news events as they unfold; people should be photographed as they really are, not as they think they should be or how they want to appear; photojournalists should concern themselves with men and women from all social backgrounds, and not with a small group of social elites; and the camera should portray life realistically.[69] Such an ideological approach to the production of news photography was certainly very different from the narrow and limited vision of the daily popular press, which pandered to the great and the good, prurience, spectacle, and sensation.

After 1933 many of the pioneering photographers left Germany. In 1934 Stefan Lorant found refuge in London, after spending six months in a Nazi prison, and helped to found the first popular weekly magazine, *Weekly Illustrated*, for Odhams Press. There were other weekly magazines, but these catered only for the upper classes, and were still tied to old traditions. Photographers Felix Mann and Kurt Hübschmann (who changed his name to Hutton) followed Lorant to Britain, and others moved on to the United States. Robert Capa and Ina Bandi settled in Paris. In Britain, from the mid-1930s, the influences that these innovators brought with them, of a new culture of journalism, were slow to take hold. The one-shot photographer still held sway over the popular daily press, and their news value culture had not changed. Lorant applied his new journalism to the *Weekly Illustrated*, and in 1937 was a joint owner of the pocket-sized weekly, *Lilliput*.

Early in 1938 Lorant was invited to create a new pictorial magazine for the newly formed Hulton Press. Its concept was to be a continuation of Lorant's earlier work in Germany and Britain. The new magazine, *Picture Post*, was to be the culmination of the development of photojournalism and the effects the practice would have on shaping the style of presentation of predominantly photographic communication. Lorant's philosophical approach was that the magazine would be representative of '... the masses, the common man ... the workers ... the intelligentsia' – it would '... print the truth and do it honestly'. The purpose would be to 'share a common knowledge' by enlightening readers about subjects they knew little of, and to do so by not talking down to them. He explained his editorial attitude to photographs as being like 'a composer uses notes', he composed stories with pictures.[70]

Before the magazine's first edition was printed, assistant editor Tom Hopkinson was asked if the magazine would be political. Hopkinson replied: 'Of course it would. All life was political ...'. He also declared that it was intended to:

> use photographs as they'd never been used before. It would treat all human beings as of equal dignity and importance. It would show the life of a charlady and the life of the big business boss, without laughing at the charlady or touching its cap to the big boss, the duke, the bishop.[71]

From the outset the *Picture Post* lived up to the promises of Lorant and Hopkinson. In the first edition on 1 October 1938, photographs included a picture story by Kurt Hutton about the history of corset making. The front cover carried a full-page picture of two girl skaters leaping through the air, a picture full of vitality and lightheartedness. The hard news value of immediacy was evident in the first edition also. A change to the front page of the picture magazine was made during the print run, and a substitute photograph of Neville Chamberlain with Hitler at their second meeting in Godesberg was used. On 8 October the famous daring picture (for its time) of two girls at the fun fair, one with her hair blowing in the wind and skirt billowing around her waist, added glamour and vitality; it was a picture of ordinary people, enjoying the fun of life. But *Picture Post* also dealt with the serious side of life. In the edition dated 26 November, two double-paged-spreads carried pictures of the Nazi leaders of Germany, with 'evidential force' images of the damaged properties of Jewish people, and twelve portrait photographs of world-famous Jews. This topic was to become a long-running story. The magazine was an instant success, with sales of the first issue reaching nearly 706 000. In six months sales had soared to 1.7 million copies.[72]

The successful editorial policy of *Picture Post* was arguably due to the fulfilment of the pledges of Lorant and Hopkinson to represent as wide a vision of British society as possible. Importantly, there was a socially aware use of photographic and written materials, with the former dominating the publication's pages as first order messages of news information, and the latter fully cooperating with, and complementing, the images that offered a wider diffusion of knowledge about the life experiences of the people of Britain and the wider world.[73]

Conclusions

With the institutionalisation of news photography, the popular daily press failed to truly represent the interests of a large majority of readers, merely reflecting the interests of proprietors and the cultural tradition of professional journalism. The popular press picture newspapers started out with good intentions, bringing photographic 'realism' to their readers, and presenting them with photographic evidence of sights they could only previously have imagined. During the interwar years, however, popular press photography did not interest itself with the more pressing social concerns of the majority of people. From the beginning of the twentieth century, when the illustration of news became institutionalised by the popular daily press and was consolidated as a genre of photographic practice, photographers pursued royalty, the rich, the famous and infamous, presenting readers with a facade of 'realism', other than the very rare occasions when the cameras focused more sharply on a wider spectrum of the people of Britain and their daily lived experiences.

The practice of press photography was driven by the value judgements of the culture of popular press journalism, which was brash, sensationalist, and guileful. Novelty was the name for frivolity. Press photographer 'hunters' sought out their prey, at the cost of personal privacy, and deference to an elite. They pandered to the readers' interests in the name of the 'scoop'. Northcliffe's astuteness, and that of other proprietors of the popular press daily newspapers who followed in his wake in order to compete in the market place, no doubt recognised that answering the needs of readers' curiosity – or even prurience. Their financial risk-taking adventures in journalism paid back handsomely. This created a blinkered approach to news-gathering practices until the gradual emergence of a new kind of news photography in the mid- to late 1920s. However, the popular daily press did not pretend anything other than to represent a limited view of British society and the wider world, and the demands and expectations of its readers for its news photography products.

The philosophy of the new photography led to fresh approaches to considerations of news values in the practice of photojournalism in the late 1920s and early 1930s. These new approaches encouraged the photographic telling of stories of ordinary people, as well as the great and the good. Photographers told their stories as their cameras witnessed the unfolding of events; stories were told as the camera witnessed them, and not in the posed or contrived ways practised by the daily popular press photographers. Émigré photographers brought about the creation of a new style of popular picture magazines in Britain during the 1930s. These publications, amongst which *Picture Post* was most prominent, were the culmination of a new trend in pictorial story-telling. The news photographs published in *Picture Post* fulfilled a promise, to represent a much wider socially diffused readership than that catered for by the popular dailies. In doing so, the magazine sharply focused the camera lenses on the more pressing social and economic concerns of the majority of people, bringing a sharper visual democracy to the representation of their lives in the British press.

In the fresh approach to news photography, visual stories became primary sources of communications and the written word functioned as a secondary, or supplementary, source. The outstanding success of *Picture Post*, was to be found in its catering for a wide range of photographic information interests. Visual education and entertainment were communicated in the picture magazines, answering public need and expectations. In the case of *Picture Post*, its philosophy was to visually inform readers in a truthful way, whilst its ideology was the politics of all classes of people; and these policies were captured in its photographs. Nevertheless, the news photographs that press photographers and modern photojournalists of the interwar years have bequeathed are historical documents that show us how it was – to a lesser or greater degree.

Notes

1   The term 'circles of confusion' is a camera optics explanation of lens focus: 'When a distant object casts a sharp image on a film the image of a closer object will not be sharply in focus for it will be cast sharply behind the film ...'. Eric De Maré, *Photography* (Harmondsworth: Penguin, 1962), pp. 91–2. The analogy with the practice of press photography is apposite, in terms of the limited focus of news values – their characteristics and categories – that is determined by the culture of professional journalism. The focus of news values in this sense might be said to rely on 'distant' subject–objects; while those 'closer' to the press photographer remain out of focus, or more critically, out of sight. The news focus of popular daily press photography can in this sense be said to be out of focus, and its images 'circles of confusion' in the representation of society.

2   The word 'paparazzi' is derived from a character in Frederico Fellini's film *La Dolce Vita*. The character, Paparazzo, was named after a buzzing, stinging, unpleasant insect, and was a photographer who preyed on celebrities and sold their photographs to the popular press and magazines. The film character drew on the early 1950s activities of photographer Tazio Secchiaroli 'the Wolf of the Via Venito' who, touring the streets of Rome on a motor scooter after dark searched out the rich and the famous at play. Tim Gidal, *Modern Photojournalism: Origin and Evolution, 1910–1933* (New York: Macmillan, 1973), p. 17; and Richard Williams, in 'Spying for Fellini', *The Independent on Sunday Review*, 6 December 1998, pp. 15–20.

3   The term 'press photography' entered the language of professional journalism at the end of nineteenth century. In the context of this chapter it is used to describe the singular practice of photography, specifically for the newspaper press media – the daily popular press and the weekly illustrated magazines. A distinction has to be made between this term and that of 'photojournalism', coined by the Dean of the University of Missouri, School of Journalism, in 1924. Under this definition, a new form of photographic reportage, emerging in the mid-1920s, was designated to mean an individual's combined talents as a reporter, and a skilled photographic communicator for newspapers and magazines. A. McDougall, in Leslie Stroebel and Richard Zakia (eds), *The Focal Encyclopedia of Photography* (3rd edn), (London: Focal Press, 1993), p. 599.

4   *Weekly Illustrated, Coronation Souvenir and Guide*, 12 May 1937, p. 54; Gidal, *Modern Photojournalism* p. 17; Harold Evans, *Pictures on a Page: Photo-journalism, Graphics and Picture Editing* (London, Heinemann, 1978), introduction.

5 For these purposes the popular press is taken to mean those daily published national newspapers and weekly illustrated magazines which
   appealed to a wide-ranging majority of readers in Britain during the
   period under review. They are specifically those publications that, in the
   early part of the twentieth century, were referred to as 'picture papers',
   and adopted a tabloid format, such as the *Daily Mirror, Daily Graphic,*
   and *Daily Sketch.* These are distinguished from the larger broadsheet
   'serious' newspapers. Picture paper is a term that did not readily apply to
   the popular weekly illustrated magazines that were launched in the early
   to mid-1930s in Britain, although there was a gradual shift from drawn
   illustrations to the use of photography as the 1930s progressed.

6 J.M. Bulloch (ed.), C.K. Shorter, *An Autobiography: a Fragment by Himself*
   (London: Constable, 1927), pp. 84–5.

7 G. Binney Dibblee, *The Newspaper* (London: Williams & Norgate, 1913),
   pp. 10, 16–17.

8 Mason Jackson, *The Pictorial Press: Its Origin and Progress* (London: Hurst
   & Blackett, 1885), p. 2. H. Simonis, *The Street of Ink,* (London: Cassell,
   1917), pp. 9–22.

9 Cited in Tom Clarke, *Northcliffe in History* (London: Hutchinson, 1950),
   pp. 86–7.

10 To his staff, Harmsworth (Lord Northcliffe) was always referred to as 'the
   Chief'. Tom Clarke, *My Northcliffe Diary* (London: Victor Gollancz, 1931),
   pp. 23, 44.

11 R.D. Blumenfeld, *The Press in My Time* (London: Rich & Cowan, 1933),
   pp. 34–8.

12 Harold Herd, *The March of Journalism: The Story of the British Press from 1622
   to the Present Day,* (London: George Allen & Unwin, 1952), pp. 240–1, 262
   f.n. 1. Kurt von Stutterheim, *The Press in England* (Translated by W.H.
   Johnston), (London: George Allen & Unwin Ltd., 1934), pp. 92, 94.

13 Geoffrey Smith, *News and Newspapers* (London: W. & A.K. Johnston &
   G.W. Bacon, 1962), pp. 54–5.

14 Bernard Grant, *To the Four Corners: The Memoirs of a News Photographer,*
   (London: Hutchinson, 1933), p. 245. Max Pemberton, *Lord Northcliffe A
   Memoir* (London: Hodder & Stoughton, no date), pp. 88–9.

15 Tom Hopkinson, introduction to Ken Baynes (ed.) *Scoop, Scandal and
   Strife: a Study of Photography in Newspapers,* (London: Lund Humphries,
   1971), pp. 7–12; Grant, *To the Four Corners* pp. 32–49; Matthew Engel,
   Tickle the Public: One Hundred Years of the Popular Press, (London: Indigo,
   1996), p. 151–2.

16 John Given, *Making a Newspaper,* (London: George Bell & Sons, 1907), p. 48.

17 John R. Whiting, *Photography is a Language,* (Chicago: Ziff-Davis, 1946),
   p. 17.

18 Francis Williams 'Introduction' in Frank Atkinson (comp), *The English
   Newspaper Since 1900* (London: The Library Association, 1960), p. 5.

19 James Curran, 'The press as an agency of social control: an historical
   perspective.' in G. Boyce *et al. Newspaper History: from the 17th Century to
   the Present Day* (London: Constable, 1978), p. 72.

20 John Everard, *Photographs for the Papers* (London: Adam & Charles Black, 1914), p. 9.
21 The term 'black-and-white artists' was used to distinguish the newspaper illustrators from paint artists. Bulloch, C.K. Shorter, *An Autobiography* p. 85.
22 Hopkinson, in Baynes (ed.) *Scoop, Scandal and Strife*, p. 7.
23 Philip Gibbs, foreword to Bernard Grant, *To the Four Corners: The Memoirs of a News Photographer* (London: Hutchinson, 1933), p. x.
24 Alfred Barratt, 'Photography for the Press', *British Journal of Photography*, 7 May 1920, p. 284.
25 In February 1856 the reportage photographs of the Crimea War attracted enormous public interest and were said to have brought the realities of war 'practically, immediately' before the public. *Journal of the Photographic Society* 21 February 1856, p. 303. It was reported in July 1856 that 'French photographers have been very busy lately', with coverage of news events such as the baptism of an 'imperial Prince' and the flood damage in Lyon, Tarascon, and Avignon, after the river Rhone had burst its banks. *Photographic Notes*, 1(8), 17 July 1856. A decade later 'news windows' created great public attention in the main thoroughfares of cities, with their displays of photographs of the great and the good, and landscapes of faraway countries. David Lee, 'Window on 19c News' in *The British Journal of Photography*, 16 August 1985, pp. 913–14; citing *The Art Journal*, June 1864, p. 191.
26 Stuart Hall, 'The determination of news photographs' in Stanley Cohen and Jock Young (eds), *The Manufacture of News: Social Problems, Deviance and the Mass Media* (London: Constable, 1978), p. 235.
27 Harold Evans, *Pictures on a Page*, pp. 105–126.
28 Editors of *The Photogram, Photography for the Press* (London: Dawbarn & Ward, 1905), pp. 15–16.
29 Bell R. Bell, *The Complete Press Photographer* (London: Sir Isaac Pitman & Henry Greenwood, 1930), pp. 3–4.
30 Allan Bell, *The Language of News Media* (Oxford: Blackwell, 1994), pp. 14–15.
31 James Jarché, *People I Have Shot* (London: Methuen, 1934), p. 215.
32 *British Journal of Photography*, 8 February 1907, pp. 103–4; and 15 November 1907, pp. 886–7.
33 Grant, *To the Four Corners*, p. 144.
34 Jarché, *People I Have Shot*, pp. 89–91.
35 *Photographic News*, 3 August 1906, p. 613.
36 *Amateur Photographer*, 26 May 1926, p. 583.
37 Bulloch, C.K. Shorter, *An Autobiography*, p. 92.
38 Blumenfeld, *The Press in My Time*, p. 152–4. 'Focal-Plane', 'Press Photography Notes', *British Journal of Photography*, 10 February 1933. p. 76. Focal-Plane was the pseudonym of the long serving Fleet Street freelance photographer, Bell R. Bell.
39 Focal-Plane, *British Journal of Photography*, 23 March 1934, p. 171.
40 *Photographic News*, 30 June 1905, p. 405.

41   Bert Hardy, *My Life*, (London: Gordon Fraser, 1985), p. 31.
42   Ibid.
43   *British Journal of Photography*, 3 December 1920, p. 736.
45   'Over-enterprising Press Photographers', *British Journal of Photography*, 27 October 1922, p. 658.
46   Jarché, *People I Have Shot*, pp. 75–8, 144–5. After their wedding in July 1922 the Mountbattens became the focus of the popular press gossip columnists. On their honeymoon tour of the United States they were pursued each day by press photographers; Janet Morgan, *Edwina Mountbatten: A Life of Her Own* (London: Harper Collins, 1991), pp. 143–6.
47   Cecil Beaton, *Photobiography* (London: Odhams Press, 1951), pp. 84–9.
48   Focal-Plane, *British Journal of Photography*, 29 March 1929, p. 186.
49   Engel, *Tickle the Public*, p. 155.
50   Focal-Plane, *British Journal of Photography*, 10 February 1933, p. 76.
51   Engel, *Tickle the Public*, p. 155.
52   Gidal, *Modern Photojournalism*, pp. 183–9.
53   Jarché, *People I Have Shot*, pp. 183–9.
54   Ibid.; *Weekly Illustrated*, 12 May 1937.
55   Ute Eskildsen, 'Photography and the Neue Sachlichkeit Movement', in David Mellor (ed.), *Germany – The New Photography, 1927–33: Documents and Essays* (London: Lund Humphries, 1978), p. 101.
56   Focal-Plane, *British Journal of Photography*, 2 August 1929, p. 454.
57   Focal-Plane, *British Journal of Photography*, 26 January 1934, p. 49.
58   Gidal, *Modern Photojournalism*, p. 13.
59   R.J. Yeatman, 'The Pleasures of Actuality', in C.G. Holme (ed.) *Modern Photography* (London: The Studio, 1939), p. 116.
60   Gidal, *Modern Photojournalism*, p. 14.
61   Derrick Knight, 'Development', in *Scoop, Scandal and Strife*, op. cit. p. 29. Gidal, p. 13. Eskildsen, in Mellar, *Germany* p. 108.
62   Focal-Plane, *British Journal of Photography*, 9 March 1934, p. 137.
63   Knight, 'Development', op. cit.
64   Jarché, *People I Have Shot*, pp. 58, 61–2.
65   *Amateur Photographer*, 28 April 1926, p. 518.
66   Arthur Rothstein, *Photo-Journalists*, (New York: Amphoto, 1974), p. 203.
67   David Mellor, 'The Regime of Flash', in Rupert Martin (ed.), *Foods of Light: Flash Photography 1851–1981* (London: The Photographer's Gallery, 1982), p. 28.
68   Gidal, *Modern Photojournalism*, pp. 19–23.
69   C.G. Holme, 'The New Photo-journalism' in *Modern Photography* (London: The Studio, 1939), p. 115.
70   Michael Hallett, 'The Picture Post Story', *British Journal of Photography*, 2 July 1992, p. 15.
71   Tom Hopkinson, 'How Picture Post Began', *Picture Post*, 2 October 1948, p. 13.
72   Jarché, *People I Have Shot*, pp. 75–8, 144–5.
73   Michael Hallett, 'The Picture Post Story', *British Journal of Photography*, 2 July 1992, pp. 14–15; 9 and 23 July 1992, pp. 22–3, 25.

6

All the News that's Fit to Broadcast: the Popular Press *versus* the BBC, 1922–45

Siân Nicholas

Introduction

At 6 p.m. on Tuesday, 14 November 1922, the first news bulletin broadcast of the British Broadcasting Company ushered in a new era in mass communication in Britain.[1] Newspapers welcomed the 'wireless' as a fascinating curiosity, but few commentators expressed either anticipation or foreboding about what this might mean for the traditional purveyors of news to the British people, the newspapers. Within a year, however, the BBC was under attack in the popular press, heralding the start of a war between the broadcasting and print media that has never quite ceased. The abiding issue, which it took a world war to resolve, was news: who was entitled to provide the public with news, and what form should it take.[2]

This chapter investigates the complex and often fraught relationship between the broadcast and the popular print media in the early decades of broadcasting in Britain. The interwar years were a period of fierce competition between newspapers in both Fleet Street and the provinces; but the popular press also mobilised their considerable forces outwards against the BBC. In so doing they helped shape the history of mass communications in Britain this century.

The birth of broadcasting

Like so many innovations that produce profound change, radio's initial impact was muted. Compared to the public response to Alfred Harmsworth's launch of the *Daily Mail* in the same year, Marconi's

121

radio demonstrations of 1896 were seen largely as a technical curios-ity and sparked interest principally among enthusiasts who experi-mented under Post Office licence until the First World War, when radio was reserved for military needs.[3]

It was in the USA that the first wireless experiments demonstrated the true potential of the medium. Enrico Caruso's broadcast direct from the New York Metropolitan Opera in January 1910, and David Sarnoff's seventy-two-hour marathon relay of news of the sinking of the *SS Titanic* in 1912, captured the imagination of American listen-ers. The immediate postwar years saw a rapid expansion in broad-casting in the USA, consolidated by the foundation of the Radio Corporation of America (RCA) in 1919. On 31 August 1920, 8MK, the first radio station sponsored by a newspaper (the *Detroit News*), began broadcasting with news reports of the results of that day's national primary elections. In November, KDKA (Pittsburgh) came to national attention by broadcasting the results of the Harding–Cox Presidential election on its inaugural night's broadcast; and, in October 1921, WJZ (Newark, NJ) marked its arrival with another scoop, a relay of the baseball World Series between New York's Giants and Yankees. By January 1923 there were over 50 licensed sta-tions operating across the USA, owned variously by universities and colleges, department stores, city administrations, religious organisa-tions – and newspapers. In city after city newspapers – 69 in 1922 alone – launched radio stations, all broadcasting a service designed essentially to publicise the newspapers themselves, wireless news bulletins acting as teasers for the 'full stories' in the papers.[4]

In Britain, private experiments continued after the war amid increasing concern at the apparent free-for-all in the USA. The first serious venture into popular wireless broadcasting in Britain belat-edly followed the American pattern: in June 1920 Tom Clarke, news editor of the *Daily Mail*, persuaded Alfred Harmsworth (now Lord Northcliffe) to sponsor a broadcast from Chelmsford by Dame Nellie Melba. It was heard across Europe amid great publicity (not least in the *Daily Mail*).[5] Northcliffe stood alone among Fleet Street propri-etors in his recognition of the potential of wireless (though like his American counterparts he clearly envisaged radio as a marketing tool rather than an independent news medium), and for a short time in 1922 the *Daily Mail* even rented a radio station in The Hague that broadcast the first organised radio service directed at

Britain. During his world tour of 1921/2 he took a particular interest in the organisation of broadcasting in the countries he visited.[6] However, further forays into broadcasting were hampered by Northcliffe's rapid mental and physical deterioration, and a few months after his death in August 1922 the Government granted a broadcasting monopoly, not to a newspaper, but to a consortium of wireless manufacturers, the 'British Broadcasting Company' (BBC).[7]

Public service broadcasting and 'news'

The establishment of the BBC saw British broadcasting take a radically different path from the American version – although not quite in the simplistic 'public service' *versus* 'commercialism' terms often cited. Rather the BBC set out to attract as wide an audience as possible across its programme schedule in order to sell more radio sets, whereas American stations increasingly sought to match the largest possible audiences to specific programmes financed in ever larger numbers by commercial sponsorship. With the issue of broadcast news reserved by the Government for 'separate consideration', the new broadcasting organisation met with little opposition from the press. Once on-air advertising was ruled out as a source of BBC revenue, newspapers (which had feared new competition for the advertising revenue on which their profits depended) praised the creation of the BBC as a sensible, very British, means of circumventing the chaos and encroaching commercialisation of US broadcasting.[8]

Broadcasting, of course, addressed a new kind of audience: not a self-selecting readership whose age, social class, interests and opinions could be substantially predicted and catered for, but a disparate and potentially huge collection of curious listeners-in of all ages, tastes and sensibilities. Although this raised important issues about the (as yet unknown) power of radio as a medium of mass influence, in fact in almost all cases radio was initially seen as dangerous not in social or political but *commercial* terms. The music and entertainment industry's fears of the power of radio would be vividly presented during the hearings of the Broadcasting Committees of 1923 and 1925 (the Sykes and Crawford Committees).[9] The prevailing impulse of the press was, likewise, to focus on the dangers of competition.

On 11 November 1922, representatives of the four news agencies (Reuters, the Press Association, Central News and the Exchange

Telegraph Company), the Newspaper Proprietors Association (NPA, representing Fleet Street), the Newspaper Society (representing the provincial press), the Post Office and the BBC signed an agreement which specifically ruled out the BBC setting itself up as an independent news provider – specifically, from using unauthorised, uncredited, or unpaid for newspaper material in bulletins. The Postmaster-General, Neville Chamberlain, had argued for broadcast news ('a real boon and a service', especially to people in isolated areas). However, the BBC Directors – as yet there were no BBC staff – readily agreed that the BBC would obtain its news exclusively from the agencies, which would supply through Reuters (the dominant partner), a daily half-hour summary (1 200–2 000 words) of the world's news for broadcast. Payment was to be a minimum of £4 000 per annum, on a sliding scale related to the number of radios licensed. As Sir William Noble, Chairman of the BBC, told *The Times*, the BBC had no intention of 'usurping the legitimate functions of the Press' ('we want to act in such a way that broadcasting may become an incentive to the public to buy more newspapers'). Shortly after, it was agreed that to safeguard newspaper sales – particularly of the evening papers – no news *at all* would be broadcast before 7 p.m. Provisional news bulletins were permitted in the first weeks of the BBC, but the first bulletin of the new era went out at 7 p.m. on 23 December 1922. It included an on-air copyright acknowledgement to each of the four news agencies (subsequently shortened to the phrase 'copyright reserved'). The full agreement was incorporated into the Company's Licence in January 1923, with the additional proviso that if the BBC at any time broke this contract it would be subject to claims for damages by the newspaper industry.[10] By agreeing to supply the news, the press safeguarded their monopoly on newsgathering; by asserting the case for damages they characterised news as property – their property – and by insisting on scheduling restrictions they neutralised the broadcast medium's one competitive advantage: immediacy.

Conflict broke out almost immediately. The NPA demanded that the BBC pay advertising rates for programme listings in its publications – only to see BBC Managing Director John Reith outmanoeuvre them by persuading Gordon Selfridge to place BBC listings in his daily advertisement in the *Pall Mall Gazette*.[11] In turn, Reith challenged the press's prohibitive definition of news, protesting that both listeners and the BBC itself were entitled to more from broad-casting.[12] In April 1923 Lord Beaverbrook's *Daily Express* and *Evening Standard* simultaneously launched the first of their many press crusades against the BBC. The *Express* attacked the BBC's licence fee and monopoly status, singled out the news ('by far the most feeble part of the whole programme ... to anyone with the remotest sense of news value and interest') for especial condemnation, and offered to 'lead the way' with a free broadcasting service of its own. The *Standard* questioned the very practice of 'doling out news items at settled times whether there is any value in the item or not'.[13] The Sykes Committee (1923) was convened in part to address the issue of monopoly ownership raised in the Beaverbrook press; in their submission to the Committee the NPA, Newspaper Society and news agencies argued forcefully that:

> it is wrong in principle that any telegraphic corporation or other carrying system should engage in the business of collecting news and supplying it to the public. The news agencies spend very large sums in the collection and distribution of news, and they urge with justice that it would not be in the public interest that the broadcasting system ... should be allowed to publish news otherwise from authoritative and responsible sources of information.[14]

In fact, the Sykes Report strongly endorsed both the continuation of a state-regulated monopoly and the BBC's record thus far. Speculating that 'it may be that broadcasting holds social and political possibilities as great as any technical achievement of our generation', the Report tentatively agreed with Reith's position and singled out for future consideration announcements of events of universal public interest, important statements by the Government and debates in Parliament. However, it recommended for the time being only 'a gradual extension of the broadcasting of news, under proper safeguards', with more latitude given 'for the broadcasting of special events'. [15]

A new informal 'Memorandum of agreement', signed between the BBC and the newspaper representatives in September 1924, did give the BBC the right to broadcast 'ceremonies, speeches or other functions' – but only if no commentary of any kind was given. The BBC also agreed to broadcast only news items '... which do not interfere with newspaper reports' (the draft agreement, more bluntly, had prohibited the BBC from broadcasting anything 'likely to affect prejudicially the sales of newspapers'). The BBC was also permitted to broadcast news from official (i.e., government) sources at any time.[16] The Memorandum also established a four-man Press Committee comprising representatives of the BBC (Reith), the NPA (Lord Riddell, Chairman of the *News of the World*), the Newspaper Society and the news agencies, to consider breaches of or extensions to the agreement.

Notwithstanding the apparently 'extraordinary response' from *Express* readers to its call to 'free the air',[17] the opportunity for American-style cross-media ownership appeared to have passed. Although for a time Lord Beaverbrook sought to influence the development of broadcasting through the newly formed Wireless League, in general the popular press contended itself with blocking Reith's pleas for more latitude and criticising the BBC's 'dull' and 'useless' programmes.[18] Indeed, press fears that radio might prove a rival on their own territory dissipated. At a time when even the fastidious *Daily Herald* was beginning to accommodate the sensational human interest story,[19] the BBC's concern for the sensibilities of their listeners bordered on the obsessive. As early as December 1923, Reuters agreed to eliminate from their radio summaries all 'harrowing, unpleasant or distressing details' after BBC Director of Programmes A.R. Burrows asked them to 'recognise the difference between *reading* and *listening* to news':

> We are discovering that a certain class of person is very sensitive to this sort of thing. ... The hanging of a criminal, the burning to death of a child, or the assaulting of a woman are not news items suited to a broadcast service, except, of course, where such an item would protect other listeners from moral or bodily injury.[20]

While, for instance, the Beaverbrook press operated under the principle that 'people like to know what diseases a man dies of', the BBC warned Reuters to take greater care in reporting illnesses after a report of a death from sleeping sickness prompted a single letter from a man whose sister had the disease and had been distressed by the report.[21]

Meanwhile, disputes within the Press Committee centred on restricting eye-witness coverage, notably in sports news. In 1925 a proposal from Reith that the BBC be permitted to broadcast the first half of the forthcoming England–Scotland rugby international, a 'sound impression' (i.e., no commentary) of the Derby, and 'coded narratives' of the Boat Race and the FA Cup Final, met heated opposition from the press representatives, unconvinced by Reith's ingenious argument that newspapers themselves would benefit (i.e., people would buy more papers in order to learn the codes and results). Sir James Owen forcefully outlined the Newspaper Society's position:

> We say the BBC can do anything which involves the reproduction of … natural sounds. They can put a microphone on the racecourse, they can give the clattering of the horses' hoofs, the cries of the crowd, anything they can get through the microphone, but they have no right to say, 'The horses are now at the post; they're off; now reaching Tattenham Corner; so-and-so is leading.' We say they are not entitled to do that. Or with the Boat Race.

To the Postmaster-General the press representatives argued a case largely based on obligation. The BBC owed its success to favourable press publicity and therefore had a moral obligation not to 'interfere unreasonably with our business'. The newspapers had a public duty to police the BBC's monopoly. Their arguments were also tinged with hints of conspiracy (Riddell: 'I can quite understand the desire of certain persons to establish another Agency which will compete with the Press. I can quite understand that persons who suffer under the lash of the Press are very anxious to get another lash which will not be under the same control…').[22] In 1926 the BBC did broadcast the Derby under the Press Committee's conditions: the 'sound impression', in driving rain, was a disaster.[23]

Unsurprisingly, the newspaper industry's submission to the Crawford Committee (1925) renewed its indictment of the power of broadcasting. However, its argument was weakened by the maverick voice of Hamilton Fyfe, editor of the *Daily Herald*, who submitted that radio's victory over the daily newspaper was not merely inevitable ('I suppose, within a short time, we shall all carry earphones about with us and be able to pick up messages wherever we may happen to be') but a positive good, both to the general public ('Those who regard newspapers merely as a help to passing time, will find wireless news enough for them') and to journalism ('This will change the newspapers from collectors of entertaining scraps to organs of opinion, purveyors of intelligence for those who study events at home and abroad'). In his oral evidence he cited American findings that broadcast news *increased* newspaper sales, and happily acknowledged being utterly out of step with his journalistic confrères on the whole issue.[24] Moreover, while in 1923 the press industry had received a disinterested hearing from the committee Chairman Sir Frederick Sykes (Conservative MP, former Chief of the Air Staff, and subsequent member of both the *Daily Mail* and *Daily Express* boards[25]), their position in 1925 was far weaker. Not only had the principles of public service broadcasting already been broadly accepted by the committee, but David Lindsay, twenty-seventh Earl of Crawford, heir to a family of celebrated bibliophiles and a leading cultural figure in his own right, matched Reith himself in his belief in enlightened public service. He brought to the committee proceedings a visceral dislike of the popular press in general, whose influence on public life in Britain he considered wholly malign, and of the press barons in particular, whom he considered 'vulgar and ostentatious'.[26] Oddly, Reith, whose relationship with Lord Beaverbrook was tempestuous, had struck up a close friendship with Riddell with whom he now regularly dined.[27] Crawford, however, was neither friendly nor sympathetic to Riddell (whose *News of the World* he considered 'infamous') and, far from discounting Riddell's apocalyptic visions, appears to have hoped they would come true ('The world would be all the better for a violent purging of these vile sheets').[28] The report itself, published on 7 March 1926, advocated the public incorporation of the BBC and suggested that the press would have to face up to the reality of broadcast competition ('this country cannot withhold privileges so widely enjoyed without restriction elsewhere').[29] To Crawford the BBC appears to have represented, among other things, a political and even moral triumph over the popular press, and he dismissed *Daily Telegraph* criticisms of the Report with the comment, 'Respectable papers won't suffer'.[30] On 14 July the government accepted the Report's main recommendations, notably the formation of a British Broadcasting Corporation by Royal Charter. In the interim period, the General Strike had seen Fleet Street come almost to a standstill, the agencies waive the terms of their agreement with the BBC, and the BBC (placed by Reith at the service of the Government) broadcast news throughout the day.

The establishment of the British Broadcasting Corporation on 1 January 1927, coming so soon after the BBC's success as a news medium during the General Strike, marked a new stage in broadcast news. In theory the new Corporation had no restrictions on its news gathering (the BBC's Royal Charter authorised it 'to collect news of and information relating to current events in any part of the world and in any manner that may be thought fit and to establish and subscribe to news agencies'), and the historian of Reuters notes a new assertiveness in the Corporation's dealings with the agencies.[31] Yet the new BBC's first dealings with the press saw it *renewing* its agreement with the agencies in return for a handful of concessions: permission to move the 'First News' to 6 p.m., to broadcast (at any time of day) up to 400 eye-witness descriptions per year, and to write its own news bulletins from a 5 000-word agency digest.[32]

The following years saw the new BBC 'News Section' (initially comprising just two members, Geoffrey Strutt and Lance Sieveking) gradually increase in strength and (qualified) independence under the aegis of the Talks Department. Hilda Matheson, Director of Talks from 1927 to 1932, was convinced that the BBC's distinctive news policy was 'not only sound, but also good business', to the extent that she discouraged the appointment of anyone with 'ordinary popular journalistic experience'.[33] However, anticipating further extensions of the BBC's news remit, in 1928 she commissioned an internal critique of BBC news output from Philip Macer-Wright, news editor of the *Westminster Gazette*. Suggesting practical means by which BBC news might position itself, Macer-Wright concluded that news bulletins must seek to provide as 'complete a summary as possible of the day's outstanding facts'. They should endeavour to inform, not simply edify, and to contain 'something for everyone'. They should have 'news value' ('contained in new or hitherto unknown facts about personalities, places and things [as well as unusual and outstanding events] that are of interest to large classes and groups of people'). They should be written and arranged for the ear, not the eye. Were news to be established as a full BBC Department in its own right its service might extend 'far beyond its present range of usefulness and influence...perhaps to become the most important News Service in the country, indeed in Northern Europe.[34]

The Press Committee still retained the power to prohibit broadcast news reports: in 1929 it agreed to let the BBC broadcast the

General Election results till 4 a.m. on the night of the count but refused to allow an update on the state of the parties at 10 a.m. the following morning ('we feel there is no occasion for this').[35] However, one of Macer-Wright's most urgent recommendations was realised in December 1929 when the news agencies finally conceded to the BBC the right to gather and write its own bulletins from the agencies' full tape services. In consequence the BBC news staff was increased to six: four news editors, plus records clerk and part-time office boy. But the BBC's new freedom to write the news did not necessarily mean an extension of news coverage: it is to the Corporation's own news values that we must credit the BBC's notorious single-line news bulletin of Good Friday 1930, 'There is no news'. [36]

During the 1930s the popular press abandoned their formal attempts to control broadcast news and the news agencies were left to defend their position alone. The BBC was soon alerted to their delaying tactics, such as the addition of 'not for broadcasting' captions (first introduced by government departments during the financial crisis of 1931) to permit newspaper scoops. [37] In November 1931 the Press Committee agreed to let the BBC broadcast earlier than 6 p.m. selected news items not covered by existing arrangements ('eg., lunchtime Test Match scores and unforeseen events of importance').[38] From 1934 the BBC News Section was established as a Department in its own right and for the first time employed staff with journalistic experience (though not from the popular press).[39] In their submissions to the Ullswater Committee on Broadcasting (1935), the press industry's opposition to broadcasting focused principally on the commercial challenge represented by the pirate station Radio Luxembourg, and on the declining circulations of evening newspapers; while Reuters chairman Sir Roderick Jones restated the agencies' property right in all news broadcast from their sources over the BBC for as 'long as it has news value'.[40] Following the Ullswater Report's (1936) anticipation of future relaxations to the restrictions on broadcast news, BBC news steadily expanded, for instance in parliamentary coverage (where special parliamentary 'observers' reported on important debates) and topical affairs coverage (albeit tentatively, and with an eye to avoiding 'controversy'). The appointment in 1936 of Richard Dimbleby, an experienced young journalist with a distinct and enthusiastic vision of broadcast news, heralded a more innovative use of eyewitness accounts in news bulletins.[41] In March 1938 a new agreement was signed between the NPA, Newspaper Society and BBC alone, which not only allowed the BBC yet more latitude in compiling news bulletins, but allowed for the provision of daytime news broadcasts in cases of 'events of urgent national importance or of exceptional public interest'.[42]

However, the BBC's increased *capacity* to exploit the medium for news did not necessarily mean it sought to take advantage of the opportunity, and the press ridiculed as well as encouraged the clear distinction in both scope and character between popular newspaper and radio news. In fact both would play strongly to the BBC's advantage.

'News value': the character of broadcast news

From its earlier years, BBC news staff had paid close attention to the tone and scope of broadcast news. Reuters had lost patience when in September 1924 the BBC criticised a headline on a bus disaster in Nuneaton – 'Seven lives lost in blazing bus' – as sensationalist,[43] and Macer-Wright had singled out as a travesty of genuine news values the BBC news editors' objection to reporting the murder of the popular and widely known elephant driver at the London Zoo. According to a *News Chronicle* survey in 1933, the most read news in popular dailies were stories about accidents, crime, divorce and human interest.[44] Yet the BBC did not consider its approach to be more restrictive so much as inherently superior to that of the popular press. As Strutt outlined in 1926:

> Newspapers, to keep up their income from advertising etc. must print ... what their public wants to read. The BBC ... need only give such news as it wants to give. ... [I]f (A) we are recognised as the chief official channel through which the Government shall communicate to HM subjects ... and (B) provided the accuracy of our news remains unimpaired, then a very large percentage of our listeners will listen to and appreciate our news bulletins ... even though they lack the 'sensation' of the press. ... 'If it came through the BBC it is so' should be our aim. ... our responsibility here is greater than any that has arisen since Adam's fateful choice.[45]

It is unfortunate that there are no listening figures available for BBC radio news in this period to judge the effect of this approach.

Certainly, throughout the 1920s and 1930s BBC news was the constant butt of press jokes and criticism. Yet the News Section and its successor the News Department maintained that not only was it transforming listeners' general knowledge of public affairs,[46] but that the very existence of broadcast news acted in the public interest as a check on the worst excesses of the popular press (which, Matheson argued, 'having commercial ends in view, have succeeded in putting over a conception of news which even intelligent people have been induced to accept at its face value').[47] During the 1930s the BBC News Department slowly began to adopt more commercial news values (more attractive presentation, more human interest stories), and Richard Dimbleby waged a steady one-man war for more lively news coverage, which included a celebrated attempt to interview a prize-winning cow.[48] But the BBC's refusal to give licence-payers simply 'what they want', and the elevation of this policy to not only a principle but a defining virtue, differentiated broadcast news utterly from popular newspaper journalism.

In fact this approach gave BBC news unexpected advantages in several areas of proven 'news value', nowhere more clearly than in those who subject areas central to popular media success in the twentieth century, 'royal news' and sport. The first 'royal broadcast', George V's speech opening the 1924 Wembley Empire Exhibition, was heard by an estimated ten million listeners, and several newspapers, including the *Daily Mail*, organised public relays of the broadcast. The BBC was highly sensitive both to the accuracy and tone of royal bulletins, laboriously double-checking with Buckingham Palace that agency stories were correct for broadcasting, and seeking to avoid either overfamiliarity or excessive sycophancy. Thus the BBC objected to the 'film-star' tone of agency reports of the Prince of Wales's American tour in 1924, while at the same time criticising gushing descriptions of Princess Mary's babies as likely to inspire 'feelings akin to bolshevism'.[49] Assiduous cultivation of royal contacts resulted in arrangements for regular bulletins direct from Buckingham Palace during George V's illness in late 1928 (including on Christmas Day and Boxing Day, when no newspapers were printed).[50] In 1932 Reith finally persuaded the King to give his first Christmas broadcast; this was followed by a succession of broadcasts of royal events, including the wedding of the Duke of Kent and Princess Marina in 1934 and the Silver Jubilee in 1935. Although newspaper 'death editions' were on the London streets within half an hour of George V's death in January 1936, it was the BBC, working directly with Buckingham Palace, which had announced to the nation that the monarch's life was drawing 'peacefully to a close'.[51] Neither the press nor, of course, the BBC reported the story of Edward VIII's relationship with Wallis Simpson until the Abdication Crisis was in its last throes; however, while the 'gentleman's' agreement across the British press'[52] looked like complicity, it was the kind of story listeners would *never* have expected to hear on the BBC. The nation listened-in as the King gave up his throne, and listened-in again as a new King was crowned. If the renewed mystique of the British monarchy in the 1930s was connived at by both the popular press and the newsreel companies, it was secured through the close ties between Reith and Buckingham Palace.

Meanwhile, at a time when sports coverage was becoming an increasingly important feature in popular newspapers,[53] the Corporation took full advantage of the concessions with respect to 'eyewitness' coverage gained in its 1927 agreement with the news agencies, and instituted broadcast commentaries of the Five Nations rugby union, the Grand National, Lincoln and Derby, the Boat Race, the FA Cup Final, test match cricket and the Wimbledon tennis championships; all of which soon became established as integral features of the broadcast year. Sports results were among the most popular items in news broadcasts, and individual sporting organizations actively sought BBC coverage. The press continued to assert that radio sport was killing evening papers and the National Union of Newsvendors appealed in vain to the BBC to withdraw its results service ('The broadcasting of Football Results on Saturdays at 6.15 ... has often ruined the prospects of a Sunday dinner for the newsvendor and his family'). However, *Newspaper World* challenged claims that broadcasting had, for instance, 'killed' special results editions, suggesting that BBC sports reports had galvanised the prompt publication of Boat Race or Derby results.[54] When in 1936 the BBC requested the right to cover the Berlin Olympics, the agencies deployed their only remaining weapon, demanding a £150 special fee for broadcast rights to their reports. The BBC professed outrage – and knocked them down to a hundred guineas.[55]

Press priority was undermined in other ways. As early as 1924 Reith had offered his services to the Ministry of Agriculture and

Fisheries during an outbreak of foot and mouth disease, and in the years after the General Strike, despite the thwarting of Reith's ambitions to broadcast from Parliament, the BBC increasingly assumed the role of official news source linking government and people. When in early 1930 the BBC broadcast a Home Office denial of statements attributed to the Home Secretary in that evening's papers, it set a precedent whereby government departments periodically used BBC news to 'clarify' or to deny unwelcome press stories, and the BBC likewise sought guidance from government departments in compiling news reports (most notoriously from the Foreign Office regarding overseas news coverage).[56] Ironically, rather than undermining public perceptions of the BBC's independence, this usage only enhanced its air of authority.

Above all, however stilted and restrictive its normal practice, the BBC always had in the last resort the unrivalled quality of *immediacy*. The press's stratagems undermining or circumventing the BBC's use of this advantage had fatal limitations. For instance, the BBC was permitted to interrupt its regular schedules for stop press announcements, and although this power was infrequently exercised, its impact was considerable. While news stories of 1929–30 which merited such announcements included Lindbergh's successful solo flight across the Atlantic, the birth of Princess Margaret, the result of the Americas Cup and Anglo-American Polo, Dimbleby took breaking news a step further in 1936 by broadcasting a live report of the Crystal Palace fire from a public telephone near the fire scene. In early 1939 he showed what the medium could do with a live broadcast into the news from the fighting on the Franco–Spanish border.[57]

This unique combination of immediacy and authoritativeness ensured that, at moments of national crisis, the nation turned increasingly to the BBC. Three news stories of the interwar years underline the BBC's growing status as the nation's prime news provider. During the General Strike, with regular press distribution disrupted, for the first time the British public received its news principally from the BBC. Reith placed the BBC at the service of the Government, partly because his own constitutional beliefs demanded it, but partly because he knew the BBC had no other choice if it wished to safeguard any form of independence in future. The BBC broadcast five strike bulletins a day, as well as Baldwin's speeches to the nation (some of the most celebrated parts were drafted by Reith himself) which cast the strikers unequivocally as enemies of the British constitution. Despite Reith's refusal of air-time to advocates of conciliation, such as Ramsay MacDonald and the Archbishop of Canterbury, the BBC's regular service and measured tone during the strike raised both the profile of its news and (with some exceptions) public confidence in its new operation. The demand for newspapers during the strike was heavy and many newspapers across the country published emergency bulletins or special editions (according to one commentator, 'Things heard were not fully believed until they could be read in cold print'), but these often were simply reprinted BBC bulletins. Reith, who had himself announced to the British people both the start and the end of the strike, saw the BBC's role during the strike in terms of averting revolution – not a claim the Government's inflammatory strike newspaper the *British Gazette* could readily have made.[58]

Second, during the 1931 political crisis the BBC broadcast the first news of the formation of the National Government (including the names of the new Cabinet, telephoned through from Downing Street), 'objective and non-sensational' accounts (its own words) of the sterling crisis and special talks by 'prominent public men during the critical period', not only maintaining 'its high position as a supplier of unbiased information', but also 'by means of its news service...contribut[ing] materially to the steadying of public opinion'. By contrast, the press was blamed in some quarters for having sparked off the run on the pound in the first place by its hysterical reporting of the Invergordon naval mutiny.[59] Third, while the Munich Crisis marked, in one press historian's words, 'the most inglorious period in the history of the British press', raising questions about government/press relations that the 1949 Royal Commission on the Press would eventually seek to address,[60] the BBC for the first time exercised its powers 'in time of national emergency' to take centre stage, broadcasting government statements, civil defence announcements, news flashes, and, in successive news bulletins on the evening of 30 September, an account of Chamberlain's triumphal progress from Heston Airport to Buckingham Palace. The BBC News Department's acceptance of Foreign Office 'advice' and its failure to provide the nation with adequate foreign news prior to the crisis – its own 'conspiracy of silence', according to Coatman[61] – was the catalyst of considerable internal recrimination. Although this criticism focused largely on the inadequacies of Reuters' 'too populist' foreign news service, the Department committed itself to develop more authoritative and independent foreign news sources in future.[62] Yet again, however, the BBC's coverage was considered to have compared well with Fleet Street's inflammatory mixture of 'shrill' anti-Nazi invective (e.g., the *News Chronicle* and *Daily Herald*) or 'unrestrained adulation' of Chamberlain (the *Mail* and *Express*), and again the BBC was credited – and indeed credited itself – with having kept the nation calm under fire.[63] After Munich the press attempted to tighten its embargo procedure: BBC Senior News Editor R.T. Clark estimated that a 'newspaper vendetta' had seen the number of messages marked 'not for broadcast' increase by a third between the crisis and February 1939. But the days of such restrictions were numbered. Instructions to delay the broadcasting of particular news stories were already 'invariably disregarded' by BBC news staff (now over 30 strong).[64] News bulletins were now enlivened by short topical talks, regular outside broadcast commentaries of sport and state occasions, and eyewitness accounts from the two formally accredited 'BBC news observers', Richard Dimbleby and David Howarth. From October 1938 the 9 o'clock News was permanently established as the news cornerstone of the broadcast day.

'A useful auxiliary'? The impact of broadcast news on the press

The end of the popular press's attempts to control broadcast news did not mean the two media went their separate ways. The impact of broadcasting on the press was considerable. As early as 1927 the trade publication *Newspaper World* had suggested that broadcast news, far from being a threat, would prove a 'useful auxiliary' to the press, indeed that the morning papers might benefit from an extension of evening news broadcasts (wireless news 'whets rather than satisfies' the curiosity of the listeners').[65] While the newspapers were probably correct in their insistence that people preferred to read news stories at leisure, the BBC was also correct in asserting that radio news fulfilled the demand for immediate news but encouraged listeners to read further. The evidence for the adverse affect of wireless on newspaper circulation figures increasingly tended to the anecdotal, as the interwar years saw a spectacular rise in both radio listening and newspaper circulation.[66]

The effect of broadcasting on the news *content* of newspapers was another matter. In 1928 commentator St John Ervine, following Hamilton Fyfe, suggested not only that 'impartiality...be forced upon the press by the BBC', but that newspaper news itself would evolve through the influence of broadcasting. As wireless continued to disseminate 'straight' news, a newspaper would 'become more an organ of opinion'. He suggested that Beaverbrook's *Daily Express* was already moving in this direction.[67] Although the *Express*, for instance, did not term its leader articles 'opinion', it was not opinion but entertainment that increasingly superseded 'straight news' in popular newspapers in the 1930s. As Curran notes, popular newspapers, financially dependent on advertising, increasingly sought material with an universal appeal. By 1936, of the principal Fleet Street popular dailies, only the *Daily Herald* devoted more space to public affairs than human interest. The ailing *Daily Mirror*'s relaunch in 1933 as a paper for a younger, more working-class and more female readership (according to Curran, 'a key moment in the incorporation of the press by the entertainment industry') saw public affairs content slashed to 6 per cent of total news coverage, sport increased to 21 per cent and human interest to over 30 per cent, as the paper highlighted 'features, sex and crime stories' in its pages. Further, by the 1930s the popular press had abandoned traditional grammatical forms and formal vocabulary to mimic the rhythms, clichés and slang terms of ordinary speech, and the 1930s saw newspaper editors increasingly master the visual layout of their papers, integrating headlines, photographs and competing stories in an ever more eye-catching fashion. The changing interwar appearance of newspapers (lower density of print and clearer presentation, bolder headlines, shorter sentences and more concise paragraphs) has been directly ascribed to the brevity and clarity of radio bulletins.[68]

Above all, in the late 1930s both broadcasters and the 'quality' press alike used the BBC's contribution to news in Britain to attack the popular press and the power of the press barons. In an address to the Institute of Journalists in October 1937, BBC Public Relations Director Sir Stephen Tallents announced that in this 'age of News'... the British broadcast news service is the ally of responsible journalism everywhere...a newspaper with a private axe to grind cannot now invent or suppress news so easily as it could before wireless came...'[69] In a Penguin Special in 1938, broadcaster and former *Times* editor Wickham Steed put it more powerfully still:

> the advent of wireless broadcasting, the broadcasting of news and views, is one of the most wholesome influences that could possibly have come into our public life... in the long run, it may help to save the press itself from some of the evils and dangers which now beset honest journalism.[70]

These statements (whether or not actually *true*) served yet again to enhance the prestige of broadcasting at the expense of the press. Few if any commentators speculated until war was nearly upon them on the effect on the British people's understanding of the world around them of a monopoly wireless organisation too fearful of controversy, an elite press too closely associated with the establishment and a popular press too mindful of its profit margins to offer serious domestic and foreign news coverage.

It may be impossible to disentangle the effects upon newspaper content respectively of competition from broadcasting and from within the newspaper industry itself, but in one respect above all the influence of the BBC on newspaper contents is clear: to the popular press, the BBC itself was news. This was true whether reporting the machinations of BBC mandarins or the outcome of BBC SOS messages – the latter, of course equally newsworthy whether family members reached a dying relative in time ('Called Back after 16 Years. Aged Mother and Son Reunited after Broadcast SOS') or tragically failed to do so ('SOS and Race to Dying Wife; Luck Turns too Late').[71] Special weekly radio pages were first instituted in the early 1930s (the *Daily Express*, for instance, considered them invaluable both as page fillers and revenue boosters), and the *Daily Mail's* radio correspondent Collie Knox made a name for himself with his steady stream of invective against the institution that had once brutally turned him down for a job.[72] Whether laudatory or critical, news of BBC policy decisions, reviews of BBC programmes or gossip about radio personalities had the dual effect of attracting newspaper readers and advertising the BBC itself. Thus the popular press itself helped make the BBC both a household name and a national institution.

War and news, 1939–45

During the Second World War the commercial interests of the press suddenly found themselves pitted against not just the BBC's definition of public service but the national interest itself. With the ever increasing demand for authoritative and immediate news, radio news underwent an expansion that the press was powerless to prevent.[73]

In recognition of the state of emergency, the BBC immediately instituted morning, lunchtime and afternoon bulletins on the wartime 'Home Service'. Within a week, however, the *Glasgow Herald* was suggesting that only the press should report war news (the BBC should confine itself to government announcements and 'distractive entertainment'), and soon newspaper editorials were warning that the public was becoming unhealthily addicted to radio bulletins and that newspapers alone provided sufficiently reasoned comment and analysis. They also accused the BBC of plans to broadcast live from the battlefields – something the BBC strenuously denied.[74] Press pressure ensured the establishment of the notorious wartime embargo system by which the BBC agreed to use no news received after 5 p.m. in bulletins until the following 7 a.m. broadcast, and none received between midnight and 5 a.m. before 4 p.m. that afternoon (thus allowing respectively the morning and evening newspapers to break news). However, NPA calls for an end to morning news bulletins altogether were rejected by the BBC, secure in its argument that not only public morale but national prestige was at stake, and that if the British public was denied BBC news it would turn to news on German stations.[75] Although during the 'phoney war' BBC news came under severe criticism for its limited and repetitive character, by the end of August 1940 three-quarters of respondents in a Mass-Observation survey claimed to have more confidence in BBC news than newspaper news. [76]

The British press began the war with its morale and reputation in tatters (the *Daily Express* in particular haunted by its assertion 'There will be no European war'). Over the course of the war, despite shortages of newsprint, disruption of supplies, censorship and other handicaps, newspaper circulations rose to unprecedented levels, especially for the popular London dailies. Yet compared to the BBC, newspapers had a bad war. Although eager for good news in preference to bad, readers were quick to condemn the frequent examples of over-optimism in their newspapers. In comparison, the BBC maintained almost complete national wavelength coverage and the reputation of BBC news reports (always more circumspect than press accounts) survived instances of over-optimism unscathed. Indeed, listeners tended to blame the BBC's official sources, not the BBC itself.[77] Emboldened by public feeling, the BBC increasingly bypassed the press's embargo policy by seeking out independent confirmation of agency news stories, which then ceased to be agency 'property', and by broadcasting any news that had already been reported on foreign stations. Audiences for every news bulletin rose throughout the war: by 1944 the average audience for the 9 o'clock news was 54 per cent of the adult population, over sixteen million listeners (compared with a combined daily *Mirror/Express/Mail/Herald* circulation of under ten million).[78] In February 1941 BBC Listener Research found that nearly two-thirds of respondents considered BBC news '100% reliable'. Most gratifying for the BBC, several respondents remarked that 'I heard it on the wireless' tended to be the last word in any dispute about the news – accompanied by the corollary: 'it has not been on the wireless, so it is probably newspaper talk'.[79] Newspaper assertions that the British public *dis*liked news bulletins, the Institute of Journalists's call on the BBC to abandon its early morning bulletins, and rumours that the NPA might be given a radio wavelength of its own (since 'the BBC is becoming an increasing rival to Fleet Street'), only confirmed the BBC's news strength as a news medium.[80]

Two things marked the decisive shift from press to BBC priority in news. First, the BBC began at last systematically to exploit the powers of the medium. From Charles Gardner's commentary of a dogfight over Dover to Bruce Belfrage trailing the latest despatch from Cairo with the preface 'It's a cracking good one', the BBC was modified its formal tone and became more 'human'. More popular presentation styles included a greater emphasis on commentary and explanation, as well as an attempt to emulate American drama-documentary techniques in topical war features. The use of eyewitness accounts exemplified the BBC's new confidence in war reporting, as Godfrey Talbot (with the British tank advance at the start of the Battle of El Alamein), Richard Dimbleby (in a bomber over Germany) and the ever increasing band of war reporters set out, armed with the latest recording technology, to find the human interest news behind the war and to broadcast from as near the battlefront as was technically feasible.[81]

The D-Day landings confirmed this change.[82] The Americans had given their radio networks extensive access to the front line; if the BBC did not match American coverage, British, American, even world audiences might conclude that the Americans were doing most of the fighting.[83] A dramatic change in official perceptions of the news providers thus saw for the first time the BBC formally accorded priority in access to news. From D-Day to the end of the war BBC correspondents were given unprecedented access to front line news and facilities. British listeners followed the Normandy campaign day by day with the BBC's 62-strong War Reporting Unit. The nightly news programme *War Report* attracted audience figures regularly over 50 per cent (even greater than for *ITMA*).[84] At first the press was unusually generous in its praise of the BBC's coverage, reassured by the 'astonishing' demand for newspapers (especially evening papers) since D-Day. But they soon recognised the significance of the change; by January 1945 press journalists were complaining that the authorities now routinely held war news back, not for the evening papers, but for release in the BBC 9 o'clock news. The newspapers which performed best in the last years of the war (most spectacularly the *Daily Mirror*), did so by highlighting their entertainment not their news content.[85]

In July 1945 the BBC unilaterally terminated its prewar scheduling agreement with the press ('Listeners are now in the habit of morning and mid-day news'). The Corporation, under its new Director-General William Haley – former editor of *The Times* – was already planning a peacetime service with eleven daily bulletins across two networks, starting at 7 a.m.[86] The war ended with the press and broadcasting now equivalent and mutually independent news providers for the first time.

Conclusions

Given the way in which the BBC was instituted and structured, the press and broadcast media were destined to have an uneasy competitive relationship. In 1922 it seemed to all concerned that a state-organised monopoly institution was preferable to American-style commercialism; the press, who had seen radio as a threat rather than an opportunity, realised too late that they had effectively shut themselves out from broadcasting in Britain. The result was conflict between a single monopoly radio broadcaster and a diverse set of press interests united in their belief that news should remain the property of the print media.

The subsequent development of radio news was coloured both by these initial misperceptions and by the press's concerted attempts to undermine radio's innate competitive advantage of immediacy. The two media appeared in the interwar years to have reached some kind of accommodation, mutually benefiting from the new public interest in news of all kinds and together fostering areas of mass public interest. But ironically, the restraints placed on the interwar BBC served above all to mark out its position in an already crowded market-place: its rationed bulletins, impersonal and unsensational tone, its discriminating approach to 'important' and 'accurate' news, and its close structural ties with, yet semi-independence from, government, all served to give the medium of broadcasting in Britain an unique air of authority and integrity which distanced it from the irresponsible, partisan and increasingly entertainment-led popular press. The increase in circulation of popular newspapers was largely at the expense of news content; people turned to radio for information.

Although by the late 1930s the BBC had done much to extend its news operation, the Second World War was decisive in redefining the relationship between print and broadcasting. The press could only look on as the BBC abandoned scheduling controls, embraced new technology and presentation techniques, and for the first time exploited the radio medium to its limit in bringing the British people authoritative round-the-clock news coverage. The BBC would of course trade on its wartime image for the next 50 years; but the different status popularly accorded to print and broadcast news (including, from 1955, Independent Television News: lighter and brighter but still a recognisable version of the BBC original) would remain one of the most characteristic features of the British news media in the twentieth century.

Notes

1 The bulletin reported, first in normal speech, then at dictation speed, the final election speeches before the following day's General Election; a train robber; the sale of a Shakespearean first folio; a London fog; and the latest billiards score. Reuters Archive, London [hereafter Reuters]: 1/902721 LN492, Leonard Miall, 'Here is the News', typescript, 30 June 1980, p. 1.

2 While historians of the BBC have noted the role of the press in the development of broadcast news, historians of the press have largely ignored the effects of broadcasting on the press. For broadcast news, see Asa Briggs. *The Birth of Broadcasting* (London: Oxford University Press, 1961) and *The Golden Age of Wireless* (London: Oxford University Press, 1965), passim; Paddy Scannell and David Cardiff. *A Social History of British Broadcasting, Volume I, 1922–30: Serving the Nation* (Oxford: Basil Blackwell, 1991), Chapters 2, 3, 6. Press histories barely mention the coming of broadcasting: Stephen Koss, *The Rise and Fall of the Political Press in Britain* (London: Fontana, 1990), for instance, dismisses its effects in less than two pages (pp. 827–8); James Curran and Jean Seaton, *Power Without Responsibility: the Press and Broadcasting in Britain* (London: Routledge, various edns) discusses the two media separately.

3 Briggs, *Birth of Broadcasting*, Part II.

4 See Erik Barnouw, *A Tower in Babel: a History of Broadcasting in the United States, Volume I: to 1933* (New York: Oxford University Press, 1966), chapters 1–3.

5 See *Daily Mail*, 16 June 1920; Tom Clarke, *My Northcliffe Diary* (London: Victor Gollancz, 1931), pp. 149–51; S.J. Taylor, *The Great Outsiders: Northcliffe, Rothermere and the* Daily Mail (London: Weidenfeld and Nicolson, 1996), pp. 201–2; Briggs, *Birth of Broadcasting*, pp. 46–7.

6 A.P. Ryan, *Lord Northcliffe* (London: Collins, 1953), pp. 149–52; Clarke, however, describes Northcliffe's 'suspicion' of radio. Clark, *My Northcliffe Diary*, pp. 140, 274–5, 297.

7 Briggs, *Birth of Broadcasting*, pp. 21, 110.

8 See Briggs, *Birth of Broadcasting*, p. 97; *The Times*, 15 November 1922.

9 See, for instance, Crawford Committee minutes, BBC Written Archive Centre, Caversham [BBC WAC]: files R4/28/4-12, R4/29/1-3, R4/30/1, passim. As late as 1929 BBC critics were banned from some West End theatres, since 'a broadcast criticism is a totally different thing from a newspaper criticism ... a good play may be utterly doomed by the voice of a single critic'. *Popular Wireless*, 5 October 1929.

10 BBC WAC: R28/154/1, Broadcasting Committee minutes, 12 October 1922; Minutes of Conference with representatives of the Press, News Agencies and the BBC, 26 October 1922; Agreement of 11 November 1922, Minutes of meeting of 12 December 1922. *The Times*, 15 November 1922.

11 The *Gazette's* circulation rose in consequence. See BBC WAC: S60/5/2/1 Reith diary, 23 January–20 February 1923, and Briggs, *Birth of Broadcasting*, p. 142.

12 See J.C.W. Reith, *Into the Wind* (London: Hodder and Stoughton, 1949), pp. 93–4.

13 *Daily Express*, 5 April 1923; *Evening Standard*, 5 April 1925. See also *Daily Mail* 13–18 January 1928.

14 Reith, *Into the Wind*, p. 90; *Report of the Broadcasting Committee, 1923*, Cmd. 1951 (London: HMSO, 1923), p. 31.

15 Ibid., pp. 5–6, 36.

16 BBC WAC: R28/154/1, Memorandum of agreement, 16 September 1924, and draft June 1924.

17 According, at any rate, to the *Daily Express*, 6 April 1923.

18 *Evening News*, 27 February 1925; *Daily Mail*, 28 February 1925. For Wireless League, see Mark Pegg, *Broadcasting and Society 1918–1939* (London: Croom Helm, 1983), pp. 82–7. Beaverbrook 'had made up his mind there must be monopoly in Broadcasting, but that he had to be in it'. BBC WAC: S60/5/2/1, Reith dairy, 23 March, 1923.

19 Huw Richards, *The Bloody Circus: the* Daily Herald *and the Left* (London: Pluto Press, 1997), p. 89.

20 BBC WAC: R28/169, Clements to Carpendale, 15 February 1924; Burrows to Broadcasting editor, Reuters, 6 December 1923 (his italics).

21 Beaverbook, quoted in Curran and Seaton, p. 55. BBC WAC R28/169 Palmer to Reuters, 27 May 1924.

22 BBC WAC: R28/154/1, Minutes of meeting of Press Committee, 20 February 1925; transcript of meeting with Postmaster-General, 13 March 1925. See also Reuters: 1/876002, LN91, Minutes Book, 20 February 1925.

23 Scannell and Cardiff, *A Social History of British Broadcasting*, pp. 25–6.

24 BBC WAC: R4/29/3, Broadcasting Committee 1925, Paper No. 77, Hamilton Fyfe, 'Wireless and the Press' R4/28/11, Minutes of twelfth meeting of Broadcasting Committee, 3 February 1925.

25 House of Lords Record Office [HLRO]: Beaverbrook Papers (BBK) H/56, correspondence October–December 1928.

26 Record of conversation with Baldwin, 22 December 1922, in John Vincent (ed.), *The Crawford Papers: the Journals of David Lindsay, Twenty-Seventh Earl of Crawford and Tenth Earl of Balcarres, 1871–1940, during the Years 1892 to 1940* (Manchester: Manchester University Press, 1984), p. 510.

27 For Reith on Beaverbrook see Hugh Cudlipp, *The Prerogative of the Harlot: Press Barons and Power* (London: Bodley Head, 1980), p. 232, Ian McIntyre, *The Expense of Glory: a life of John Reith* (London: HarperCollins, 1993), pp. 123, 136, 260, 263, HLRO: BBK C/273 (Reith correspondence), passim. For Reith on Riddell, see Reith, pp. 93–4, BBC WAC: S60/5/2/1, Reith diary, 8 March 1923, 10 March 1925 (Riddell introduced to Reith's mother), etc.

28 *Vincent, The Crawford Papers*, pp. 504–6.

29 *Report of the Broadcasting Committee, 1925*, Cmd. 2599 (London, HMSO, 1926), p. 11.

30 Vincent, *The Crawford Papers*, pp. 3, 505.

31 Briggs, *Birth of Broadcasting*, p. 359; Donald Read, *The Power of News: the History of Reuters 1849–1989* (London: Oxford University Press, 1992), pp. 202–4.

32 BBC WAC: R28/154/2: News agreements 31 January 1927, 22 February 1927, 18 September 1928.

33 BBC WAC: R28/169, Matheson to Eckersley, 4 May 1928; R28/177/1, Matheson to Reith, 18 October 1927.

34 BBC WAC: R28/177/2, Philip Macer-Wright, 'Suggestions for the improvement of the BBC News Service', 24 September 1928.

35 BBC WAC: R28/154/3, Riddell to Reith, 11 May 1929.

36 '[T]here was no news of the normal type or standard for broadcasting'. BBC WAC:R28/79, News Service Review of the Year 1930. See also Reuters: Miall transcript, p. 8, Scannell and Cardiff, p. 118.

37 Scannell and Cardiff, *A Social History of British Broadcasting* pp. 48–50.

38 BBC WAC: R28/79, 'News', undated memorandum (1940?).

39 For instance, Kenneth Adam and R.T. Clarke *(Manchester Guardian)*, Tony Wigan *(Belfast Telegraph)*. Jonathan Dimbleby, *Richard Dimbleby: a Biography* (London: Hodder and Stoughton, 1975, pp. 70–1.

40 See BBC WAC: R4/7/18/6, R4/7/18/5, Minutes of Evidence of Broadcasting Committee 1935.

41 For 'controversy' see Scannell and Cardiff, *A Social History of British Broadcasting*, Part I, passim. For Dimbleby's prewar BBC career, see Dimbleby, *Richard Dimbleby*. Ch. 3.

42 BBC WAC: R28/159, News Agreement , 25 March 1938.

43 BBC WAC: R28/169, Murray to Burrows, 2 September 1924.

44 Curran and Seaton, *Power Without Responsibility*, p. 55.

45 'This is vital for our Country'. BBC WAC: R28/154/2, Strutt to Stobart, 29 September 1926; see also Briggs, *Birth of Broadcasting*, p. 267.

46 BBC WAC: R28/177/2. Matheson to Eckersley, 4 May 1928.

47 BBC WAC: R28/172, Matheson to Reith, 10 June 1932.

48 Dimbleby, *Richard Dimbleby*, p. 73.

49 See Scannell and Cardiff, *A Social History of British Broadcasting*, p. 281; BBC WAC: R28/169, Burrows to Murray, 3 September 1924; R28/170, Burrows to Carey Clements, 7 November 1924; and R28/225/1 passim.

50 See *Sunday Graphic*, 25 November 1928, *The Times*, 20–21 December 1928.

51 See HLRO: BBK H/108, Night Circulation Report, 21 January 1936, Briggs, *Golden Age*, p. 505.

52 See Koss, *The Rise and Fall of the Political Press in Britain*, pp. 1000–5.

53 For instance, between 1927 and 1937 *Daily Mail* sports coverage rose from 27 to 36 per cent of its total news content, while home news content fell from 10 to 6 per cent. Curran and Seaton *Power Without Responsibility*, p. 57.

54 See BBC WAC: R28/171 passim; R28/137, John Syme (National Union of Newsvendors) to the Secretary, BBC, 6 July 1934; *Morning Post*, 17 June 1927; *Newspaper World*, 18 June 1927.

55 BBC WAC:R28/152/2, Murray–Jardine–Brown correspondence 13–31 July 1936.

56 Reuters: Miall transcript, pp. 6–7; BBC WAC: R28/79, News Service Review of the Year, 1930; Scannell and Cardiff, *A Social History of British Broadcasting*, pp. 44–5.

57 BBC WAC: R28/79, News Service Review of the Year, 1930; Dimbleby, *Richard Dimbleby*, pp. 77, 85–6.

58 Wickham Steed, *The Press* (London, Penguin Special, 1938), p. 213; BBC WAC: S60/5/2/1, Reith dairy, May 1926; Lord Reith, 'Forsan...', *Parliamentary Affairs*, 17/1, 1963/4, p. 30.

59 See BBC WAC: R28/79, 1931 Review of the Year; St. John Ervine, *Time and Tide* , 10 October 1931.

60 James Margach, *The Abuse of Power: The War Between Downing Street and the Media from Lloyd George to Callaghan* (London: W.H. Allen, 1978), p. 60. Richard Cockett, *Twilight of Truth: Chamberlain, Appeasement and the Manipulation of the Press* (London: Weidenfeld and Nicolson, 1989), p. 1.

61 BBC WAC: R34/325, John Coatman, 'The BBC and National defence', 5 October 1938.

62 Briggs, *Golden Age*, pp. 645–7; Scannell and Cardiff, *A Social History of British Broadcasting*, pp. 125–7, 130–2. Compare Coatman's scathing memorandum, above, to Clarke's more complacent assessment: BBC WAC: R28/218, Clarke to Nicolls, 4 November 1938.

63 Cockett, *Twilight of Truth*, pp. 74, 80, and Chapter 2 passim; *The Listener* , 6 October 1938 ('Broadcasting... satisfies that hunger for news which siezes the population during critical hours... [it] scotches rumour... [helps] maintain order and guide action').

64 BBC WAC: R28/184, Clark to Tallents, 10 February 1939; R28/177/4, Clark to Nicolls, 19 August 1938.

65 See *Newspaper World*, 11 June 1927 19 November 1927, 26 November 1927, 9 April 1929.

66 For radio licence figures see Pegg, *Broadcasting and Society 1918–1939*, p. 7; for press circulation see PEP (Political and Economic Planning) *Report on the British Press* (London, PEP, 1938), p. 84.

67 *Time and Tide*, 24 February 1928.

68 Curran and Seaton, *Power Without Responsibility* pp. 57, 115, 67; D.L. Lemahieu, *A Culture for Democracy: Mass-Communication and the Cultivated Mind in Britain Between the Wars* (Oxford: Clarendon Press 1988), pp. 30–2, 43, 69–80; Pegg, *Broadcasting and Society 1918–1939*, pp. 150–1.

69 BBC WAC:R28/79, Tallents, 'Fleet Street and Portland Place', 12 October 1937.

70 Steed, *The Press*, pp. 209, 220, 223.

71 *Daily Chronicle*, 27 March 1928; *Evening News*, 9 February 1929.

72 See HLRO: BBK H/84, John Gordon to Beaverbrook, 17 July 1931; Collie Knox, *It Might Have Been You* (London: Chapman and Hall, 1938), pp. 286–90, 363–409.

73 For BBC news during the war, see Siân Nicholas, *The Echo of War: Home Front Propaganda and the Wartime BBC 1939–45* (Manchester: Manchester University Press, 1996), chapter 6.

74 *Glasgow Herald*, 5 September 1939; *News of the World*, 1 October 1939; *The Listener*, 12 October 1939, p. 706.

75 BBC WAC: R28/121/1, Wellington to Nicolls, 19 September 1939; agreement between BBC and Newspapers and Periodicals Emergency Council, 25 September 1939. R28/184, note of meeting between BBC and NPA/Newspaper Society, 7 December 1939.

76 Mass-Observation Archive, University of Sussex [M-O A]: File Report [FR] 375, Tom Harrisson, 'The Popular Press?', article for *Horizon*, August 1940.

77 Ibid.; A.D. Wadsworth, *Newspaper Circulations 1800–1954* (Manchester: Norbury, Lockwood and Co., 1955), p. 35; M-O A: FR 1914, 'Fortnightly bulletin', 15 September 1943.

78 BBC WAC: R9/9/7, LR/2440, 3 March 1944; Wadsworth, p. 35.

79 BBC WAC: R9/9/5, LR/217, 10 February 1941. See also R9/9/7, LR/1644, 6 April 1943.

80 *Newspaper World*, 27 September 1941.

81 Nicholas, *The Echo of War*, pp. 197, 202–5.

82 Between 1942 and 1944 the BBC had played down the second front. This seems to have been, in part at least, because news editors were reluctant to give Lord Beaverbrook, spokesman of the 'Second Front Now' movement and long-time adversary of the BBC, any more publicity than necessary. See BBC WAC: R28/88/2, European News Editor to North American Station Director, 25 April 1942.

83 BBC WAC: R/28/280/1, Graves to Radcliffe, 2 October 1942; R28/280/2, Ryan to Brendan Bracken, 8 February 1943.

84 For *War Report*, see Nicholas, *The Echo of War*, pp. 211–8 and Desmond Hawkins, *War Report, D-Day to VE-Day* (London: BBC/Ariel Books, 1985).

85 *Newspaper World*, 13 January 1945; Wadsworth, p. 29.

86 See BBC WAC: R28/88/4, Ryan note, 2 January 1945, and note of meeting to discuss Ryan note, 6 February 1945.

7

The Relationship of Reuters and other News Agencies with the British Press 1858–1984: Service at Cost or Business for Profit?

Donald Read

News and news agencies

The financial relationship between the British press and the news agencies which have supplied it with news has been more than a matter of money payments. The circumstances of such payments have raised important questions of principle and practice in the conduct of journalism.

Could or should news agencies expect to make significant profits out of selling their news? Is news a commodity or a public service? If a commodity, should agencies always sell at the highest price that the market will bear? If a service to the public, does this mean selling at the lowest price? Does it also mean that Governments are entitled to intervene in what they declare to be the national interest? Should Governments therefore offer subsidies to news agencies? Should agencies ever accept such payments? Or should they insist upon maintaining standards of independence and truth in newsgathering, even if there are damaging financial consequences, refusing to colour their news to suit either their media customers or national Governments? But what if the price of such purity is likely to be bankruptcy?

These questions were (and are) difficult to answer conclusively. Whenever possible, news agency managers have avoided asking them; sometimes, however, usually at times of crisis, they have had to commit themselves to answers, if not explicitly at least implicitly. The same questions about service or profit can of course be asked about the newspapers themselves, in the past and in the present.

Lofty claims have been made about the role of the 'fourth estate', not least with regard to its part in fostering good international relations by keeping readers fully informed. The mission of the press, exclaimed James Grant, a Victorian newspaper editor and author of *The Newspaper Press* (1871), was 'to Enlighten, to Civilize and to Morally Transform the World'. Francis Williams, a leading British journalist of a later generation, made the same claim in a 1953 Unesco booklet on *Transmitting World News*. Williams wrote of the responsibility borne by a free press to spend money upon foreign correspondents. 'Newspapers must pay their way. But they must be prepared to include in their overall budget a public service of world news reporting which may be relatively less profitable than national news and feature services'.[1]

Williams made this point still more strongly with regard to news agencies, and he added an important gloss about the need for reduced news charges for the media of the Third World:

> Upon the world news agencies this conception of public responsibility imposes a special duty – the obligation to report news from and to less-developed and relatively less-profitable areas of the world, as well as to those where large newspaper concentrations bring substantial returns.

Williams was of course here anticipating the 'New World Information Order' debate of two decades later.

This global dimension of responsibility is not the present concern. Responsibility begins at home, and we are interested here in discussing the terms, both financial and moral, upon which overseas news has been supplied to the British press (and later to radio and television) by the news agencies, and in particular by Reuters, the London-based news agency.

Reuters started in 1851. Thanks to the new overland telegraph and undersea cable networks, developed from the 1840s onwards, mid-Victorian newspapers were beginning to have access to foreign and imperial news in minutes and hours, whereas previously delivery had taken days and weeks. But the cost to each newspaper of collecting such news for itself was very high. Only *The Times* maintained a full network of correspondents and stringers in Europe and beyond. By accepting news through Reuters, the London newspapers came to realise that they could obtain a much fuller supply of material than they were each able to collect for themselves. And yet they remained free to appoint their own resident correspondents in the major news capitals, and they could send special correspondents to report wars or particular events. Crucially, they found that their readers did not complain because the same Reuters' telegrams were appearing in other newspapers.

Success encouraged imitation. At different periods Reuters was to face strong competition from other British or foreign news agencies. Among its London-based competitors, the Central News (1871), the Exchange Telegraph (Extel) (1872) and the British United Press (BUP) (1922) were the most enduring. These rivals threatened at various times to overtake Reuters, but never quite did so. Central News and Extel concentrated upon supplying overseas news to Britain only, and did not generally compete with the outward services of Reuters to the British Empire and elsewhere. In addition, Central News and Extel reported domestic British news, whereas Reuters left this to its ally, the Press Association (PA) (1868). In 1937 Extel and the PA took over Central News, which had been losing money for years, and its overseas news operation was closed down. Extel itself had ceased to be a serious competitor for Reuters by the end of the Second World War, and its foreign news service was stopped at the end of 1956, losing £20 000 a year. After that war, two foreign news agencies emerged (and remain) as strong rivals to Reuters in selling news to the British and world media – firstly, the Associated Press (AP), the big American agency based in New York; and soon also Agence France-Presse (AFP), the Paris-based agency. In 1992 the *Daily Telegraph* gave up subscribing to Reuters in favour of AFP.[2]

Since the time of Havas, which had begun in Paris in the 1830s as the first of all news agencies, few if any of them have made regular profits from the sale of news. Havas made money by acting as an advertising agency and was, in any case, subsidised by the French Government. AFP, the successor to Havas, is still subsidised. Another basis for prosperity has been co-operative ownership. The Press Association in Britain is owned by the provincial papers, while the Associated Press in the United States is the property of the American media. The first purpose of both the PA and the AP has been to collect news for their respective owners as cheaply as possible. BUP, a strong competitor of Reuters between the wars, was an offshoot of the United Press (UP), started in the United States in 1907 to compete with AP. UP aimed to make a commercial profit, and for over 50 years it was apparently successful in this purpose. Indeed, UP was nominated in its company history in 1957 as perhaps the first news agency to have made money from the sale of news rather than from subsidiary non-journalistic activities. In that year UP merged with the International News Service to become United Press International (UPI); but it subsequently began to lose ground, and by the 1980s was in danger of collapse.[3]

AP and UP enjoyed the advantage of serving the huge American home market, whereas non-American agencies have had to operate with much smaller home bases. A memorandum entitled 'AFP and International Public Information' by P.L. Bret, AFP's director-general, was submitted in 1948 to the United Nations. Bret argued that it was impossible to run an international news agency anywhere in Western Europe at a commercial profit because the press base in each country was too small: 'from the time an agency has passed a certain stage of development and, in particular, it has gone beyond the phase where it simply covers national information, it can no longer meet the whole of its cost with the resources of its press alone'. It then had no choice, claimed Bret in tacit justification of AFP's own French Government subsidy, but to seek official help. Yet interestingly, the memorandum went on to suggest an alternative course. This would be to create independent news agencies financed by the automatic transfer by governments of the proceeds of an expenditure tax, rather as the BBC automatically received its licence revenue. Each of these agencies could then offer its own factual 'public interest service', free from official influence. 'This bare, neutral and impersonal information cannot be produced except in the absence of any kind of pressure'. Control of news, continued Bret, assumed that readers needed direction in their reading; in contrast, objective news of the kind which he was recommending sought to treat citizens 'as being of age', letting them make up their own minds. Eventually, concluded Bret, if news agencies with complete financial and editorial independence were created in different countries, they might begin to work together, producing 'largely identical news'. The existence of such a common news service would then encourage international unity. Bret's piece was a rare and stimulating instance of the head of a news agency thinking in the abstract about problems of finance and control, and how to solve them.

Reuters 1858–1918

Against this background, what then has been the position of Reuters in response to the 'service or profit' question and related issues? The short answer is that its position down the years has been variable – sometimes emphasising profit, sometimes service, and often both at the same time.

In 1858, after seven years of frustration, Julius Reuter finally succeeded in selling his news to the London daily papers. *The Times* tried to stand out, but had to subscribe when all the other London dailies started to do so. Reuter had given the papers a fortnight's free trial, and they had quickly found his service of telegrams from overseas to be indispensable. Reuter news became even more valuable when it was extended to include regular and full reports from America, Asia and Africa, as well as from Europe. As his geographical range widened, Reuter increased his subscription charges. The earliest surviving cash book (for 1862) shows *The Times* paying £100 per month, the *Morning Chronicle* and *Morning Herald* £83 6s. 8d., the *Daily News* £75 and the *Daily Telegraph* and the *Morning Advertiser* £66 13s. 4d. It is unclear whether these differing payments reflected differing telegram usage, or whether Reuter had been raising his charges as contracts came up for renewal, probably the latter.

James Grant of the *Morning Advertiser* had been the first London editor to subscribe to Reuter telegrams in 1858. In his History of *The Newspaper Press*, published in 1871, Grant recalled how when one paper agreed to accept telegrams from a fresh part of the world at additional charge, 'the others were compelled to follow at any cost'. To calm the apprehensions of the London editors, Reuter did eventually promise not to go on demanding increases. By the end of the 1860s subscriptions for all the London morning dailies had been equalised at £1600 each per annum. This was a substantial figure, equivalent to well over £60 000 a year at the end of the twentieth century.

The feeling persisted in journalistic circles that 'Reuters' (as the agency had become known) was doing too well out of its position of dominance. There was speculation about the level of profits being made by the new Reuter's Telegram Company, which had been formed as a private limited company in 1865. Grant suggested in his *History* that the company was making £25 000 per annum, partly from charging the British press highly but even more from selling telegrams to the Continent, the United States and the colonies. Grant's was a fair guess. Profits reached a peak of nearly £32 000 in 1868, and the company paid a comfortable 10 per cent dividend until 1875.[4]

Julius Reuter never pretended that he was doing other than making as much money as he could out of the sale of news. In old age he was said to have often remarked: 'If I did give them something for nothing at the beginning, I've made thousands of pounds out of them since'.[5] Did this mean that he felt no sense of obligation? Not entirely. From the first, he had committed himself to maintaining high standards of accuracy and to being first with the news. He also took care to be impartial in the distribution of his telegrams, never selling them exclusively. His 1865 contract as managing director bound him to act 'without giving priority to any one over any other'. A *Vanity Fair* cartoon of Reuter in its 'Men of the Day' series (14 December 1872) recognised that, although his telegrams had given him 'command of public opinion on foreign affairs', he had never used them to gain unfair advantage for himself or any individual or country. He had thus established commendable standards of news agency service. But in another meaning of the word, he never felt a duty of public service in the sense of selling his news to the papers at less than the full market price. On the contrary, we have seen how, as his news gained in reputation for reliability and range, he charged the maximum that the London papers were grumblingly prepared to pay.

Yet there were already connections building up which were making Reuters into a semi-official national and imperial institution; and throughout the later-Victorian and Edwardian periods, as well as seeking to make money, the agency was keen to maintain this favoured status. Julius Reuter cultivated the acquaintance of leading ministers, including Lord Palmerston, the Prime Minister in 1855–8 and 1859–65. On several occasions Julius personally delivered important early news to Downing Street. Reuters was emerging as the news agency of the British Empire and, as such, it began to perform a visible public service day by day. It opened offices with full-time managers in the main cities of the formal and informal Empire, starting with Alexandria in 1865 and Bombay in 1866. Against this background, the word 'service' came into use inside the agency in a further sense. Senior staff began to regard themselves as on a level with senior home and colonial civil servants, doing essential work in support of the British cause worldwide. Reuters' managers, correspondents and editors at home and overseas started to be described as 'officers' within the Reuters' 'service'.[6]

This was a major responsibility, but one which required steadily increasing expenditure. Expansion had to be undertaken without commensurate growth in revenue either at home or from the colonies. Spending upon 'telegrams and agencies' grew from just over £27000 in 1866 to nearly £60000 in 1878, the year of Julius Reuter's retirement. The net profit for that year was £5 627, less than one-fifth the figure of ten years earlier. The dividend dropped to 5 per cent. Shareholders were told that these difficulties resulted from the high costs of colonial war reporting. No dividend at all was paid for 1885, the year of the failure of the Gordon relief expedition to Khartoum. Spending upon news collection and delivery peaked in 1900 during the Boer War at more than £160000 for the year.

The management of Reuters now regretfully accepted that it could not expect to make a significant overall profit out of news. Baron Herbert de Reuter, who had succeeded his father as managing director in 1878 and continued until 1915, searched with mixed success down the years for alternative sources of revenue and profit. Two non-journalistic sidelines did well – the transmission of private telegrams, and the remittance of money for private firms and individuals. Both services depended upon word-saving Reuter cable codes. Started respectively in 1871 and 1891, they were conducted between London and places throughout the British Empire, and also between places within the Empire. Because the two services were made available over the counter in local Reuters offices, they constituted a direct retail service. As soon as the First World War broke out, however, both services were disrupted by the Admiralty's refusal to permit the use of cable codes. Reuters pressed unsuccessfully for compensation, revealing that its immediate pre-war profit from private telegram and remittance traffic for the period March 1913 to July 1914 had been £6 500.

The collection of news by Reuters for the press was sometimes openly undertaken at a loss. Baron Herbert told shareholders in 1903 that in order to cover the Somaliland expedition, for which most newspapers were depending entirely upon Reuters, 'the expense in camels, servants, runners and supplies of all sorts' was 'out of all proportion to the amount of intelligence received'. By the time of the 1909 shareholders' meeting, the chairman was complaining about the continuous demands of the news department: 'before one excitement has subsided it is succeeded by another, so that for purveyors of the world's intelligence the day appears to have passed by when it was possible to recoup in quiet times for heavy expenditure during periods of political activity'.

On the eve of the outbreak of the First World War in 1914 Reuters was heading towards a major financial crisis and possible bankruptcy. One problem was the declining interest in foreign news among British newspaper readers, an attitude which of course seems remarkable in view of what was to happen in August 1914. A Home University Library book on *The Newspaper*, published in 1913, commented that 'the public at present takes less and less interest every year in either foreign or war correspondence'.[7] In this knowledge, the British newspapers were beginning to press for cuts in their subscriptions to Reuters. Early in 1914, first the *Daily Mirror* and then the *Daily Graphic* demanded reductions. The *Mirror* secured a reduction of one half in its £1 600 payment; but in a desperate attempt to maintain the appearance of equal contributions by all the other London morning papers, the *Graphic* was persuaded to continue paying £1 600 in return for a commitment by Reuters to supply it with £800 worth of advertisements from overseas.

Reuters was saved from its impending financial crisis by the British Government. During the First World War the authorities needed access to the world-wide Reuters' network in order to fight the propaganda war. Various Reuters' news services were given subsidies, and the ownership of the company itself was re-constructed with the help of a secret Government guarantee of £550 000 (equivalent to over £16 000 000 at the end of the century). In other words, in the middle of the greatest war in history there was no doubt in the mind of the British Government that Reuters existed to perform a national service. And Reuters itself, under the new management of Sir Roderick Jones, readily accepted this, although Jones always liked to claim that Reuters had maintained its independence.

Reuters and the British press

After the war, with much Government support removed, and with the private telegram and remittance services in rapid decline, Reuters was once more vulnerable – not perhaps to immediate collapse, but to gradual decay. Once again general news was demonstrating that it could not be sold to the British press at a price sufficient to make much money. In a background briefing for a director, dated 20 April 1931, Jones pointed out that news costs had risen over 20 per cent in the previous five years, whereas income from the British press had actually fallen because of a reduction in the number of newspapers. The Reuters' news service, wrote Jones, 'costs rather more than four times as much as the newspapers are called upon to pay'. Ten years later the position had not changed. The general managers pointed out in a memorandum for the board (8 September 1941) that simply from India alone – where Reuters, as well as supplying overseas news, owned the main internal news service used by the Indian press – revenue was greater than the total revenue received from the entire British press, national and provincial. 'Newspapers abroad are being disproportionately taxed to provide a service cheaply for the British newspapers'.

To help compensate for this imbalance, Jones had found a new prop. From 1920 he had encouraged a rapid and profitable expansion of the Reuters' commercial service of stock and commodity prices and information, both to and from London and to and from India, China, Egypt, Australia and South Africa. At successive annual general meetings Jones described how the commercial service was cushioning losses on the editorial side. By 1933, the profit from the commercial service was running at £23000 per annum. In that year, commercial subscriptions from the Far East alone were worth nearly £60000. This was £11000 more than the total of all British newspaper subscriptions.

In the early postwar period, Jones had virtually owned Reuters. But he always recognised that, in order to ensure the long-term survival of the agency, it needed a broader foundation; it needed to belong not to individuals as shareholders, but to the British press collectively. This switch in ownership was achieved in two stages. Firstly, in 1926 and 1930 the Press Association, representing the provincial papers, bought up the company for £313000; and then in 1941 the PA was joined as a partner by the Newspaper Proprietors Association, representing the national newspaper groups. In becoming the owners of Reuters in 1926, the Press Association could claim to be performing a public service by providing the agency with the protection of a newspaper co-operative. But the PA expected to receive not only its news from Reuters cheaply, but also to be paid an annual dividend. A recurring theme from Jones at annual general meetings was that the owners were getting 'a first-rate foreign service seriously below cost price' (1940). At the same time they were receiving an annual dividend, which totalled nearly £300 000 between 1926 and 1940. A history of the PA, written for internal circulation in 1946, described this dividend as a 'vital element' in its finances.[8]

So Reuters was still expecting to earn money for sharing out among its new owners – even though the PA was a co-operative, and even though Reuters could consequently claim to be itself co-operatively controlled. In a public announcement of the deal (3 December 1925), Jones described it as intended 'to ensure both the permanence of the Agency's relationship with the British Press and its inviolability against outside influences beyond the period of his own personal administration'.[9]

After 1926, in negotiations with Kent Cooper, the manager of the Associated Press, the great American co-operative, Jones liked to emphasise strongly that Reuters was now as much a co-operative news agency as AP itself. And yet in discussions with Karl Bickel of United Press, AP's main American competitor, which was run as a commercial concern, Jones claimed an affinity with UP rather than with AP. Bickel recollected this in a 1943 letter to Cooper. 'He [Jones] always insisted that inasmuch as we were a "dividend" conscious group we understood each other better than Reuters and the AP'. Jones was being characteristically two-faced, but each face did exist within Reuters. Acceptance of obligations of service to the British provincial press, and subsequently to the national press, was demonstrated by the way Reuters supplied them with cheap overseas news; and yet this acceptance existed alongside an aspiration to make a good business profit.[10]

Not that such a good profit-level was ever achieved by Reuters during the 1930s. There was never sufficient money available to pay not only a dividend to the PA and to provide the British papers with news cheaply, but also to modernise the news services fully. Reuters was falling behind in the face of increasing competition from its international rivals. Many of these were subsidised by their respective Governments, and Jones turned with increasing urgency to the British Government for help. The Government, for its part, began to complain about the shortcomings of Reuters in projecting the British point of view abroad. In a memorandum for the Foreign Office (16 January 1935) Jones explained that 'the state-subsidised services of other countries, like France and Germany, and the commercially-privileged services of the United States, are gravely threatening the unsubsidised and the commercially-unprivileged services conducted by Reuters'. Jones wanted indirect subsidies (though he did not like to use the word), such as generous official subscriptions, and reduced cable and radio transmission charges. Reuters' news, he remarked without any sense of contradiction, was 'objective, but thoroughly British in character and tone'.[11]

The Foreign Office accepted the need for Reuters to be made more competitive, but concluded that this would require the removal of Jones himself. His ejection was not finally contrived until 1941. In that year, Reuters was reformed. At the same time as the NPA joined with the PA in the ownership of Reuters, the Reuter Trust was created. The idea of running newspapers under the protection of trusts, intended to ensure editorial independence in the publication of news and views, had come to the fore between the wars – notably, to protect such respected titles as *The Times*, the *Observer* and the *Manchester Guardian*. Trust-protected newspapers remained commercial enterprises to the extent that they were free to seek profit in order to finance their own development. So much was obviously desirable. But in practice profitability often proved unattainable, and the three papers mentioned each had to be more or less subsidised from other sources, such as the profits made by other titles within the same group. C.P. Scott, whose family name was given to the *Manchester Guardian* trust, had declared explicitly in 1926 that 'the paper is carried on as a public service and not for profit'; and yet he knew that the *Guardian* was being sustained by the money earned by the *Manchester Evening News*. Trust protection could not in itself save a newspaper or a news agency, as the failure of the *News Chronicle* later demonstrated.[12]

The 1941 Reuter Trust deed was largely drafted by William Haley, a PA/Reuter director who, as a director of the *Manchester Guardian* group, had already been involved in the creation of the Scott Trust. The Reuter Trust guidelines required 'that no effort shall be spared to expand, develop and adapt the business of Reuters in order to maintain in every event its position as the leading world news agency'. The assumption was that money would be spent upon modernisation, and that profits would be earned for such a purpose. The PA regretfully accepted that it could no longer expect to receive a dividend from Reuters, and none was paid for 40 years. The owners settled for a policy of balancing the books. At the 1958 trustees' meeting W.A. Hawkins from the PA raised Reuters as 'a model operation' because the turnover was well over £2 000 000 'and yet it operated on a profit or loss margin within 2 per cent'.The newspapers did continue to expect, however, that they would be supplied with their overseas news cheaply. Another trustee at the 1958 meeting exclaimed ingenuously that 'Reuters is a magnificent investment. Even if the owners did not pay themselves profits in the form of dividends they certainly got them in the low cost of the news services'. The owners were also aware that any dividends would be taxed, whereas cheap news was not. Haley, the prime author of the Reuter Trust document, had himself given countenance to the existence of this lower material motivation alongside the high purpose of ensuring truth in news from Reuters. Asked during the 1941 negotiations what return the national newspaper proprietors could expect from buying into the company, he had replied: 'the establishment of Reuters as incontestably the greatest news agency in the world; and the use of its steadily improving services at gradually lower prices'. Haley recalled in a letter to the chairman forty years later (18 March 1984) that this had closed the discussion.

An analysis of the company's trading account by Christopher Chancellor, the general manager, submitted to the Reuters' board on 10 June 1947, said plainly that 'provision of a complete news service for members' was 'the basic activity of Reuters'. Beyond that, however, Chancellor suggested that the agency had an obligation to distribute its news as widely as possible, because the Trust guidelines required Reuters 'to maintain in every event its position as the leading world news agency'. This wider involvement, noted Chancellor, brought both prestige and profit. In addition, continued Chancellor brusquely, Reuters conducted its commercial service. 'This is run for the sole purpose of subsidising the news service. If it ceased to show a profit we should discontinue it'.

Finally, Chancellor included a financial overview as at April 1947. This showed an annual deficit of £92 000 on news provided for the press of the countries sharing in the ownership of Reuters. The

Australian Associated Press and the New Zealand Press Association had recently become junior partners alongside the PA and NPA. This deficit on news supplied to their various 'home' territories was cushioned but not completely eliminated by a total of £70 000 received in chief part as news broadcasting subscriptions from the BBC and the Australian Broadcasting Commission. The deficit on news contrasted with a commercial service surplus of £48 000 world-wide, although this was costed marginally, without charge for use of the Reuters' network. Overall, Chancellor recorded an annual trading profit of £36 000 before tax (see Appendix). This margin left the owners without any qualms about taking their news on terms so generous as to amount to the provision by Reuters of an indirect public service to and through the press.

On the occasion of the centenary of Reuters, *The Times* of 12 July 1951 published a leader which directly addressed the 'service or profit' question in the handling of news. It concluded that, although service was the higher purpose, profit must also be an objective:

> News gathering is a business to the extent that, unless it can be made to pay, it loses freedom to tell the truth, but it cannot be regarded merely as a business. Too much is at stake. Unless the common man, upon whom so much responsibility rests nowadays, knows what is happening in world-affairs, he is a citizen blindfold. He depends on the independent gatherers of news to qualify him to vote and to act with free will... What comes from Reuters is a valuable supplement to the truth flowing into newspapers even when they can afford the costly service of a staff of correspondents of their own.

The Times expressed satisfaction that Reuters was now owned by the press, and that it was protected by a trust similar to those established to protect some newspapers 'from falling into unprofessional hands'.

The fact remained, however, that throughout the 1950s and early 1960s Reuters was still struggling to make enough money to finance long-term development, even though no dividend was being paid. The weak financial position of Reuters led it in 1954 into involvement with the Arab News Agency (ANA), despite the knowledge that this organisation was covertly subsidised by the British Government. Reuters handed over to the ANA the distribution of its news throughout most of the Middle East, although still retaining its own news-gathering network. In addition, the ANA paid Reuters a generous subscription as a subsidy – £28 800 in 1960, the fourth highest overseas subscription. The operational connection with the ANA was not terminated until 1969; and even then, the subsidy was covertly continued by quadrupling the BBC external services subscription from £20 000 to £80 000. After John Burgess of the PA had become chairman of Reuters in 1959 he pressed the board to accumulate a surplus 'placed to reserve for capital expenditure and for financing new services during their early non-productive life'. Burgess admitted (7 October 1959) that the owners might feel aggrieved 'at having to subsidise more than is immediately necessary and then see half of the excess going in taxes'. But he argued that it was in the long-term interest of the owners that Reuters should be run efficiently.

The provincial dailies and the London evenings were the steadiest publishers of news from Reuters in these postwar years. The attitude of most of the London dailies was more distant. A 1975 analysis of newspaper content for the Royal Commission on the Press found that only 15 per cent of foreign news in British national newspapers was credited to news agencies at all. The nationals liked to give the impression that they always had their own correspondents in places where important stories were breaking. The *Express*, *Mail*, *Mirror* and *Sun* virtually never credited a foreign affairs story to a news agency. This applied equally to news from Reuters, even though these same papers were part-owners of the agency through the NPA and even though all the national dailies paid the same 'assessments' to Reuters on the assumption of comparable news usage.[13]

From news agency to commercial information systems

'Assessments' were the yearly contributions made by the owners to help pay for the running of Reuters. In 1947 the assessments from the PA, NPA, AAP and NZPA totalled £264 000 (equivalent to about £5 500 000 at the end of the century). Every few years, overall losses were incurred, the last such year being 1967. After each bad year the owners raised their assessments, although they did so without enthusiasm. They regarded their payments as a burden which they carried for the sake of maintaining an assured supply of world news from a British source. They felt themselves to be servicing a service, even though their contributions were the minimum necessary to keep Reuters in business. The Reuters' management, for its part, tried to keep the owners in check. Each autumn, if more than a modest profit on the year seemed to be in prospect, senior staff were quietly urged to increase their spending. The fear was that, if too much came down to the bottom line the owners would at best leave the assessments unchanged, and at worst might even contemplate reductions.

During the 1960s this minimalist attitude began to be abandoned. The owners were persuaded by Burgess, the chairman, in alliance with successive general managers, to start paying realistic assessments in support of the new policy of creating a surplus for development. This change was noticed on 21 March 1967 in a letter to the British Foreign Office from Gerald Long, the general manager 1963–81. Long described the current position and prospects:

Reuters, as you know, does not pay dividends to its owners nor does it seek to make a profit in the commercially accepted sense of the word. We nevertheless must ensure that our trading activities produce an adequate surplus to meet the increasing competition from the other international agencies, and to provide for essential investment in automation and advanced communication techniques.

The owners were now paying assessments totalling £713 600, which (Long conceded) was 'at least twice as much as the British press would have to pay if they were not concerned with the maintenance of a British owned international news agency'. Yet this substantial payment was still not enough. Nigel Judah, the company secretary, had written to Long on 24 June 1966 demonstrating that additional long-term capital was much needed, and arguing that the owners should provide it. Judah pointed out that they were pledged under the terms of the Reuter Trust document to maintain Reuters 'as the leading world news agency'. He recommended that the owners should subscribe for additional ordinary stock to produce a capital injection of £250 000. They refused to do so. Instead, they agreed, albeit faintheartedly, to allow heavy borrowing. Given the exposed financial position of Reuters, Judah did well to secure two successive loans from Morgan Guaranty Trust ($430 000 and $864 000), and one from Credit Suisse (£375 000). At the end of 1973 outstanding borrowing from all sources totalled £1 400 230, only 14 per cent secured.

But by this date Reuters had started to change dramatically. It was ceasing to be an old-style general news agency living on the financial brink. While still selling general news to the media, it moved into the provision of computerised information for traders worldwide. New products introduced by Reuters Economic Services – in particular, Stockmaster (1964) and Monitor (1973) – began to make unprecedented profits. The global economy was opening up, a process which Reuters assisted. After 1980 annual profits began to double and redouble. By 1984 they were passing £74 million. In 1981 Reuters paid a dividend to its owners for the first time since 1940: £1 924 000 was distributed in that year, £5 817 000 in 1982 and £7 799 000 in 1983. The owners now realised that their individual shareholdings in the company, long treated as burdensome, had acquired great financial value. If Reuters were floated on the stock exchange as a public company, these holdings could be sold, or be used to back borrowing. The newspapers could then employ the capital so raised to finance their own long-overdue modernisation. Reuters duly went public in June 1984.

An article in the *Guardian* of 10 June 1982 had published the new position of Reuters. 'It was as if a hidden treasure had been discovered in the loft'. Yet twenty years earlier the same paper's manager, Laurence Scott, had grumbled about its £3 600 Reuter assessment, imposed when the *Guardian* joined the NPA after transferring to London from Manchester. 'These thieves in the NPA. Do they think I'm made of money'. Now the *Guardian's* obligation had turned into a great asset. By 1990 the Guardian group had cashed in Reuter holdings worth over £70 000 000, and had paid off all its debts and mortgages.[14]

Up to 1984, British politicians still insisted upon regarding Reuters as a provider of a public service. They feared that the new company would not be free to take up this responsibility; that a public company would, paradoxically, be less interested in public service, because its first commitment must be to the making of money for its shareholders, many of whom would not be British. A debate took place in the House of Commons on 27 January 1984 when some of these fears were aired. One member, Nicholas Soames, Churchill's grandson, spoke of Reuters in the old vein as 'a splendid British institution'; but Austin Mitchell, the Labour MP who had introduced the motion, recognised that Reuters no longer wished to be regarded in this way. It was now an international organisation, still with its headquarters in London but serving many publics in many parts of the world. Mitchell wanted to be reassured that any new company would not only maintain traditional Reuters' standards of news handling, but would at the same time be allowed by shareholders and Ministers to serve what he called 'the public interest worldwide'. Here was a novel definition of 'public interest', no longer equating it with 'national interest'. In reply, Kenneth Baker, the Minister for Information Technology, deftly reconciled the Soames and Mitchell lines by describing Reuters as 'a national asset' because it was a successful international company and yet one based in Britain. It was the more an asset, continued Baker, because it was unconnected with the British Government. He declared himself satisfied that the Board and trustees of Reuters would preserve its independence after flotation.

Conclusions

In the 1990s, the Reuter Trust principles are still given prominence within each annual report. Reuters assumes that the guidelines and restrictions which the Trust deed spells out are reconcilable with the successful running of a public company. Since 1984 Reuters has been extremely successful commercially, with profits running into hundreds of millions each year. Such success has blunted the question whether care for the bottom line might one day lead to the abandonment of any or all news services which were not making money. Media services – textual news, pictures, film, radio, television – now produce only some 5 per cent of total Reuter revenue. Yet the collection of general news can never be abandoned, for it is not really detachable. A political assassination is general news, but it may affect markets: a market fall becomes of general interest if the fall is big enough. So the distinction between general news on the one hand, and economic information and data on the other, cannot be sharply drawn.

Nevertheless, living within a company which is driven by the bottom line has made Reuters' media services keen to be at least (and at last) self-supporting. Peter Job, the chief executive, admitted in a 1998 internal circular to staff that it had been 'difficult to balance the books in media business for most of the 34 years I have worked with the company'; but he told employees that it was 'now possible for us to stem our media losses and talk about profits'. The rise of the Internet, Job explained, had opened up alternative approaches towards the sale of news. 'We have gained the ability to deliver target news according to the recipients' desired profile'. And such customised news could be profitable. For example, by the late-1990s Reuters Business Briefing was able to collect news and business information from thousands of sources and to serve individual subscribers at four different levels of content, customisation and interactivity. Has Reuters therefore reached a turning point on the media side? If it were ever to announce that it was making steady and substantial profits out of its media services, it would be back where it has not been since Julius Reuter's heyday.

But by way of epilogue, perhaps we need to ask a fresh question. We have suggested that news agency managers have been variously motivated – sometimes by ideas of public service, sometimes by a less lofty search for profit, often by both. Yet has there also been a third influence at work? A 1933 *Fortune* article about UP, the American news agency, may have relevance for other news agencies. The article remarked that, although UP was clearly being run for profit and not as a charity, yet among its staff there existed 'another motive which drives them quite as strongly'. UP employees showed great enthusiasm; they displayed what the article called 'an actual and genuine love of the game'. Perhaps love of the game – organising and selling news services, setting up communications, finding fresh stories every day, supplying economic information with ever more sophistication, watching for reaction, beating competitors – perhaps this has been the strongest motivation of all.[15]

Notes

Unless otherwise indicated, source material used in this article is kept in the Reuters Archive, 85 Fleet Street, London.

1 J. Grant, *The Newspaper Press* (London: Tinsley Bros, 1871), I, p. vi; F. Williams, *Transmitting World News* (Paris: UNESCO, 1953), pp. 80–1.

2 On Reuters, see D. Read, *The Power of News, The History of Reuters* (Oxford: Oxford University Press, second edn, 1999); on the Press Association, see G. Scott, *Reporter Anonymous, The Story of the Press Association* (London: Hutchinson & Co., 1968); on the Central News, see H.G. Hart, *The Central News Diamond Jubilee Souvenir* (London: Central News, 1931); on the Exchange Telegraph, see J.M. Scott, *Extel 100, The Centenary History of the Exchange Telegraph Company* (London: Ernest Benn, 1972).

3 J.A. Morris, *Deadline Every Minute, The Story of the United Press* (New York: Doubleday, 1957), p. 36.

4 Grant, *Newspaper Press*, II, pp. 334–7.

5 *Riviera Daily*, 26 February 1899.

6 See D. Read, 'Reuters: News Agency of the British Empire', *Contemporary Record*, 8(2), 1994, pp. 195–212.

7 G. Binney Dibblee, *The Newspaper* (London: Williams & Norgate, 1913), pp. 71–2.

8 E.W. Davies, A Short History of the Press Association, Prepared for the Confidential Information of the Board of Directors by the General Manager, typescript (1946, revised 1960), pp. 15, 42–3.

9 Sir R. Jones, *A life in Reuters* (London: Hodder & Stoughton, 1951), chs XXVIII–XXXI.

10 Lilly Library, Indiana University, Manuscript Collections, Cooper Mss. 11, Karl Bickel to Kent Cooper, 16 January 1943. [I owe this reference to Professor Terhi Rantanen.]

11 Public Record Office, Kew: OF 395/527.

12 J.L. Hammond, *C.P. Scott of the Manchester Guardian* (London: G. Bell & Sons, 1934), p. 96. See also F. Williams, *Dangerous Estate* (London: Longmans, Green & Co., 1957), pp. 252–3; and G. Taylor, *Changing Faces: a History of the Guardian 1956–88* (London: Fourth Estate, 1993), ch. 24.

13 Royal Commission on the Press, Research Series 4 (Cmnd. 6810–4), *Analysis of Newspaper Content*, by D. McQuail (1977), pp. 271, 275.

14 Taylor, *Changing Faces*, pp. 297–8.

15 Morris, *Deadline Every Minute*, p. 179.

Appendix

Analysis of the trading account of Reuters (£) (April 1947)

1. *News service*

Cost		356 000
Assessments from PA, NPA, AAP, NZPA		264 000
	Direct deficit	92 000
From non-members (BBC, ABC, etc.) in home territory of owners		70 000
	Overall deficit	22 000

2. *Profit-making activities*

Commercial service		48 000
South African remittance business		7 000
	Surplus	55 000

3. *News distribution overseas*

	Surplus	80 000

4. *Administration overheads*

	Net cost	77 000

5. *Trading profit before tax*

	36 000

8
The Fall and Fall of the Third
Daily Herald, 1930–64

Adrian Smith

'Everybody's *still* talking about the *Daily Herald!*'

For a newspaper that folded over 30 years ago, the *Daily Herald* continues to exert a peculiar fascination over academics and journalists. Huw Richards is only the latest member of the fourth estate to write about the paper's early travails, albeit the first to rely on scholarship rather than recollection.[1] Fleet Street veterans have, since the late 1920s, either waxed lyrical about the passion of George Lansbury and the drive of Ernie Bevin, or retold mildly amusing anecdotes about Elias the eccentric owner, *or*, if from a different camp recounted with relish the *Herald's* final demise and miserable reincarnation as the pre-Murdoch *Sun*. Recycled press clippings laced with personal reminiscences have been a recipe for insiders' stories which, when read individually appeal to connoisseurs of the 'I was there' school of newspaper history; but when consumed *en masse* they strongly suggest that, if journalists enjoy an obvious advantage over academics in understanding what took place and why, they are handicapped by meeting publishers' demands for tight deadlines and good copy. This is what trailblazers of the popular press like Cecil King and Hugh Cudlipp were good at, of course, so we should scarcely be surprised if, in order to boost their superannuation, pages of prejudice and inflated ego poured forth from their Remingtons and Imperials.[2] Today, marketing not methodology remains the name of the game, so that even such an attractive and well-written book as Matthew Engel's *Tickle the Public: One Hundred Years of the Popular Press* relies heavily upon the same old stories.[3]

Francis Williams first chronicled the *Herald*'s glory prewar days of circulation battles and 2 million readers when recalling his decade-long tenure as City editor and then editor, and in so doing he provided former colleagues, old rivals and a future generation of hacks and campus scribblers with all they ever needed to know about Julius Elias, the benevolent but bland Viscount Southwood. As Chairman of Odhams Press, which from 1929 had a 51 per cent stake in the *Herald* leaving the TUC as minority partner, Elias belied his public image of a well-intentioned but extremely dull public benefactor by privately berating his editors for an absence of upbeat reporting in their coverage of economic depression at home and tension abroad. The Pooterish, unintentionally ironic, authorised biography of Labour's premier press baron, full of reconstructed dialogue and reverent commentary, provides the cynical 1990s researcher with a further fund of recyclable stories on topics as diverse as Elias's talent for doodling (photograph naturally included) and his posthumous control of the Odhams board via a medium. His prewar pref-erence for investing in promotional gimmicks and gifts rather than foreign correspondents, and his much-publicised rivalry with Beaverbrook, whose reverse priorities were ultimately vindicated, are treated far more generously than in any other assessment of Elias's record as a newspaper proprietor.[4]

On the whole, academics writing about the *Herald* have rightly been wary of relying overmuch on ceaselessly repackaged anecdote and hearsay. Thus, when Richard Cockett, explaining Elias's disapproval of Francis Williams's largely anti-appeasement line, berated the proprietor's 'essential commercial rapaciousness – this was his governing ethos, to which considerations of politics came second', he looked for evidence beyond Douglas Jay's recollection that putting a positive gloss on international relations and world trade was deemed necessary to boost much-needed advertising revenue.[5] Similarly, Colin Seymour-Ure, in his pioneering essay 'The Press and the Party System between the Wars', drew heavily upon data generated by the 1947 and 1961 Royal Commissions on the Press, sources also tapped by James Curran and Jeremy Tunstall once quantitative analysis was seen as helping to explain why the *Herald* failed.[6] Attention henceforth often focused upon the debate over whether advertising has the capacity to determine a national newspaper's editorial content and financial stability. The argument that the

Herald was discriminated against on commercial grounds – because major advertisers judged its political standpoint hostile and its ABC1 readers too few, too old, and too thrifty – was first expounded in a lengthy essay by James Curran; he sought to demonstrate that the postwar decades had witnessed an accelerating 'deradicalisation' and 'depoliticalisation' of left-of-centre popular newspapers, culminating in the *Daily Mirror*'s efforts to match the *Sun*'s success as a flagship of aggressively downmarket tabloid journalism.[7]

By concluding that advertisers had not only destabilised the *Herald* by judging its readers' 'purchasing power and influence' marginal, but 'also directly influenced the political content of the national press by influencing the market strategies adopted by publishers to maximise revenue', Curran ensured the paper's lasting presence in the burgeoning literature of media studies. Cockett, in explaining Elias's *de facto* censuring of anti-appeasement leaders, could draw comfort from Curran's thesis, while a more sceptical Huw Richards could ask why 'the impeccably Tory *Daily Sketch*' suffered a similar fate in 1971. Cognizant of the influence of *Power Without Responsibility* on successive cohorts of students, Ralph Negrine in *his* textbook insisted that Curran had failed to explore alternative or complementary factors in explaining why the *Herald* had not adapted to rapidly changing circumstances, witness the impact of rival media, most notably television:[8]

> To argue, therefore, that changes in newspapers – in their content, style, readership, etc. – may be undesirable (e.g. 'deradicalisation', 'depoliticisation') is to confuse that which one may desire (and which may be socially desirable) with the actual and real choices which individuals and groups make in the market place. Such choices may be exploited, and fed, by commercial considerations but they ultimately reflect an actual desire for a specific type of medium.[9]

Negrine went on to suggest that *Sun* readers fail to find any appeal in *The Times*'s presumed superiority (whatever the cover price) because, 'in a complex social and psychological way', their paper satisfies their particular needs. To imply Curran advanced a purely monocausal explanation of why the *Herald* failed was to distort his argument; but Negrine was surely right in stressing that newspapers only survive by continuing to evolve: once a paper ceases meeting the twin challenges of constant flux, and of its readers' ever-changing demands and expectations, then it starts to die.[10] This is what happened to the *Herald*, starting almost as soon as it was so spectacularly relaunched in March 1930, and by the time Odhams and the TUC celebrated its silver jubilee the writing was already on the wall.

So why, taking due account of the corrosive effect of inadequate advertising supply, did the *Herald* fail? Richards rightly suggests that the paper failed to re-establish a strong identity after 1922 when the General Council stepped in to sanitise – some would say silence – Lansbury's decade-old voice of Direct Action and shopfloor socialism: the *Herald* ceased membership of the awkward squad once the upper echelons of the Labour movement gained access to the books, and if Ernie Bevin only had time to scan the leaders then from 1930 the future Viscount Southwood could always be relied upon to draw the line.[11] Clearly this failure to develop a clear identify warrants further exploration, but it needs to be placed in a wider context, notably those problems peculiar to any paper indissolubly linked with a particular party, and the implications for the *Herald*'s marketing potential of the impact of mid-century societal changes upon Labour's core support.

Nothing so strange

Francis Williams's memoirs were aptly titled as nothing was so strange as the financial and legal relationship agreed by the TUC and Odhams in the summer of 1929, and restated in 1957 following talk of a *Herald–News Chronicle* merger. Although Elias surrendered ultimate control of political and industrial policy to the TUC's four 'A' directors, his company retained a 4:5 majority on the board of Daily Herald (1929), with himself as Chairman. Other than at moments of national crisis, such as August 1931 or September 1938, vice-chairman Bevin and, to a lesser extent, the other General Council nominees simply kept an eye on editorial content. Day-to-day management of the paper's affairs they left almost entirely to the presumed experts. Neither partner in the original agreement were natural allies, and for Elias it was clearly a marriage of convenience: Tory by inclination, he had already courted the *Morning Post* and then the *Daily Chronicle*. The attraction of the *Herald* was that it suffered from chronic under-investment and poor marketing, but could be printed cheaply on *The People*'s presses – and had a huge target audience among the eight million voters prepared to return a second Labour government.[12]

With sales of the old *Herald* languishing at a feeble 250 000, the general secretary of the T & GWU relied on personal charisma and a network of loyal Labour canvassers to attract fresh subscribers. Like Lansbury and Arthur Henderson before him, Bevin bluntly informed the party rank and file that they had a duty to support 'their' paper: the *Herald* would no longer be a liability, but an opportunity. Thus, for three months, he toured the country putting the political case for a pro-Labour mass circulation penny paper. Elias, while recognising the importance of a successful *Herald* to the TUC and the Labour Party, saw the title's future in strictly commercial terms: the party loyalties of canvassers, and more importantly of readers, were irrelevant so long as the revamped paper thrived; any form of promotion no matter how tacky was justified; and the principal objective was to topple the *Daily Mail* not the Tory Party. The TUC and Odhams collaborated brilliantly during the 'Million Campaign' of 1929–30, culminating in spectacular relaunches in London and Manchester (with endorsement by Ramsay MacDonald and Gracie Fields respectively), and a steady million-plus circulation, partly thanks to the collapse of the new-look *Daily Chronicle*'s parallel campaign. Nevertheless, both parties had very different agendas, and very different aims.[13]

Bevin wanted no more than to guarantee the Labour movement direct access to 'our people' at a time when the popular press was still seen by many as the most effective medium of mass communication.[14] Quiet and modest, Elias was nevertheless driven by a far greater ambition. He saw Odhams' diverse publishing interests, and undoubted expertise in aggressive promotion, as the means by which *his* newspaper could achieve a circulation of two million. Not only would Rothermere and Beaverbrook have to eat humble pie, but the *Herald* might at last attract enough advertising revenue to secure self-sufficiency, and thus start making money. In June 1933 the *Herald* won the battle, but by the end of the 1930s it was clear that the *Express*, with daily sales of 2.4 million, had won the war. The *Herald* in 1939 was struggling to retain readers, with only the narrowest of profit margins and an editorial staff still playing second fiddle to a publicity department which at one stage had been 'investing' a pound in every new subscriber. Richards has suggested that Bevin and his colleagues were indifferent to the means by which the two million sale was achieved and maintained: here were guaranteed readers of pro-Labour news, many of whom could ill-afford a second paper advancing an alternative viewpoint.[15] However, even if Labour leaders had been concerned about the methods adopted, and the cost entailed, there was precious little that they could have done about it. In practice it was the Odhams directors, to be specific Elias and his lieutenants John Dunbar and Surrey Dane, who ran the *Herald* in the 1930s and 1940s; and it was their short-termism and poor management which inflicted lasting damage on the paper. Selling techniques appropriate to the *People* in the 1920s, notably free insurance and cheap books, were singularly inappropriate for a national daily, hence the repeated efforts of Elias's rivals to call a truce: the quality of journalism and the potential to attract advertising revenue, rather than promotional ingenuity, had to remain definitive performance criteria, or eventually losses would become intolerable and the whole industry collapse.[16]

Bevin had every reason to trust Elias's presumed good judgement in that, from the TUC's point of view, the relaunched *Herald* had passed its first great test with flying colours. In August 1931 it provided saturation coverage of the sterling crisis, consistently defending the actions of the General Council, the NEC and those MPs who followed Henderson into opposition. Hostile to the National Government from the outset, leaders, commentaries, and front page stories paid scant attention to the new administration while lauding loyal former ministers as heroes, and of course blaming it all on the banks. Readers were left with an absurdly one-sided view of what was going on; although successive leaders were by no means out of touch with the real world, drawing heavily on Bevin and G.D.H. Cole's by now familiar alternatives to crude retrenchment, most notably, protection and the suspension of the Sinking Fund.[17] Hugh Dalton's diary reveals Bevin's key role in determining the *Herald*'s editorial line at the outset, and not surprisingly his Birmingham speech of 30 August 1931 attracted a full half-page report:[18]

> Mr Bevin said that he was proud to have played his part during the last week as a director of the 'Daily Herald' which was the only

paper in the country that had tried to protect the very poor. When the choice came between the defence of the poor and the support of the rich, the 'Daily Herald' would stand by the poor every time.[19]

Elias's spirits must surely have risen at the news of Baldwin's return from the south of France and MacDonald's remarkable audience with the King, yet he remained silent as Long Acre effectively surrendered direction of the *Herald* to Transport House. Once the crisis had passed, and a now trusting Bevin again became preoccupied with more pressing matters, so Elias and Dunbar consolidated their control over the paper.

Since its purchase by Odhams the content of the *People* had been subject to close scrutiny, and Elias relied upon its all too acquiescent editor, Harry Ainsworth, to brief him every day on the deficiencies of the *Daily Herald*. Ainsworth's morning memorandum coincided with Francis Williams's tenure as editor, from late 1935 to his replacement by Percy Cudlipp in the summer of 1940.[20] Space prevents detailed consideration of the stormy relationship between Elias and Williams, the latter loyally supported by his successor on the City desk, Douglas Jay; and anyway both editors have left detailed if highly jaundiced accounts of their Long Acre years. The gist of their complaint was that Elias regularly sought to temper the prevailing editorial line on appeasement, namely that Labour had to heed the message of Dalton and Bevin, and agree on a pro-rearmament platform that assumed genuine equality of sacrifice, and the conscription of wealth and resources as well as of manpower. Dalton, singularly unimpressed by the previous editor, William Stevenson, and the *Herald*'s veteran diplomatic correspondent Norman Ewer, liaised closely with Williams and Jay, fellow members of that informal but in retrospect highly influential dining group, the XYZ Club.[21] Bevin could have protected Williams from Elias's constant carping, but he never wholly trusted him, and anyway he preferred to hammer out party policy on the conference floor: he eschewed back-stairs politicking, and smoke-filled rooms were where you negotiated pay deals. Exasperation with the Labour leadership, exceeded only by his scorn for Bevan and Cripps in their pursuit of a popular front, left Bevin reluctant to do little other than regularly instruct the *Herald*'s editor in the ways of the world. Lloyd George's assertion that, 'Bevin controlled the *Daily Herald*, and one had to turn to the *News Chronicle* to know what the Labour Party was really up to,' may have been correct in 1931 but later in the decade required heavy qualification. Bevin's correspondence reveals him as sensitive if not always sympathetic to Labour activists' frequent complaints about the *Herald*, but clearly reluctant to become involved in any controversy concerning the paper's future direction.[22]

Williams complained not just that Elias was wrong in demanding more cheerful news, particularly with regard to events in Europe, but that he was undermining the long-term future of the paper by refusing to fund a decent foreign service. Unlike Beaverbrook, Elias saw no reason to 'waste money on foreign correspondents when he could get all the news from Reuters'. Throughout the 1930s the *Herald*'s global coverage was very poor, being scarcely more than a page and heavily dependent on the agencies, the same being true for the token grainy shots 'from around the world' on the back cover. For connoisseurs of reportage, the contrast with the *Daily Express* could scarcely have been starker. Nevertheless, Elias and Dunbar continued to use the *Express* as a benchmark for judging Williams's performance.[23] Without investment they were fighting a losing battle, and Beaverbrook's flagship had an even greater incentive to surge ahead of the *Herald* in sales and profitability once Elias had rejected an alliance in support of Edward VIII. Baldwin rewarded Elias with a peerage, but there was never any doubt where the *Herald* stood over the prospect of a divorced queen given Attlee and Bevin's insistence that, 'Our people won't 'ave it.'[24]

Beyond the most senior members of the General Council, Williams was not that well known within the TUC, and there was scant protest at his sacking in April 1940. The Odhams directors ignored Citrine's objections, and, although Bevin was away, there is no evidence that he would or could have prevented Percy Cudlipp, 'with the Beaverbrook glow still on him', assuming the editorship. Williams paid the price for advocating a more aggressive pursuit of the war. In difficult and trying circumstances he had done a good job, and he was highly regarded by both editorial and production staff, but Southwood was determined that he should go. Once again Odhams bore direct responsibility for a damaging management decision, with the TUC either indifferent or powerless.[25] Ironically, the trade unions' most vocal representative on the board took a far keener interest in day-to-day editorial content once appointed to the Ministry of Labour. The *Herald's* wartime reluctance to act as a campaigning, dissenting voice of the shopfloor and the barracks was partially attributable to natural caution, and partially the consequence of Labour ministers' prominence on the Home Front. By the end of 1941 Bevin was probably second only to Churchill in power and influence, but long before then he was clashing with Southwood over editorial criticism of the Prime Minister. There is a delicious irony in the idea of Julias Elias as a defender of editorial freedom, but the truth of the matter is that Bevin was over-reacting, and the *Herald's* attacks on the coalition were tame and timid by comparison with those of the 'pugnaciously populist' *Daily Mirror*.[26]

To be fair, Cudlipp proved no proprietor's poodle, and his repeated calls for Churchill to sack Chamberlain prevented the new Prime Minister from inviting Lloyd George to join the War Cabinet. On 6 June 1940, Chamberlain made clear to his successor that, 'I cannot allow it to be said that his [Lloyd George] inclusion in the Government is part of a bargain between you & me in return for which you have agreed to protect me.' At the *Mirror*, Cecil King, convinced Churchill could defy his backbenchers and dispense with 'political liabilities' such as Chamberlain and Halifax, heard that Downing Street had 'fixed the *Herald* through Bevin'. A precedent had been set, and yet only a few weeks later Cudlipp nearly did unseat a minister – ironically, Duff Cooper, the only cabinet member to resign over Munich. Ritchie Calder's exposé of the work of the Wartime Social Survey as intrusive and counter-productive prompted a signed leader on why Duff Cooper was ill-suited to head the Ministry of Information. The Beaverbrook press was eager to enter the fray, and virulent attacks upon the minister's competence necessitated a virtuoso Commons performance in order for him to survive. Nevertheless, Bevin was clearly a very handy channel of communication, even if in October 1940, following press criticism of the ill-fated Dakar expedition, Southwood had been part of a Newspaper Proprietors' Association delegation infuriated by Beaverbrook and Attlee's message from the War Cabinet that supposedly irresponsible editorials would provoke compulsory censorship.[27]

Following the fall of Singapore Churchill complained of the *Herald's* contribution to a wider campaign in the popular press 'calculated to undermine the Army'.[28] Yet when publication of Philip Zec's famous cartoon, 'The price of petrol has been increased by one penny – official', on 6 March 1942 brought the *Mirror* close to suppression under Defence Regulation 2D, the *Herald* was more concerned with maintaining the principle of press freedom than with defending its rival: the cartoon was innocuous, but the language of the *Mirror's* leader columns was invariably 'highpitched and distasteful'. According to King, while Herbert Morrison had done no more than threaten, Bevin was 'in favour of suppression without warning – presumably because of our support of Cripps'. Bevin had no need to put pressure on the *Herald* in March 1942 as it was obvious the paper had no incentive to go out on a limb in supporting the *Mirror*; but the same month saw him and Dalton seek cabinet approval of coal rationing in the face of backbench Tory opposition. At a time when the *Daily Herald* was leading a grassroots Labour campaign for the nationalisation of coal, many Conservative backbenchers saw rationing as the thin end of the wedge. Pressure on Cudlipp must have been considerable, just as six months earlier Bevin had publicly condemned 'a paper that I helped to build' for 'carrying on a nagging, Quisling policy now every day of our lives'. These were strong words indeed, and the issue on that occasion was the TUC's insistence that industry should have priority over the services in recruiting skilled men. Despite Attlee's efforts to take the heat out of the matter, Citrine and Bevin quarrelled bitterly over the latter's insistence that the *Herald* had not only invented his use of the word 'Quisling', but, far worse, had been engaged in an 'insidious' campaign of 'suggestion and innuendo' against the Ministry of Labour for the past five months. This was a ridiculous charge, reflecting the fact that Bevin was over-sensitive to cabinet colleagues' and civil servants' complaints about a newspaper he had so closely been associated with since 1919.[29]

The truth of the matter is that, compared with the *Mirror*, the *Herald* had a quiet war, fully bearing out Cecil King and Hugh Cudlipp's claim that for 30 years it was:

> obliged to appraise and advocate Labour policy in an entirely uncritical manner – a deadly dull mission. The pudding appeared in the (Labour) *Herald*, and the sauce in the (Labour) *Daily Mirror*.[30]

Colin Seymour-Ure was right to quote the *Herald* as a classic example of how party managers in the 1930s 'lost control over the

finances of the press – and therefore over press personnel and policies', but in practice it did not make that much difference.[31] The
Odhams-owned *Herald*'s absence from the awkward squad before,
during, and even more especially after the Second World War is
highlighted by the contrasting experience – and commercial success
– of the *Mirror*.

'We are all in it together'

Throughout the war the *Mirror* kept insisting that 'We are all in it
together', but its skilfully-blended package of special features,
human-interest stories, sports reporting, and mild titillation, coun-
terbalanced by hard news and columnists with a healthy disrespect
for established authority, was targeted at a large but very specific
audience: that untapped working-class readership identified after
1935 as the means by which an outmoded guide to suburban gen-
teelness could be transformed into a dynamic, mass circulation
tabloid. With the emphasis on visual appeal, entertainment, and a
populist approach to key issues of the day, the *Mirror* created for
itself a fresh, youthful image. The proportion of space devoted to
hard news may have halved, hence Curran identifying 'depoliticalisation' even prewar, but the identity of the paper became more
sharply defined – 'Tell the *Daily Mirror* the Facts, Mr Baldwin, not
any old newspaper'.[32]

King and Bartholomew's American-inspired creation articulated
the hopes and concerns of those still suffering from the worst effects
of the Depression, but the secret of its success was an embryonic
working-class consumerism in those areas and occupations beginning to benefit from modest economic recovery. At the same time,
avoidance of any dramatic shift leftwards meant *Mirror* executives
could reassure major advertisers that many of its older, more affluent readers had remained loyal. On the eve of the war the *Mirror*
claimed a net increase of 670 columns of display advertising, with
a circulation up to around 1 750 000. All newspapers, even the
fast fading *Daily Mail*, benefited from 1940s paper rationing and
pegged circulations, and the *Herald* climbed steadily after 1942 to
peak at 2.1 million five years later; but between 1943 and 1946
audited sales of the *Mirror* rose from 2 to 3 million, an astonishing
achievement.[33]

By moving leftwards without losing its middle-class readership, the *Mirror* was a potential threat to the *Herald* even before the outbreak of hostilities. The onset of the 'People's War' saw the *Mirror*, its profit margins guaranteed as a consequence of rationing and the advertisers' 'space famine', foster a more radical, and a more consciously proletarian, image. Not only did it have immediate visual impact – even bigger headlines and plenty of girls in uniform (or in comic-strip Jane's case, usually out of uniform) – but it was lively, punchy, and above all irreverent. The *Mirror*'s convenient tabloid format, its forthright but easily digestible views, and its ability to articulate the feelings of factory workers and other-rankers, rendered it highly attractive to many long-standing, Labour-voting *Herald* readers, particularly if young and/or female. Mass Observation highlighted the *Herald*'s failure to attract freshly-recruited munitions workers, many of them women. Also, although all copies were sold, often it was purchased as a last resort. There was a growing perception that the *Herald* was hard work to read, certainly by comparison with a *Mirror* catering for short tea-breaks and even shorter attention spans. Even worse, the *Herald* was seen by its critics as boring and unchallenging: for all Percy Cudlipp's efforts to voice the concerns of party rank-and-file, his paper was naturally associated with the views of the Labour leadership, from May 1940 pillars of the new status quo. Not even the commencement of Michael Foot's long association with the *Herald* in August 1944 countered the impression that it was far too worthy and intense.[34]

In the 1945 general election campaign the pro-Labour daily press accounted for around 35 per cent of national circulation, with the *Herald* and the *Mirror* in the vanguard of campaigning. Nobody today talks about the *Herald*'s contribution to Labour's victory, if only because the *Mirror* was that much more credible, and that much more effective. The *Herald*'s partisanship was so extreme and so absurd that its propaganda in the end proved counterproductive. Its coverage was tedious and relentless, with screaming front-page headlines such as 'A Vote for Churchill is a Vote for Franco' day after day throughout the month-long campaign. Under the umbrella of the TUC, it even organised an election rally at the Albert Hall.[35] Eight years later, Hugh Cudlipp contrasted 'the *Telegraph* of the Left' with his own paper, 'unencumbered by any obligation to deaden its columns with extravagant publicity for the orations of Transport

House matters. Nor was it impelled to defend the Labour Party right or wrong. The influence of the official and sycophantic Socialist newspaper was therefore swiftly dwarfed.' Citrine and his fellow 'A' directors complained about the *Mirror*'s 'counterfeit proletarianism', implicitly disapproving of its witty, relatively goodhumoured, but nevertheless persuasive, demolition of Churchill's case for re-election. Half a century later, mind-numbed by exposure to the *Herald*'s ceaseless exhortations to vote Labour, one sympathises with Hugh Cudlipp's description of the *Mirror* as a 'flourishing, independent, national newspaper of the Left – without the straightjacket of Party overlordship or the enforced insincerities of Party affiliation'. Many readers at the time could see this: they did not need to be told time and again how to vote, and as a result they came to appreciate the *Mirror*'s independent voice. The *Herald* was more and more living on borrowed time, and the end of pegged circulation on 3 January 1949 brought the first signs of nemesis: according to Stephen Koss, on the first day of 'free sale', the *Herald* lost around 100 000 sales and the *Mirror* gained approximately half a million. Huw Richards questions these figures, pointing out that sales *rose* by 13 000 in March and April 1949. He sees 1951 as the real watershed for the *Herald*, with 'a massive loss of 121 000 taking the paper below the psychologically important two million mark ... Why 1951? Labour lost power that year, a rare example of the *Herald*'s fortunes running parallel with rather than against electoral fortunes ...'.[36]

'Socialism is what a Labour Government does'

Herbert Morrison, author of the most famous (infamous?) definition of mid-century British socialism, could never have exerted very much influence over the *Herald*, if only because Ernie Bevin's dead body would have been in the way. Yet Morrison, archetypal party manager, was the model *Daily Herald* Labour politician: male, middle-aged, moderate, and convinced of the state's capacity to enhance working people's standard of living and quality of life. Secure control of the workings of the state, and the New Jerusalem would be built, as agreed by Conference, the NEC, the General Council, and the Parliamentary Committee. This was a world of composite motions and complex agendas which the *Mirror* rarely got bogged down in, but was food and drink for postwar *Herald* reporters such as Leslie Hunter, Deryck Winterton, and Hugh Pilcher: lobby correspondents only a taxi ride from Smith Square or Hampstead, whose idea of getting away from it all was a September break in Blackpool.[37] It was this narrow, inflexible, incestuous approach to party politics which, for all Foot's twice-weekly passion, made the *Herald's* news reports and leaders attractive only to the most dedicated follower of life at Westminster and inside Transport House (the sort of newspaper which would devote its front page to the election of Party Treasurer – and rioting at a Liberace concert). No wonder Attlee treated it like an in-house bulletin, begrudgingly reading it to find out what the chaps were up to before turning with relief to the overwhelmingly superior cricket coverage in *The Times*.[38]

The quality of the football reporting and the reliability of the racing tipsters were probably the main reasons why many men carried on buying the *Herald*. The editor of the sports pages knew what his readers wanted, but his colleagues on features failed to appreciate that there might be a world beyond Mum and Dad living on a nice new estate in Dagenham and looking forward to the Festival of Britain. Scanning the back half of the *Daily Herald* across the 1950s, the feeling is that this was a deeply conservative newspaper trapped in a late 1940s timewarp. During the Suez crisis, the enemy within was rock'n'roll, and above all the malevolent ghost of James Dean, busy subverting teenage girls and inciting teddy boys to trash milk bars; with 'Hound Dog' at number three, and Bill Haley and Lonnie Donegan sharing three other Top 10 places, the *Herald* was preoccupied with Vera Lynn's winter tour and Ted Heath's new lineup. The real question regarding the *Herald* between 1947 and 1960 is not, why did sales drop by 700 000 at a time when its rivals were gaining readers, but how did such a boring newspaper cling on to a circulation of around 1.3 million?[39]

The answer of course is that the *Herald's* core audience was slowly ebbing away, but had by no means disappeared. For all the *Mirror's* appeal to the young, and the growing challenge of television, the *Herald* retained a substantial proportion of sales gained in the 1930s, and both newspaper and readers entered middle-age in harmony.[40] In this case middle-age meant still voting Labour, but with loyalty tested by arcane internal wranglings and Tory reassurances of continued affluence; Dad enjoying job security, and everyone appreciating better housing; and Dad determining most facets of family life, not least leisure and recreation – *and* he paid the papers. Editorial content consistently reflected longstanding readers' interests and concerns, and as such proved singularly unattractive to those reaching adulthood in a world where Herbert Morrison or Vera Lynn were no longer ideal role models. In 1939 80 per cent of the *Herald*'s readers were over 24, of whom 42 per cent were in the 25–44 age range, and thus well into middle-age two decades later; 91 per cent were in classes C and D. By the early 1960s, when an astonishing 59 per cent of all readers were male, little had changed in terms of social composition: 87 per cent of readers were classified as working-class (of whom 83 per cent were Labour supporters, which was not surprising given the diet of news they were fed).[41]

The caricature *Herald* reader in the late 1950s lived in a council house outside London and the south-east, had been a trade unionist for over 30 years, spent Saturday afternoon on the terraces, and drank in the local Labour club. This was very definitely a caricature, but as James Curran has demonstrated, it was a set of assumptions and prejudices which had a crippling effect upon the *Herald*'s capacity in the 1950s and early 1960s to attract profitable upmarket advertising; particularly after newsprint rationing ended in 1956 and advertisers were no longer forced to spread their spending over a range of titles. Having exceeded both the *Express* and the *Mail* in advertising revenue per copy sold at the end of the war, by 1964 the *Herald* was generating less than half of either paper. In 1955, just as postwar consumerism was beginning to take off, the *Herald* had an 11 per cent share of both national daily circulation and advertising revenue. By 1964, its share of circulation had dropped to 8 per cent (a by no means disgraceful 1 265 000), but critically, its share of advertising was a risible 3.5 per cent. Yet, like all other national dailies, the *Herald* needed to maximise its advertising potential in order to cover escalating production and delivery costs. Not only was it unable to parallel the *Mirror*'s success in consistently achieving a full advertisement quota on a 28 or 32 page paper, but both its fixed and variable costs were higher.[42]

From carthorse control to 'King's cross'

As early as 1953 Hugh Cudlipp had mocked the *Herald* for aping the *Mirror* in seeking to widen its appeal, a largely unsuccessful strategy that complemented a half-hearted campaign to convince advertisers that working-class readers on good wages were potentially heavy-spending consumers. In Curran's words, the *Herald* needed to break out of its 'working-class ghetto' and 'upgrade the paper's reader-ship'.[43] One possibility was to accept the *News Chronicle*'s reluctant suggestion of a merger, and immediately inherit a largely middle-class readership as loyal to their newspaper as the *Herald*'s working-class readers were to theirs. A formal approach to Odhams was made early in 1957, in the knowledge that Hugh Gaitskell was by no means hostile to the idea.[44]

Clearly in debt to the *Herald* for its saturation coverage of the Suez crisis, and in particular his role in opposing military action, Gaitskell nevertheless viewed the paper with a good deal of distrust. He had a poor opinion of its editor in the mid-1950s, Sydney Elliott, and was wrongly convinced that foreign correspondent Basil Davidson, despite his bravery in reporting from Budapest, was a Communist. Although most of the Bevanites saw the *Herald* as a tool of the party leadership, Gaitskell frequently complained that Elliott was anti-American and pro-Russian. In 1954–5 he had pri-vately lobbied 'A' directors such as the NUGMW's Tom Williamson to ensure the paper did not align itself with *Tribune* and the *New Statesman*, and to support Nye Bevan's expulsion for opposing German rearmament. In this respect, Gaitskell had more in common with MacDonald than with Attlee, the latter retaining a characteristi-cally relaxed view of the *Herald*'s standing and influence within the party. Gaitskell's view was that the *Herald* was *ipso facto* the Labour Party's official mouthpiece, and hence the principal channel through which the leader should address policy issues, either in the form of an article or an 'interview' with Deryck Winterton. For this reason he had turned down the *Mirror*'s invitation to contribute, albeit agreeing to the occasional interview if paid.[45]

Gaitskell therefore had an obvious incentive to see his message get across to a more representative cross-section of the electorate, and his close alliance with senior trade unionists gave him every reason to believe they would accept an amalgamation of the *Herald* and the *News Chronicle*. However, he was wrong, and the TUC refused to release Odhams from its 1929 undertaking. Instead, in July 1957 the historic link was reaffirmed, with the *Herald* confidently asserting that, 'our future as Labour's daily newspaper is assured': no threat to the paper's political identity, but equally, no move upmarket to attract AB-targeting advertisers. A condition of Gaitskell's support had been that the merged paper was still 100 per cent Labour. He held the *News Chronicle* in especially low esteem, and was only too pleased when it ceased publication in October 1960, hoping that its traditionally pro-Liberal readers would belatedly embrace the *Herald*. In practice, a good number took no action when having purchased and immediately closed the *News Chronicle*, the *Daily Mail*, with the old title in small type on the masthead, fell through their letterboxes the following day. In the medium-term, however, the *Mail* failed to capitalise on the *News Chronicle*'s pre-closure circulation of 1.2 million, its sales falling well below 2 million over the next ten years.[46]

The Cadbury family had shocked many in the industry with their readiness to reverse a century-old tradition of subsidising Liberal newspapers by selling the *News Chronicle* and the *Star* with only minimal protection for loyal staff, all of whom had been kept in the dark about the proposed sale. That these by now dimly glimmering lights of Liberalism should be blown out by Associated Newspapers seemed especially galling, but in 1960 the by now tiny parliamentary party could do little more than galvanise protest among a much wider left-of-centre constituency. The demise of the *News Chronicle* did, however, have two short-term effects: it fuelled demands for a second Royal Commission on the Press, acceded to by Macmillan in 1961; and it warned Labour that any future sale of the *Herald* could not be an exercise in removing competition and in asset-stripping, but had to entail the new owner guaranteeing the paper's survival.[47]

Not surprisingly therefore, Odhams' proposed sale of the *Herald* in early 1961 generated fierce debate within senior echelons of the Labour movement over which was the most reassuring offer. After 1957, when the *quid pro quo* of Odhams reiterating the *Herald*'s political identity was the TUC gradually relinquishing ultimate editorial control (formally confirmed in August 1960), the paper had deliberately sought to distance itself from the party leadership. One demonstration of this supposed newly-acquired independence occurred during the Commons debate on the 1958 Defence White Paper: Douglas Machray, Elliott's successor as editor, not only published a letter from 65 backbenchers calling for Labour to promise an end to the manufacture of nuclear weapons and the closure of US missile bases, but in a front-page leader endorsed their demand. With the

Labour leadership eager to hammer out a compromise policy well in advance of the next general election, there was uproar within both the parliamentary party and the trade unions. Hugh Cudlipp took advantage of the *Herald*'s 'H-Bomb hysterics' to pledge the *Mirror*'s unequivocal support for official party policy, not out of any concern for Gaitskell's embarrassment but because he wanted to pick up any unhappy readers.[48]

The *Herald*'s flirtation with unilateralism ended abruptly in August 1960 with the appointment of John Beavan, a Labour right-winger and longtime editor of the *Manchester Evening News* whom Crossman dismissed as a 'complacent sod' eager to create a '*Daily Mail* of the Left' and curry favour with Gaitskell. Beavan's remit was to embrace the new meritocracy and move the *Herald* upmarket, with features and reviews likely to attract a widening middle class: books and ballet were in, bowls and ballroom dancing were out. Luckily, the sports pages continued to focus on Turf Moor not Twickenham so no readers were lost, but then precious few were gained. At the same time, solid support for Gaitskell at a particularly low point in Labour's post-1959 election fortunes, did little to convince ex-*News Chronicle* readers that here was a genuinely independent newspaper.[49]

The *Herald* was ripe for takeover, but in the event Odhams Press was acquired in its entirety by the Mirror Group in April 1961. Cecil King initiated the takeover, partly because having already acquired Amalgamated Press he wanted to rationalise and restructure the magazine market (Odhams owned the highly profitable *Woman* and *Woman's Own*), and partly because he could not resist the temptation to counterbid Roy Thomson, with whom Odhams were already discussing a merger. Gaitskell had encouraged the new Odhams chairman, Sir Christopher Chancellor, to make a pre-emptive approach to Thomson on the grounds that better a distant Canadian media mogul than a 'dominating and unpredictable friend like King'. In the light of their subsequent clash over the Common Market, Gaitskell was right, and indeed the enjoyed support from the *Herald*'s NUJ Chapel and many MPs, all of whom feared a Mirror Group monopoly of Labour-supporting dailies. At the end of the day, however, Gaitskell was reluctant to antagonise King and Cudlipp, particularly as his deputy, George Brown, and the TGWU's Frank Cousins, were both arguing strongly in favour of the Mirror Group bid. This was an uncomfortably public debate, with Labour's differences regularly aired in Parliament and exploited by the party opposite. Furthermore, the decision on whether to refer Mirror Group's takeover of Odhams to the Monopolies Commission rested in the hands of the Government; although to everyone's relief Macmillan merely indicated that the whole episode should be closely scrutinised by the Royal Commission.[50]

Gaitskell cut his losses, and, with Brown and Cousins, used the approval of the TUC as a means of securing from King first a two year, and then a seven year, guarantee of the *Herald*'s autonomous existence. Ironically, well before that period was up the TUC was to surrender its 49 per cent shareholding to IPC, King's corporate successor to the Mirror Group. Hugh Cudlipp, who drafted for King a signed leader in the *Mirror* promising to respect its rival's independence, and who memorably described the *Herald* as 'the Editors' Passchendaele', later recalled that:

I know of no other occasion on which the man about to be hanged was given the privilege of selecting his own rope and specifying the time he should spend in the death cell before the definitive act.[51]

The swiftly-labelled 'King's cross' was in practice Cudlipp's personal nightmare, yet Cecil King inspired the first big clash with Gaitskell, a mere two months after taking over the *Herald* .

King saw a joint *Herald–Mirror* campaign in support of Britain's entry into the Common Market as an ideal issue on which to attack Express Newspapers, and portray Beaverbrook as a senile outdated imperialist. Indifferent to Gaitskell's views on the matter, and with no serious objection from Beavan, King launched the *Herald* into uncharted waters – sustained criticism of the party leader, culminating in a front-page editorial early in 1962 that lambasted Gaitskell for his preoccupation with Clause Four, and for not embracing the Common Market as 'an act of moral courage'. The following day's front-page reply revealed the depth of Gaitskell's antipathy towards the paper's new regime. His complaint that coverage of party activities had greatly diminished was so widely endorsed that a harassed Cudlipp felt forced to take remedial action.[52] Nevertheless, he and King continued to use attacks on Gaitskell over his antipathy towards the Common Market as evidence that the *Herald* could now be as free and forthright as the *Mirror*. Dick Dinsdale, a hard-nosed tabloid veteran, had already been seconded to 'advise' Beavan, who in June 1962 was finally kicked upstairs and replaced by a major player within the Mirror Group, long-time political editor, Sydney Jacobson. It was Jacobson who, when Gaitskell threatened to denounce the *Herald* at conference, urged him to do so as 'nothing would be better for its circulation'.[53]

Jacobson and Dinsdale, reporting directly to Cudlipp, could have manufactured a clone of the *Mirror* with their eyes closed, but continued use of the old Odhams presses meant that the *Herald* had to remain a broadsheet (a key reason why the original *Sun* was not a tabloid). More importantly, any attempt to attract women and the under-thirties by making the paper livelier, lighter in its coverage of politics and the economy, and less visibly class-conscious, represented an unacceptable threat to the *Mirror*'s sales. No wonder King and Cudlipp's evidence to the Royal Commission on their plans for the *Herald* was so unconvincing, full of empty phrases ('It must look different and be different. Look like no other morning paper … Only journalism of an outstandingly original level will reverse the present trend …') and unrealistic sales projections. This 'bloated, listless boa constrictor suffering from fatty degeneration of the heart', to use Cudlipp's honest opinion of the *Herald*, was living on borrowed time.[54]

The *Sun* also rises – conclusion

The end, of course, came in an unexpected form, with the *Herald*'s relaunch on 15 September 1964 as the *Sun*. A front page declaring 'Good Morning! It's Time for a New Newspaper' was, as Matthew Engel has pointed out, scarcely a compelling reason for buying the second issue. Charles Wintour later recalled the apprehension at the *Express*, given the slickness of IPC's market research and advanced advertising, and the enormous relief when it became clear that, glitzy columnists notwithstanding, the *Sun* was not all that different from the *Herald*.[55] The *Sun*, despite its broadcast format and uninspiring layout (almost like a parody of mid-1960s modish design), clearly was different from the *Herald*, witness for example its attempt at investigative journalism. According to Michael Leapman, who wrote one of the better studies of the *Sun* pre- and post-Murdoch, the 'Insight'-inspired 'Probe' (soon nicknamed by insiders 'Grope') failed because the journalists were inexperienced, and because they were never given enough time to file a complete story. Thus, the *Sun* was handicapped by under-investment once the initial advertising budget was exhausted and the losses mounted (IPC lost £12 702 000 on the two titles between 1961 and 1969), and by executive indifference once Cudlipp realised that his gamble had not paid off.[56]

But the main reason why the first *Sun* was so very different from its successor, was that – like the *Herald* – it was never, in its own words, 'a newspaper born of the age we live in'. The costly market research had yet again focused on how to retain old *Herald* readers *and* attract the young and affluent, this time labelled 'social radicals'. Given its target audience, a left-leaning, fun-loving *Sun* appeared in the firmament at just the right moment. Unfortunately its content, particularly its feature articles, too often reflected an older generation's perception of 'young people' with O- or even A-levels, some spare cash, and a social conscience. Jacobson, Dinsdale, and the new editorial team were the equivalent of parents who loved the Beatles, but failed to understand why their offspring preferred the Stones; or in Leapman's words, they relied on 'the *Mirror* formula of the 1950s, thinly disguised in fashionable clothes'. Curran has argued that insufficient hard news and political commentary stymied any chance of forging 'a coalition of middle-class and working-class radicals', thus forfeiting a rare opportunity to establish an intelligent, progressive popular newspaper. Whether such a potential audience existed in 1964 is academic. The reality is, as Curran recognised, that Cudlipp, King, and their acolytes were more concerned with creating a new mass readership who were carers *and* consumers.[57]

The *Sun's* first issue sold over 2 million copies, but circulation had more than halved by June 1969, when the IPC board decided to cease publication in six months time: the guarantee period would be up, and the pledge not to amalgamate the *Herald* with the *Mirror* would be interpreted as applying equally to the *Sun* (if only because commercially a merger made no sense). Reluctant to close the *Sun* in case it provoked costly industrial unrest across the group, directors were already in discussions with Robert Maxwell. That autumn Maxwell was forced to pull out, and the rest is history. Hugh Cudlipp held a party on the night Murdoch's new *Sun* soared away off the presses. Scanning the brash new tabloid, he pronounced, 'We've got nothing to worry about'.[58]

It is tempting to conclude by simply saying that, like its successor, the third *Herald* failed to survive because it was a poor newspaper, and the market will always have the last word. But of course the *Herald* wasn't always dated and predictable, and even in 1964 well over a million people were still buying it every day. The problem was of course that, in terms of generating substantial advertising revenue, these were deemed the wrong sort of people. Today, it is possible to maintain a consistently left-of-centre political identity, *and* compete aggressively for upmarket, high revenue-earning advertising, if a newspaper can convincingly demonstrate that a fresh, ideally younger audience has been built up. The *Guardian* since the mid-1970s comes to mind, not least its success in persuading so much of the public sector and of the media that, if it became their premier noticeboard for recruitment, even more suitably-qualified readers might begin buying the paper: serious job-seekers would need access to relevant sections even if they were not regular subscribers.[59] Having identified a niche market and a strategy, the *Guardian's* trade press campaign in the early 1980s was a model for effective promotion and marketing, but it could only work because there was convincing evidence of a relatively youthful, leftish readership – real or potential. Here were the post-Robbins 'social radicals' that the *Herald/Sun* did not survive long enough to attract, even assuming that upwardly mobile, first-generation graduates could have been tempted away from a quality broadsheet.

The *Herald* had sought to move upmarket from the late 1950s because it had nowhere else to go. Well before the 1961 takeover, it was recognised that the *Mirror* held a tight grip on young working-class readers enjoying their first taste of consumer affluence. The *Herald's* core readership was intensely loyal, but it was rooted in increasingly obsolete occupations, and in communities which even 35 years ago risked losing touch with changing patterns of work and leisure. Just as Wilson's Labour Party had to carve out for itself a new electoral base – once the 1959 election had demonstrated how far the nation had moved on in only a decade – so the *Herald* had to remould itself as a more electric, youthful product – while not antagonising its older readers, many of whom were clearly content with Saga-style features and the well-worn phrases of veteran reporters (witness, for example, the longevity of Norman Ewer's career).

Curran complained of depoliticisation, but the *Herald*'s problem was that it had far too much political coverage, much of it dry and introspective. Power struggles within the NEC or General Council, however torrid for those directly involved, were rarely of great interest to anyone other than the most engaged party activist. Any casual reader, and no doubt many regular subscribers, must have been bored rigid by detailed treatment of 1950s infighting. Ironically, committed left-wingers considered all such reports so biased as to be largely useless, implicitly endorsing the view of many outside the party that the *Herald* was so closely identified with the Labour and TUC leaderships as to negate repeated assertions of editorial independence. Subtlety was quality scarcely recognised at Long Acre, witness the *Herald*'s coverage of the 1945 general election, and indeed even the Suez crisis. Gaitskell and Bevin were not alone in assuming editorial deference; albeit in the latter case being annoyed when Southwood, on commercial grounds, arrived at the same conclusion. The harassment of Tory appeasers even after May 1940, the half-hearted support of the *Mirror* in 1940 and 1942, and the 1958 endorsement of unilateralism, stand out because they are exceptions to the rule. In the 30 years following MacDonald's 'betrayal', the *Herald* was rarely a member of the awkward squad, and even in 1931 the paper was happy to portray Henderson's battered and beleaguered crew as eager to regain power and restore stability.

The years after 1931 revealed the conflicts of interest that bedevilled the *Herald* as a result of joint ownership. The TUC, even had it wanted to, was largely incapable of influencing Southwood's marketing strategy. Thus, throughout the 1930s the paper suffered from bad management, the legacy of which lasted well beyond the chairman's death in 1947. Circulation was artificially inflated during the race to 2 million, and then maintained only as a result of wartime controls and newsprint rationing. Francis Williams, clearly the paper's most able and dynamic editor, not only scorned costly promotional campaigns but pursued an editorial policy largely at variance with that acceptable to Southwood. The paper was bound to suffer in consequence, particularly given the board's reluctance to expand the editorial staff, at a time when comprehensive coverage of foreign affairs was paramount. Chronic under-investment of course handicapped the *Herald* throughout its whole history; the final indignity was the *Sun's* hybrid format, when relaunching the paper as a tabloid just might have signalled to a sceptical public that here was a genuinely new product. If, as Huw Richards has persuasively argued, the first two incarnations of the *Daily Herald* have a stirring tale to tell, then the history of version three is a sad story of missed opportunities, and of a devoted if shrinking band of readers who – like their newspaper – were more and more out of touch with a society that wanted to hear about short skirts not socialism, social workers not steelworkers.

Notes

1   Huw Richards, 'The Daily Herald 1912–1964', *History Today*, December 1981; idem, 'News coverage – or bingo?', *Journalism Studies Review*, July 1983, 28–31; idem, 'Mourned but not missed by the masses', *Times Higher Educational Supplement*, 15 September 1989; idem 'Constriction, Conformity and Control: the Taming of the Daily Herald 1921–1930', PhD, Open University, 1993; idem 'The Ragged Man of Fleet Street: The *Daily Herald* in the 1920s', *Contemporary Record*, **8**(2) (1994), 242–57. Richards was both methodical and very readable in recounting the history of the *Daily Herald* in its first two incarnations, 1912–22, and 1922–9. Having used his doctoral thesis as the basis for a book he has now provided a postscript to the paper's supposed 'golden age', in the final chapter of the well-received Huw Richards, *The Bloody Circus: the Daily Herald and the Left* (London, Pluto Press, 1997). On the contribution of the paper's founding father see George Lansbury, *The Miracle of Fleet Street* (London: Victoria House, 1925), and among a spate of biographies Bob Holman *Good Old George: the Life of George Lansbury* (Oxford: Lion 1990), pp. 78–93. Reminiscences of other early staffers include foreign correspondent and news editor George Slocombe, *The Tumult and the Shouting* (London: Heinemann, 1936) and 1922–6 editor Henry Hamilton Fyfe, *My Seven Selves* (London: Allen & Unwin, 1935) and *Sixty Years of Fleet Street* (London, W.H. Allen, 1949).

2   Examples over the past three decades of ex-editors retelling the story of the *Daily Herald* within memoirs or popular histories of Fleet Street include: Hugh Cudlipp, *At Your Peril* (London: Weidenfeld and Nicolson, 1962); idem, *Walking on the Water* (London: Bodley Head, 1976); Cecil King, *Strictly Personal: Some Memoirs of Cecil H. King* (London: Weidenfeld and Nicolson, 1969); Charles Wintour, *Pressure on the Press: an Editor Looks at Fleet Street* (London: André Deutsch, 1972); idem, *The Rise and Fall of Fleet Street* (London: Hutchinson, 1981). Simon Jenkins, *Newspapers: the*

Power and the Money (London: Faber, 1979) was from the pen of a once and future editor, but a better example of the genre, witness its treatment of the *Sun* before and after Rupert Murdoch, is Michael Leapman, *Treacherous Estate: the Press After Fleet Street* (London: Hodder and Stoughton, 1992).

3 Matthew Engel, *Tickle the Public: One Hundred Years of the Popular Press* (London: Gollancz, 1996).

4 Francis Williams, *Dangerous Estate: the Anatomy of Newspapers* (London: Longmans, 1957, Arrow pbk edn, 1959), pp. 150–77; idem, *Nothing So Strange: an Autobiography* (London: Cassell, 1970), pp. 62–158; R.J. Minney, *Viscount Southwood* (London: Odhams, 1954).

5 Richard Cockett, *Twilight of Truth: Chamberlain, Appeasement, and the Manipulation of the Press* (London: Weidenfeld and Nicolson, 1989), pp. 43–5; Douglas Jay, *Change and Fortune: a Political Record* (London: Hutchinson, 1980), pp. 66, 72–3, 80–1.

6 Colin Seymour-Ure, 'The Press and the Party System' in Gillian Peele and Chris Cook (eds), *The Politics of Reappraisal 1918–1939* (London, Macmillan, 1975), pp. 232–57; earlier research synthesised in Jeremy Tunstall, *Newspaper Power: the New National Press in Britain* (Oxford: Oxford University Press, 1996); James Curran, 'Advertising as a Patronage System' in Harry Christian (ed.), *The Sociology of Journalism and the Press*, Sociological Review Monograph 29 (Keele: University of Keele, 1980), pp. 71–120.

7 Ibid.

8 Cockett, *Twilight of Truth*; Richards, 'Mourned but not missed by the masses'; Ralph Negrine, *Politics and the Mass Media in Britain* (London, Routledge 2nd pbk edn, 1994), pp. 68–71.

9 Ibid., pp. 70–1.

10 Ibid., p. 70.

11 Richards, 'Mourned but not missed by the masses'; Labour's taming of the *Herald* by 1924, fuelled by MacDonald's general antipathy and his suspicion of alleged crypto-Communist journalists, is documented in Ross McKibbin, *The Evolution of the Labour Party 1910–1924* (Oxford: Oxford University Press, 1974), pp. 221–34.

12 Minney, *Viscount Southwood*, pp. 217–42; Alan Bullock, *The Life and Times of Ernest Bevin, Volume One, Trade Union Leader 1881–1940* (London: Heinemann, 1960), pp. 419–25; Stephen Koss, *The Rise and Fall of the Political Press in Britain: Volume 2, The Twentieth Century* (London: Hamish Hamilton, 1984), pp. 482–3, 496–7; Richards, 'News coverage – or bingo?', pp. 27–8.

13 Bullock, *The Life and Times of Ernest Bevin*. The launching of a northern edition had been the great unfulfilled dream of Lansbury and his successors in the 1920s, taking place on 28 June 1930. Bevin was disgusted that MacDonald attended the Farnborough Air Show instead of visiting the new Manchester offices to draft a congratulatory front-page message, just as he had done in a much-publicised visit to the capital's Long Acre presses three months earlier; Koss, *The Rise and Fall of the Political Press in Britain*, pp. 496–7.

14   As Ernest Bevin put it:

> Unless we can develop an intelligent democracy, although Labour may get votes, it will not have power...To develop an electorate from whom real power to change the existing order of things can be derived, we must so write and present our case as to produce all the enlightenment necessary.

Annual Report of TGWU General Secretary, March 1935, quoted in Peter Weiler, *Ernest Bevin* (Manchester: Manchester University Press, 1993), p. 79.

15   Richards, 'News coverage – or bingo?', pp. 27–8. Beaverbrook calculated in May 1939 that while the *Daily Express* retained 336 canvassers, the *Daily Herald* had 1056, roughly five times its editorial strength – figures quoted in Wintour, *The Rise and Fall of Fleet Street*, p. 58.

16   Regarding Bevin's reluctance to question Elias's strategy, Charles Wintour is over generous in concluding that, 'Everybody blamed the poor old TUC for the failure of the paper, but it was primarily the management's inability to understand that the journalistic quality of the paper mattered even more than the circulation gimmicks which led eventually to the death of the whole enterprise'; ibid., pp. 61–2.

17   Hannen Swaffer lauded Henderson and colleagues ('Eight Men Who Matter Today', 26 August 1931, and *'All* Have Made Sacrifices', 27 August 1931, *Daily Herald*), and Francis Williams fuelled the myth of the 'bankers' ramp (for example, 'Put the Country Before the Banks', 25 August 1931, and the double column leader 'Cabinet, Banks and People', 26 August 1931, *Daily Herald*: 'That is the fundamental fact about the new Government. It is not a people's government, but a bankers' government'). Bevin and Cole's ideas were articulated in the leaders. 'On Being British', 28 August 1931, and 'Labour's Task', 29 August 1931, *Daily Herald*. On Bevin and Cole's involvement in promoting an alternative economic strategy before and immediately after August 1931, see Adrian Smith, *The New Statesman: Portrait of a Political Weekly, 1913–1931* (London: Frank Cass, 1996), pp. 238–57. The truly bizarre issue of 29 August 1931 featured a front page headline of 'Mr Henderson as Leader of the Opposition' next to a large photograph of Carol Lombard's face; inside, Harold Laski had been asked to descend from his LSE ivory tower and contribute 'The Man in the Street Looks at the Crisis', a worthy challenger to the following page's romantic serial for lack of verisimilitude. Meanwhile, the extended special offer on Odhams' dictionaries finally ended, and cartoonist Will Dyson, by now a pale shadow of his former self, returned to disappoint older readers.

18   Hugh Dalton, *Call Back Yesterday: Memoirs 1887–1931* (London: Muller, 1953), 24 August 1931, pp. 273–4. Williams paid tribute to Bevin's leadership and clarity of thought in his account of reporting the 1931 crisis; Williams, *Nothing So Strange*, pp. 101–4.

19   'Mr Bevin blames Finance for Crisis', *Daily Herald*, 31 August 1931.

20 Wintour, *The Rise and Fall of Fleet Street*, pp. 52–3; Cudlipp, *At Your Peril*, p. 273, based on conversation with Francis Williams.

21 Williams, *Nothing So Strange*, pp. 130–33, 143–7; Jay, *Change and Fortune: a Political Record*, pp. 64–82; Ben Pimlott (ed.), *The Political Diary of Hugh Dalton 1918–40, 1945–60* (London: Jonathan Cape, 1986), 16 March 1936 and 5 June 1938, pp. 198–9, 232–4. For the *Herald*'s coverage of British foreign policy in the 1930s, see Cockett, *Twilight of Truth*, pp. 43–5, 60, 66, 75, 80 and Franklin Reid Gannon, *The British Press and Germany* (Oxford: Oxford University Press, 1971), pp. 213–18, 255–9, 297–8.

22 Williams, *Nothing So Strange*, pp. 136–9. On one occasion Bevin refused to convey the NEC's disapproval of a leader criticising Labour's creaking defence policy, just as at the 1926 Congress he had opposed a motion condemning the *Herald* for its disapproval of the TUC's role during the General Strike; ibid., pp. 134; Bullock, *The Life and Times of Ernest Bevin*, pp. 355, 589; D. Lloyd George, June 1937, quoted in Koss, *The Rise and Fall of the Political Press in Britain*, p. 556.

23 Wintour, *The Rise and Fall of Fleet Street*, p. 58; Williams, *Nothing So Strange*, pp. 132–3, 150; idem., *Dangerous Estate*, pp. 172–3; Cudlipp, *At Your Peril*, pp. 272–3. Hugh Cudlipp and Cecil King's joint written submission to the 1961 Royal Commission on the Press insisted, 'There was no security leak about the *Herald*'s foreign news service: it scarcely existed', replicated in Cudlipp, *At Your Peril*, p. 349. In 1950, not only was the *Herald* the only British national not to send a reporter to Korea, but it closed down its Paris and Berlin offices, paid off its Central European correspondent, and abolished the post of foreign editor. Richards, *The Bloody Circus*, p. 164.

24 Lord Beaverbrook, *The Abdication of King Edward VIII*, ed. A.J.P. Taylor (London, Hamish Hamilton, 1966), p. 68; Minney, *Viscount Southwood*, pp. 287–8, 293; Cudlipp, *At Your Peril*, p. 271; Williams, *Nothing So Strange*, pp. 140–3; Bullock, *The Life and Times of Ernest Bevin*, pp. 589–90. In 1931 Bevin had failed to persuade MacDonald, still sore over *John Bull*'s wartime revelation of his illegitimacy, to give Elias a peerage; ibid., p. 457. Elias is referred to henceforth by his title, Lord (from 1946, Viscount) Southwood.

25 Southwood was incensed by the *Herald*'s association with a Declaration of Human Rights proposed by H.G. Wells, but more especially by his editor's suggestion for a contingency resistance movement (later expanded into *War By Revolution*, (London: Routledge 1940). Williams, who 'came to hate him more than any man I have ever known', depicted Southwood as a keen advocate of a negotiated peace, an impression shared by Jay. Williams, *Nothing So Strange*, pp. 130–1, 152–6; Koss, *The Rise and Fall of the Political Press in Britain*, pp. 597–8; Jay, *Change and Future*, pp. 81–2.

26 The alliterative description of the *Daily Mirror* is by Koss, who quoted Oliver Harvey's April 1941 suggestion that Southwood tolerated editorial criticism of Churchill because of his sympathy for 'the remnants of

the Chamberlainites'; Koss, *The Rise and Fall of the Political Press in Britain*, pp. 608, 610. According to his biographer, Southwood's reluctance to intervene infuriated Bevin, with efforts to bring about an early reconciliation coming to nothing; Minney, *Viscount Southwood*, pp. 334–5.

27   Neville Chamberlain to Winston Churchill, 6 June 1940, Churchill papers, 20/11, quoted in Martin Gilbert, *Winston S. Churchill Volume VI Finest Hour 1939–1941* (London: Heinemann, 1983), p. 474; Cecil King, *With Malice Toward None: a War Diary*, ed. William Armstrong (London: Sidgwick and Jackson, 1970), 7 July 1940, p. 48; Ian McLane, *Ministry of Morale: Home Front Morale and the Ministry of Information in World War II* (London, George Allen and Unwin, 1979), pp. 84–6; Gilbert, pp. 830–1. Attlee was also given the thankless task of telling King and the *Mirror's* editorial director, Guy 'Bart' Bartholomew, that if it was up to Churchill they would by now be behind bars; a meeting recorded in a diary entry that is – unintentionally – very funny; see King, op. cit., 12 October 1940, pp. 80–4.

28   Martin Gilbert, *Winston S. Churchill: Volume VII, Road to Victory 1941–1946* (London: Heinemann, 1986), p. 90; in an episode reminiscent of the BBC World Service's unintentional warning of the attack on Goose Green during the 1982 Falklands War, Churchill had previously complained of the *Herald* correctly speculating upon an advance on Benghazi: 'he said very bitterly that this might well lead to death of a thousand Australians. But what did we care, if it made a good newspaper stunt!…From his point of view he has done, is doing, and will continue to do all anyone could to win the war. He feels this, and so attacks on his Government mystify and bewilder him.' King, *With Malice Toward None*, 31 July 1941, pp. 102–3.

29   The *Daily Herald's* comment on the *Daily Mirror* quoted in Hugh Cudlipp, *Publish and be Damned! The Astonishing Story of the Daily Mirror* (London, Andrew Dakars, 1953), p. 189; King, *With Malice Toward None*, 21 March 1942, p. 168; Alan Bullock, *The Life and Times of Ernest Bevin: Volume Two, Minister of Labour 1940–1945* (London: Heinemann, 1967), pp. 132–6, 166–7. Percy Cudlipp's evidence to the Royal Commission on the Press in 1947 that ministers other than Churchill sought to influence him only three times during the war surely excludes Bevin (and Attlee?); particularly given King's 1942 claim, albeit exaggerated, that, 'His leaders caused the Government more annoyance than anything else in the entire Press'; Cudlipp quoted in Koss, *Rise and Fall of the Political Press in Britain*, pp. 612–13; King, *With Malice Toward None*, Cecil King to Lady Cripps, 18 April 1942, p. 312.

30   Extract from Hugh Cudlipp and Cecil King's joint written submission to the 1961 Royal Commission on the Press, replicated in Cudlipp, *At Your Peril*, p. 349.

31   Seymour-Ure, 'The Press and the Party System', p. 243.

32   Curran, 'Advertising as a Patronage System', p. 87. In stark contrast to *Mirror* executives' prioritising of the human interest story (only 2 per cent

of editorial content devoted to commentary upon public affairs), the indirect influence of the TUC 'A' directors meant that the *Herald* devoted a larger proportion of editorial content to reporting and analysing public affairs (33 per cent) than all but the heaviest broadsheet; Curran and Seaton, *Power without Responsibility*, (London: Routledge, 1991 fourth edn) pp. 57, 67.

33 Curran, 'Advertising as a Patronage System', pp. 86–7, 99. The press barons collaborated in wartime via the Newsprint Supply Company, with common agreement on each publication's size, proportion of advertising space, and circulation. All canvassing and free insurance or gifts ceased, but were unnecessary anyway as supply (restricted by only one-fifth of normal newsprint supplies being available) could not meet increased demand. Even the *Herald*'s profitability grew, if only because advertisers were forced to spread their spending over a number of titles, and were willing to pay the higher rates now charged for what little space was available. Newspaper rationing did not end until as late as 1956, thus artificially maintaining a pattern of multiple newspaper buying which had spread from middle-class to working-class readers during the Second World War: total daily sales rose from 9 903 427 in 1937 to 15 449 410 in 1947 when 'free sale' resumed. Minney, *Viscount Southwood*, pp. 320–2; Jenkins, *Newspapers*, p. 32; sales figures quoted in Raymond Williams, *The Long Revolution* (London: Chatto and Windus, 1961, Pelican pbk edn, 1965), p. 231.

34 Curran, 'Advertising as a Patronage System', p. 87; Mass Observation quoted by Richards, 'Mourned but not missed by the masses'; on Foot's contribution to the *Herald* in the final winter of the war, see Mervyn Jones, *Michael Foot* (London: Victor Gollancz, 1994), pp. 118–19.

35 *Daily Herald*, 18 June 1945; another oft-quoted headline is 'Frauds, Cheats, Wrigglers Seek Power', *Daily Herald*, 26 June 1945, a reference to Tory parliamentary candidates, who were also often portrayed as latent fascists; Cudlipp, *Publish and be Damned!*, pp. 220, 259. For a markedly different view of the *Herald*, depicting it as from 1931 singlehandedly sowing the seeds for victory in July 1945, see Wilfred Fienburgh, *25 Momentous Years: a 25th Anniversary in the History of the Daily Herald* (London: Odhams, 1955), pp. 159–60.

36 TUC directors' view of the *Mirror* quoted in Koss, *Rise and Fall of the Political Press in Britain*, p. 626; Cudlipp, *Publish and be Damned!*, p. 220; Koss, op. cit., p. 644; Richards, *The Bloody Circus*, pp. 163–4.

37 Richards quotes Morrison's aphorism when contrasting the first *Herald*, rooted in syndicalism and guild socialism, with its successors' rigid perception of politics 'in institutional and electoral rather than cultural terms'; Richards, 'Mourned but not missed by the masses'. Hunter had been Morrison's public relations adviser and as political correspondent in the 1950s was deeply hostile to the Bevanites, who suspected him of planning stories on behalf of Attlee and Gaitskell, see Leslie Hunter, *The Road to Brighton Pier* (London: Arthur Barker, 1959) and Janet Morgan (ed.), *The Backbench Diaries of Richard Crossman* (London: Jonathan

Cape/Hamish Hamilton, 1981), 21 March 1955, pp. 406–7; Pilcher was Gaitskell's *de facto* press officer from January 1956 until after Suez, with the *Herald*'s secretarial staff and access to agency reports made available to the Labour leader following the Anglo-American intervention, see Philip M. Williams (ed.), *The Diary of Hugh Gaitskell 1945–1956* (London: Jonathan Cape, 1983), 9 January 1956, p. 406, and Tony Benn, *Years of Hope: Diaries, Papers and Letters 1940–1962*. Ruth Winstone (ed.), (London: Hutchinson, 1994), 4 November 1956, pp. 201–2; Winterton was lobby correspondent of the *Herald* throughout the 1950s.

38 *Daily Herald*, 1 October 1956 [Aneurin Bevan and George Brown were engaged in an archetypal left–right struggle]; Koss, *Rise and Fall of the Political Press in Britain*, p. 634. Cudlipp and King contrasted the *Mirror* formula of 'the left wing view at decisive moments, backed by pages of entertainment and clever writing', with the *Herald* 's obligation to publish 'with a zeal which ushered away the readers in dazed droves' such 'unpalatable ... verbiage' as 'a politician's bread and butter speech on an inauspicious occasion on a wet afternoon'; extract from Hugh Cudlipp and Cecil King's joint written submission to the 1961 Royal Commission on the Press replicated in Cudlipp, *At Your Peril*, p. 349.

39 See a shocking four day exposé of teenage worship of Dean, *Daily Herald*, 9–13 October 1956, and a truly disturbing report on the insidious effects of rock'n'roll, *Daily Herald*, 16 October 1956, i.e. five major features warning parents inside seven days. Symbolically, Marjorie Proops moved from the *Herald* to the *Mirror* in 1954, having earlier been chastised by Percy Cudlipp for writing that there were no frilly knickers in the Labour Party ('You've got to watch it, Marjorie, you're a sexy writer'); Engel, *Tickle the Public*, p. 187. Circulation figures quoted in Negrine, *Politics and the Mass Media in Britain*, p. 70.

40 Middle-market newspapers such as the *Herald* were the most damaged by television, as an inability to offer regional variation led to a loss of advertising revenue after 1955, and 'Their emphasis on topical exposure in news coverage and vivid use of pictures made them particularly vulnerable to a medium which could produce the coverage the night before and support it with moving pictures.' Jenkins, *Newspapers*, pp. 32–3.

41 Figures taken from: Tom Jeffery and Keith McClelland, 'A world fit to live in: the *Daily Mail* and the middle classes 1918–39' in James Curran *et al.* (eds), *Impacts and Influences: Essays on Media Power in the Twentieth Century* (London: Methuen, 1987), p. 39 (see pp. 32–9 for complete data on *Herald* readership in the 1930s); Curran, 'Advertising as a Patronage System', p. 96; extract from Hugh Cudlipp and Cecil King's joint written submission to the 1961 Royal Commission on the Press, replicated in Cudlipp, *At Your Peril*, p. 349.

42 Curran, 'Advertising as a Patronage System', pp. 87–94; Curran and Seaton, *Power Without Responsibility*, pp. 108–9. As well as consolidation of advertising, at the expense of the ostensibly proletarian *Herald*, the end of rationing meant newspapers increased in size, so that readers felt less necessity to make more than one purchase – and again the *Herald* suffered.

43 Cudlipp, *Publish and be Damned!*, p. 259; Curran and Seaton, *Power Without Responsibility*, p. 109.

44 Koss, *The Rise and Fall of the Political Press in Britain*, p. 652.

45 Beginning with a campaign in October 1956 to secure demobilisation, or at best leave, for all Reservists, the *Herald* articulated Labour opposition to any military resolution of the Suez crisis, using the episode as an opportunity to unite right and left within the party. From 31 October to 7 November 1956 the first four pages of every issue were devoted to anti-Government coverage of the invasion, relieved only by Davidson's first-hand account of the Hungarian uprising. Particularly noticeable were what was, for the *Herald*, an unusually inventive and adaptable layout, and the extensive, propagandist coverage of Gaitskell's attacks on Eden inside and outside Parliament. For Bevanite complaints about unfair and inaccurate reporting in the *Herald*, see Morgan (ed.), *The Backbench Diaries of Richard Crossman*, 23 October 1952, 26 February 1953, pp. 165, 205, and Michael Foot, *Aneurin Bevan 1945–1960* (London: Davis-Poynter, 1973), pp. 368, 378, 385, 393–4, 471(n). See also Philip Williams, *Hugh Gaitskell: a Political Biography* (London: Jonathan Cape, 1979), p. 320; Williams (ed.), *The Diary of Hugh Gaitskell 1945–1956*, 19 March 1955, 16 January 1956, 3 February 1956, 16 February 1956, 22 August 1956, pp. 382–3, 420, 434–5, 445, 582.

46 Koss, *The Rise and Fall of the Political Press in Britain*, pp. 652–4; Williams, *Hugh Gaitskell: a Political Biography*, p. 667; Colin Seymour-Ure, *The British Press and Broadcasting since 1945* (London: Blackwell, 1991), p. 22.

47 Koss, *The Rise and Fall of the Political Press in Britain*, pp. 654–5; Jenkins, *Newspapers*, pp. 35–7.

48 *Daily Herald*, 27 and 28 February 1958; Williams, *Hugh Gaitskell: a Political Biography*, p. 493; Morgan (ed.), *The Backbench Diaries of Richard Crossman* 28 February 1958, 19 March 1958, p. 668. Cudlipp was forever seeking ways to entice *Herald* readers to switch to the *Mirror*, hence his recruitment of Crossman as a columnist, and his once commissioning Bevan to write six articles even though he judged him a terrible journalist; Morgan *The Backbench Diaries of Richard Crossman*, 24 March 1954, p. 296.

49 Ibid., 1 September 1960, p. 870; Curran and Seaton, *Power without Responsibility* , p. 109.

50 Cudlipp, *Walking on the Water*, pp. 246–8; Williams, *Hugh Gaitskell: a Political Biography*, pp. 667–9; Koss, *The Rise and Fall of the Political Press in Britain*, p. 655; Jenkins, *Newspapers*, pp. 36–7; King, *Strictly Personal: Some Memoirs of Cecil H. King*, pp. 125–6.

51 Cudlipp, *Walking on the Water*, p. 247.

52 Maurice Edelman, *The Mirror: a Political History* (London: Hamish Hamilton, 1966), pp. 165, 168–9; 'A Nation in Search of a Party', *Daily Herald*, 31 January 1962; Hugh Gaitskell, 'A Party in Search of a Newspaper', 1 February 1962; Williams, *Hugh Gaitskell: a Political Biography*, p. 669.

53   Cudlipp, *Walking on the Water*, p. 248–9; Williams, *Hugh Gaitskell: a Political Biography*, pp. 730, 738, 669. The *Herald* could boast that its last two editors both became peers, Jacobson's title being his own name, and Beavan becoming Lord Ardwick.

54   Seymour-Ure, *The British Press and Broadcasting since 1945*, p. 22. The target circulation was 1.7 million, with an increase in the advertisement rate at 1.6 million, new readers deriving from *News Chronicle* veterans disillusioned with the *Mail* or *Express*, and the 'intelligent grammar schoolboy on the horizon'; extract from Hugh Cudlipp and Cecil King's joint written submission to the 1961 Royal Commission on the Press, replicated in Cudlipp, *At Your Peril*, pp. 350–1; idem, *Walking on the Water* , p. 249.

55   Engel, *Tickle the Public*, p. 250; Wintour, *Pressures on the Press*, p. 214; for a summary of IPC's market research, and the conclusion that age was more important than class, with 'traditional political attitudes' making way for 'the politics of the consumer', see ibid., p. 22.

56   Leapman, *Treacherous Estate*, pp. 26–33; Curran, *Walking on the Water*, p. 250.

57   Leapman, *Treacherous Estate*, p. 31; Curran, 'Advertising as a Patronage System', pp. 96–7. Those in Labour's 1964 election campaign team responsible for handling the media judged the news paper 'a disaster' (for Benn 'pages of fluffy pictures and nothing hard to bite on' signalled an early demise), with Wilson lobbying King and Cudlipp for the *Sun* to inspire Labour voters and activists as the *Herald* had always done; Tony Benn, *Out of the Wilderness: Diaries 1963–1967* (London: Hutchinson, 1987), 15 and 20 September 1964, pp. 141, 144.

58   Cudlipp, *Walking on the Water*, pp. 250–3; Engel, *Tickle the Public*, pp. 249–51; Wintour, *Pressures on the Press*, pp. 214–17; Leapman, *Treacherous Estate* p. 63.

59   Tunstall, *Newspaper Power*, pp. 93–4, 167.

9
The 'Max Factor' – a Mirror Image? Robert Maxwell and the *Daily Mirror* Tradition

James Thomas

A newspaper can act as the vehicle of another personality, whether that of editor of proprietor, only within the limits set by its own. It cannot radically alter its character without destroying itself.[1]

Introduction

It was just before the stroke of midnight began on Friday, 13 July 1984, suitably, that Robert Maxwell clinched his takeover of Mirror Group newspapers and finally fulfilled a long-frustrated ambition to become a national newspaper proprietor. It began what has been immortalised as an all too real horror story for the paper, at the hands of a man termed a 'monster' by one editor and once famously denounced by a Department of Trade and Industry report as 'not... a person who can be relied upon to exercise proper stewardship of a publicly quoted company'.[2] Aside from his plunder of the Mirror pension fund, revealed following his mysterious death in November 1991, the charge sheet about the impact of the 'Max factor' on the paper is a formidable one. The day after his takeover Maxwell had made three pledges to suspicious journalists. He offered a guarantee that editors would be free to conduct the paper 'without interference with their editorial judgment', which was complemented by a pledge to continue the paper's traditional 'broadly sympathetic approach to the Labour movement'. Finally Maxwell promised to 'restore the *Mirror* to its former glories' as Britain's leading newspaper and rescue the good name of tabloid journalism from its position, as he later put it, 'in the gutter with Rupert' and 'the lying, cheating, thieving *Sun*'.[3]

In practice, the received impression is that Maxwell ended up breaking the *Mirror* and replacing it with what critics soon dubbed the *Daily Maxwell*, as he interfered on a scale which made Citizen Kane appear a model of hands-off newspaper management. Politically his Thatcherite convictions ensured that 'the paper's sympathy for the labour movement was abandoned before the month was out', or at the very least was reduced to a tokenist support for the Labour leadership. This was accompanied by a more general 'betrayal' of the noble 'purpose' of the *Mirror* as the paper lost its serious news coverage, not to mention its humanity, decency and circulation, and became dominated by *Sun*-style 'junk journalism'.[4] This chapter will first outline and then challenge this interpretation. It will suggest that, despite the understandable tendency to present the Maxwell period as a barbaric aberration from the *Mirror's* civilised history, the overwhelming feature of the paper in these three areas was one of continuity rather than change.

The Daily Maxwell

Critics appear on firmest ground when they point to Maxwell's destruction of editorial freedom at the *Mirror*. His behaviour as almost 'a parody of the megalomaniac newspaper tycoons of fiction' has become legendary through countless accounts which all convey a personality who has grown larger in death than even in life. In 1998 Maxwell was still mentioned in the British press on more occasions than any other media figure.[5] The conventional orthodoxy is that the tycoon proved to be 'a supreme interventionist in almost every detail almost all the time...whose monstrous ego steam rollered over the protests and professional judgements of editors and executives alike'. When Maxwell bought the *Mirror* he immediately called a meeting of the paper's executives for 1.30 in the morning, offering a symbolic start to his ownership of a paper which, as his closest adviser Joe Haines put it, proved to be 'only a minor part of his business but a major part of his interest'.[6]

The tycoon constantly broke his non-interventionist pledges, summoning and phoning editors and staff at all hours, re-writing stories, and even bugging the offices of those he employed. As one of the journalists subject to his interference put it, to Maxwell 'the very phrase journalistic ethics was a joke. He would just laugh in your face if you even mentioned the phrase.' Roy Greenslade, *Daily Mirror* editor from December 1989 to March 1991, provides the most overwhelming evidence of the 'unbelievable' extent of the tycoon's constant day-by-day and even hour-by-hour interference throughout his fourteen month 'siege with the barbarian on the tenth floor'.[7] It is a portrait which an egocentric Maxwell frequently appeared to confirm, boasting that he sure as hell had 'got control' of a paper which he crudely viewed as his personal megaphone and which gave him 'the power to raise issues effectively'. He claimed he was not shy of interfering, and that he could not only do the editor's job but was actually 'rather good at designing front pages'. Under Maxwell, the editorial diversity of the era of Cecil King and Hugh Cudlipp (summed up in their encouragement to John Pilger, 'You write. We publish') now became inverted into Maxwell's orders, 'I publish. You write'.[8]

The new proprietor's interference was particularly noticeable during his first year of ownership. Readers were deluged with Maxwell-centred stories. Self-publicising acts of benevolence competed alongside laudatory reports of Maxwell's many meetings with 'the world's greatest dictators', in a style parodied in one *Private Eye* headline as 'ALL SMILES AS MAXWELL MEETS ATTILA THE HUN'. The tycoon's behaviour, 'like a child with a Meccano set', ensured, in Cudlipp's words, that anyone in Britain unaware of the paper's new proprietor after his first year 'must be deaf, dumb, blind or all three'.[9]

All this was a reflection of Maxwell's dominant personality characteristic, his narcissism – which led him to boast 'I'm not just a hero, I'm a cult figure' and, on one priceless occasion, to pull out of an arrangement to see the Queen five minutes beforehand, instructing his irate wife Betty to 'tell her I'm a busy man'.[10] But Maxwell's crude self-promotion did not entertain readers. In a near-catastrophic circulation loss, which one trade observer felt took 'something close to genius', sales of the *Mirror* declined by half a million in his first eighteen months of ownership.[11]

A Right-wing *Mirror*?

Maxwell's interference certainly extended to politics, where he openly boasted of the 'major say' he had in determining the paper's line.

In this field 'the world's most improbable Labour supporter' was regarded with deep suspicion within the party the paper had supported for 40 years. Despite, or perhaps because of, a brief and typically controversial period as a Labour MP from 1964 to 1970, Maxwell had long excited doubts about both his political credentials and his business dealings as 'the bouncing Czech'. More recently his use of Thatcherite industrial legislation against his employees had further added to his pariah status in the labour movement. Frequent attempts were made to revoke the party membership of a man viewed in some quarters as 'one of the ... most dangerous capitalists of all time'.[12]

Labour supporters' affection for Maxwell was hardly increased by his frequent praise of Margaret Thatcher as a great Prime Minister, to whom he owed his business advancement and who had 'taught the Labour party ... to discard silly and impractical policies'. She replied with her supreme compliment that he was 'really one of us'. Certainly the twice self-made millionaire seemed to epitomise the Thatcherite spirit, perhaps most crudely in 1984 when he appeared on television to launch his 'Who Dares Wins' million-pound bingo competition, mouthing the slogan 'Do you sincerely want to be rich?'[13]

Not surprisingly there were frequent rumours that the *Mirror* under Maxwell was, as one former Labour MP put it, giving the Conservative government a very soft ride.[14] A number of incidents seemed to confirm a rightward shift. Just two weeks after buying the paper Maxwell deleted the key part of an article by the paper's industrial editor Geoffrey Goodman, which traced the origins of the 1984 miners strike to Thatcher's determination to avenge the role they played in toppling the Heath government ten years earlier. He then inverted Goodman's headline, 'Digging Into a Vendetta', into the Prime Minister's own view of the miners as 'The Enemy Within'.[15] Soon after, a story by Pilger alleging that the government's Youth Training Scheme was a cover for cheap labour, was actually sent to the relevant government minister before it was allowed to be published with the minister's comments alongside. Maxwell also hired an old friend, the right-wing columnist George Gale, who was given a confidential brief to take a pro-Thatcher line. The cumulative effect of Maxwell's input was, Pilger suggests, a significant change in the character of the paper into a deep sympathy for the assumptions of the Thatcher Revolution. Continued editorial support for the Labour party was 'little more than tokenism'.[16]

A betrayal of purpose

Accompanying this change was a more general decline. Despite Maxwell's assertion that 'news comes first, second, third and last', his initiation of a million pound bingo war soon after buying the paper produced allegations of gutter tactics and of the damage to the reputation of journalism. By July 1985 the initial hopes he had inspired of better journalism had been replaced by low morale among many insiders. They considered that the paper's news coverage was worse than it had been for a very long time.[17] Pilger's writings are the most explicit of many accounts to see a 'betrayal of purpose' in the contrast between Maxwell and the *Mirror's* glory days under Bartholomew, King and Cudlipp. Together with Rupert Murdoch, Maxwell allegedly hijacked popular journalism and ripped the heart from the paper.[18] He so corrupted journalism that the *Mirror* lost its essential honesty and decency – and its commitment to serious and global news. Instead it embraced the 'voyeurism', 'junk', 'non-news' and 'page three cuties', popularised by the 'anti-journalism' of the *Sun*.[19] Maxwell and Murdoch, in sum, presided over what Cudlipp in 1988 denounced as a dark age of tabloid journalism:

> Bingo became a new journalistic art form; … when significant national and international events were nudged aside by a panting seven day and seven night news service for voyeurs on … the exclusive definitive autobiographies of kiss-and-tell nymphets aged eighteen and a half and of course, though on a marginally higher plane, the latest inanities in the Royal Soap Opera, where what is worn or accidentally revealed in a high wind is rated as vastly more important than what is said or done.[20]

This offered a marked contrast with the 'vintage years' of the paper, when the *Mirror* inspired 'pride', 'had a heart' and was devoid of the 'cynicism' of present-day journalism. According to Cudlipp, the paper was formerly run by journalists who 'used to give tabloid newspapers a good name' and who were 'really trying to do *some-thing*'.[21] This began to change under the malign downmarket influence of the *Sun* in the 1970s. But it took full effect only under Maxwell, the city crook, who for example abolished the *Daily Mirror* Readers' Service (which had helped people since the Second World War), and who apparently even showed his contempt more openly by urinating on them from his helipad on the Mirror building roof.[22]

The paper's moral and journalistic collapse reached a fitting climax with the revelations that 'THE MAN WHO SAVED THE MIRROR', as the paper had sycophantically greeted Maxwell's death, had stolen £526 million from its pension fund. The scandal was said to symbolise a great betrayal of everything the *Mirror* had always stood for. A paper which had once 'championed the weak, the poor, the disadvantaged', now became synonymous with 'fraud, humbug and hypocrisy'. Suitably it was the *Sun* which captured the position of its high-minded rival as it taunted, 'Mirror, Mirror On The Wall, Who Is The Biggest Crook Of All'.[23]

This argument, made by Pilger among many others, is a typically powerful indictment, which contains much truth. It offers a classic tabloid story of evil villains and noble heroes, as Maxwell, along with Murdoch, eclipses the once bright light of popular journalism with an indefinite age of darkness. But, like many tabloid stories, it offers a portrait which is highly selective, both about the nature of the paper's policy and the way it was determined for most of 1984 to 1991. More fundamentally, it locates the paper in what Michael Williams describes as 'a nebulous golden era'.[24] By juxtaposing the reign of Bad King Bob with a past golden age, it offers a one-sided picture of both the Maxwell period and the *Mirror's* history, which ignores the fact that in many respects the dominant characteristic under Maxwell was continuity rather than change.

More Copper than Kane

Firstly, a concentration on Maxwell's editorial interference provides just one perspective on the way policy was actually determined. Inverting the dominant impression, it has even been argued that for the bulk of his period as owner of the *Mirror*, the paper actually had a strong and relatively independent editor in Richard Stott (1985–9, 1991–2). Stott, when he took over in 1985, claims to have told Maxwell that he must 'have control' of the paper. In practice, Maxwell did indeed usually if not always concede this power, both to Stott and to the paper's senior journalists. Coverage of their proprietor's activities was largely restricted to a 'page two only' agreement. The paper's first editor under Maxwell, Mike Molloy, also claimed that 'the editors were quite tough with Maxwell; he did not walk all over them'. Others would dismiss these claims as pure illusion, arguing that 'working for Maxwell and having independence' were 'simply two fundamentally conflicting principles'.[25]

Regardless of these contrasting accounts, it is clear that even during the periods of Maxwell's more intense intervention his actual effect on the paper's content, if not on its morale or image, was more limited than the impression conveyed. One of the main reason's for this was that while Maxwell's very personality inclined him to try and assert control, it simultaneously militated against its achievement in practice. As his chief of staff Peter Jay recalls, the tycoon operated from one minute to the next in a condition of 'whirling chaos', in which one issue could occupy him as quickly as it would be forgotten again. He had what senior journalists unanimously considered to be 'the attention span of a gadfly – three or four seconds and it would be forgotten'. He hardly ever bothered to read the paper, in complete contrast to the man with whom he was fond of comparing himself, Lord Beaverbrook.[26] He was a man who often could not even remember whom he had sacked – or even the names of his most famous journalists, such as Anne Robinson.[27] Ian Watson, then an editorial director of *The European*, recalls one revealing episode when Maxwell told him:

> 'Mr Editor, I want you to sack our entire Brussels office.' I said: 'First of all Bob, I'm not your editor, you sacked me six months ago, and secondly we have only recently opened our office in Brussels. We have one person working there and they are doing a very good job.' He looked at me and said: 'Never mind, just get on with it.'[28]

This provides one glimpse of a 'quite lunatic' and 'utterly surreal' 'world of Maxwellia' where 'reality could be whatever he said it was'.[29] Moreover, Maxwell's vanity meant that it was probably more important to him to be seen in control and issuing orders than in ensuring that they were carried out. The contrast between image and reality at the *Mirror* was demonstrated in July 1985, when Maxwell was filmed for TV making alterations to Geoffrey Goodman's copy. Later, when the cameras were off, Goodman restored the original.[30] The effectiveness of Maxwell's control was also limited by the fact that, despite his boasts, he bordered on the subnormal in his journalistic ability and was utterly ignorant of newspaper production or 'how a tabloid newspaper operated', in complete contrast to Murdoch, the man he was manically obsessed with.[31] Maxwell, indeed, had an almost endearing innocence in this area. Molloy recalls:

> He used to come down and see me ... and he'd say, 'Let's go out and look', because he *loved* to look at it ... And he was always disappointed at looking at the newsroom, and he'd say 'Where are they all ... where are all the journalists?' – *'They're out reporting.'* He couldn't understand this. Bob wanted a room full of people like a film set. He wanted the front page effect. He was like a child.[32]

These were hardly the personal characteristics to produce the effective proprietorial control exercised by Murdoch, with whom he is so often misleadingly twinned. Maxwell was clearly not so much one of the 'Lords of the Global Village', as Ben Bagdikian describes him, as the Village Idiot – viewed by his fellow proprietors as a 'ludicrous' if sometimes rather entertaining 'total buffoon', with a distant grip on reality. His role was less akin to the omnipotent Citizen Kane than to the blundering and out of touch Lord Copper in Evelyn Waugh's *Scoop*.[33] All this meant that editors and journalists could frequently agree with their proprietor 'up to a point' but 'pull the wool over his eyes', 'baffle him with bullshit', frustrate his interventions and retain real control.[34]

Resistance from the paper's journalists or editors could take various forms. At one extreme it included a near suicidal gesture by the cartoonist Griffin, who inserted the minuscule but clear comment, 'Fuck Maxwell', into one cartoon. More routinely, Stott recalls that if Maxwell 'wanted to run a loony leader' he would get Haines, on whom Maxwell relied heavily for political advice, to talk him out of it.[35] Equally the tycoon's ludicrous interventions could be stalled until it was too late for them to appear, or he could be shown a piece of copy for his approval which never made it into the newspaper.[36] One such example came in May 1990, when the proprietor suddenly made a rare appearance on the editorial floor and insisted the paper publish a big story about his receipt of an honorary degree from Washington University. He proceeded to write the story himself, 'like a child's essay'. His ignorance of newspaper deadlines, along with the manoeuvres of the paper's night editor, ensured that the story appeared in only a couple of thousand papers out of the three million actually printed.[37]

If all this failed to divert Maxwell, the evidence suggests that the paper's journalists for the most part did not lose control of the news coverage. Most of the time Maxwell's interventions were restricted to the editorials – which he considered so important but which relatively few readers bothered to scrutinise.[38] Even here, Haines's skill in handling Maxwell would ensure that the effectiveness of his directions was limited. According to Goodman, Haines could re-write editorials in such a way that they 'still retained the basic thrust of what he had done originally, but would contain the odd phrase or one sentence which paid some recognition to what Maxwell was complaining about.[39]

Similarly, under Greenslade's editorship, the proprietor's attempts to retake control of his 'trainset' had only limited success. His most blatant attempt to dictate coverage came in January 1991, when he demanded a pro-Gorbachev spin after the Soviet leader sent tanks into Lithuania. Maxwell accused his editor of 'talking nonsense' in his reports about government-inspired bloodshed, claiming that 'Gorbachev wouldn't do anything without talking to me first'. Yet, apart from the leading article, this intervention had virtually no effect, and the paper reported that it was 'BACK TO THE BAD OLD DAYS' as 'Gorby soldiers massacre 13 in night of blood'. Indeed proprietorial pressure on such occasions spurred a determined editor to ensure his own editorial direction was maintained. As Diamond noted of the editor's accounts of Maxwell's constant interference, 'Each story would start "Maxwell demanded ..." and end 'I refused"'.[40]

More generally, the impression often given that the paper's journalists suffered a reign of terror under Maxwell is also misleading. The publisher was viewed on the one hand as a 'tyrant' and a 'monster', but equally his charm, courage and charisma could inspire affection and loyalty, and 'it was sometimes difficult not to like him'.[41] Life could be difficult in 'the mad mad world of Maxwellia', but it could also be fun, not to mention financially rewarding for the senior staff. Equally, for many journalists lower down, life continued much as before. [42]

In any case, the contrast between a Maxwell autocracy and a pre-tycoon era of journalistic freedom is misleading. Maxwell's interference had a rich heritage in a paper founded by Northcliffe and Rothermere, and transformed by Bartholomew, on the basis of an advertising agency report, with the help of two future autocrats, King and Cudlipp. Maxwell may have derived his idea of spying on staff from the equally tyrannical, crude, unpredictable, yet sometimes charming Bart, who even outdid his eventual successor in not only listening to their phone calls but also opening their letters.[43] Maxwell was only the latest in a long line of newspaper proprietors to fall victim to the occupational disease of megalomania. In him, it was only in the early stages, compared with King, the man who ousted Bartholomew. King saw 'nothing wrong with monopoly as long as I'm the fellow who holds it', and he sought vainly in the 1960s to implement this principle to the governing of the country as well as of the *Daily Mirror*.

Molloy certainly had history on his side, when as editor he would meet complaints about Maxwell's interference by recalling the similarities with King and Cudlipp, whose control was 'as autocratic as could possibly be imagined ... it wasn't a question of them interfering in the paper, it was that they allowed the staff to interfere'. Indeed, their complete preoccupation with the *Mirror* actually meant that 'it was much more liberal in many ways under Maxwell, oddly enough, because he was so busy trying to buy the world that he did not have time'.[44] Moreover, their journalistic ability made their editorial direction far more effective.

Walworth Road's *Pravda*?

Maxwell's control of the paper's political line was also subject to much the same limitations. For instance, perhaps the most famous example of Maxwell's political interference, his altering of Goodman's article on the miners' strike, in one respect illustrated continued control of the paper's journalists. Maxwell's changes only appeared in the middle editions of the paper, and were then reversed without his knowledge by the editor after protests from Goodman.[45] The evidence again suggests that the paper's proprietor was incapable of fashioning its political policy in any coherent way, given that 'as a political thinker Maxwell was mindless, simplistic and childlike' and his knowledge of British politics was 'as weak as his understanding of newspapers'.[46] This meant that, despite his occasional manic interventions, Maxwell would usually defer to wiser counsels, and while he 'liked to read the leader on the big issues, the number of times he decided to interfere was minimal'. Day-to-day political decisions continued as before to be taken by agreement between the editor, Haines, and the paper's political and industrial editors.[47]

More importantly, to argue about whether the paper's policy between 1984–91 was determined fundamentally by the paper's journalists or its proprietor rather misses the point, and ignores a deeper force which constantly informed policy decision. As the 1947 *Royal Commission on the Press* observed, newspapers may have 'personality' and operate within a set of unspoken assumptions about policy. As Cudlipp told its successor inquiry, 'we know each other's minds and the policies of our papers have been settled for very many years; we're not suddenly going to become Right Wing instead of Left Wing, or unilateralists instead of multilateralists'. 'The tablets', Cudlipp agreed, had long since been 'brought down from the mountain'.[48] This meant, as senior staff recall, that decisions were always made within a fixed framework where 'the broad policy was always laid down' and had been for forty years. [49]

Proprietors suggest that their impact on their paper lies not so much in determining day-to-day policy as in their wider power of 'setting the agenda' which informs those decisions.[50] While he frequently sought to interfere in the day-to-day direction Maxwell had no desire, nor even the ability, fundamentally to alter the paper's wider agenda. There was at work a reinforcing fusion between the *Mirror*'s traditions and the proprietor's own declared political stance, along with his desire to court the Labour leadership, which meant that this side to the paper continued largely unchanged. Such continuity must also have been heavily influenced by the obvious commercial importance of continuing the appeal to moderate Labour supporters. These overwhelmingly chose to buy the *Mirror*, given its 'unique selling point' in the 1980s as the only anti-Thatcher popular daily newspaper.[51]

The seamless continuity of the *Mirror*'s political stance under Maxwell can be demonstrated by the fact that the key challenge to the political loyalty of both paper and tycoon had come earlier in the 1980s. In November 1981, Cudlipp announced despondently that he was joining the newly formed SDP, due to Labour's 'disastrous' policies on defence and Europe and to the dominance of a Militant Tendency that was 'tearing the movement apart'. But, after some initial equivocation, the *Mirror* itself stayed loyal. It demonstrated this emphatically in the 1983 election, despite the fact that its traditional stance placed it much nearer the SDP than to the radical Labour programme.[52]

Much the same loyalty was shown by Maxwell, who later claimed that he had personally resisted the courtship of the SDP, 'to be one of the leaders of the party', but who insisted that 'he was born a socialist' and was 'not a turncoat'.[53] He certainly illustrated this in 1983, when he gave Michael Foot £38 500 to fund an unsuccessful court challenge to the electorally damaging findings of the Boundary Commission. He also discussed with the Labour leader the possibility of publishing a Labour-supporting election newspaper, at a time when the party was advocating policies on Europe, defence and domestic policy, to which he, like the *Mirror*, stood fundamentally opposed.[54]

The continuity after Maxwell bought the paper was aided by the fact that the paper's senior journalists, for all their opposition to Maxwell as 'a liar and a crook' with whom they were not prepared to work, did just that when he assumed control. In particular Maxwell quickly enlisted the support of Haines, his most vociferous opponent. Haines has frequently been singled out for criticism for his close connection with the tycoon, although inside accounts argue that his portrayal as Maxwell's 'swooning poodle is unfair and suggest that the tycoon had a huge respect for Joe' and took care not to push him 'beyond the limits of tolerance'. Haines in turn 'was always very tough with Maxwell', and would have resigned if forced to write anything he disagreed with.[55] Whatever the case, there was little to disagree about politically. Maxwell, at his meeting with Haines, gave the journalist a guarantee of non-interference in his work, but told him that one of the conditions of his employment was continued support of the Labour party. To the staunch Labour loyalist Haines, 'anything else would have been unthinkable'. Certainly the key role which the journalist played, given his outstanding leader-writing skills and 'very, very astute political brain', ensured that the paper continued with a powerful advocacy of the Labour cause.[56]

This support was very clearly shown only ten days after Maxwell bought the paper. The *Mirror* launched a 'FIGHT FOR THE LABOUR PARTY' – a four day 'Cudlipp-style' blitz, which produced a glorious

'KINNOCK VICTORY' against 'the subversion of democracy' by 'the fanatics' of the hard left'. Tony Benn in turn was to accuse the paper of eulogising Kinnock. He was particularly indignant at 'the most scandalous cartoon' of a horrific giant 'toothless figure with spectacles and wild hair', symbolising the triumph of the 'lunatic left'.[57] This very public pledge of loyalty to a suspicious Labour leadership continued throughout Maxwell's ownership of the paper, even if one could be forgiven for concluding from the tycoon's boasts that he, rather than Kinnock, had singlehandedly 'got rid of the militants out of the Labour movement' and produced the transformation to what he called 'my way of running the Labour party'. It was again shown in the 1987 election, when the *Mirror* fought 'its weightiest campaign for many a year'. This echoed its famous 1945 election coverage, in urging readers to 'VOTE FOR THEM' – the underprivileged, the sick, old, unemployed and young, and to fight the 'PRIVILEGE AND POVERTY' engrained in Thatcher's Britain.[58]

There is absolutely no evidence from such coverage of any concession to a new Thatcherite agenda. Indeed the biggest criticism of the *Mirror*'s election propaganda was that it was *too* traditional, and that it did not reflect the changed political landscape of the 1980s. For good or bad, there are certainly uncanny similarities between the much lauded Cudlipp-inspired 'IS THIS THE PROMISED LAND?' edition in 1964, and a ten-page *Mirror* 'shock issue' in 1987, exposing the 'pain and privilege' of a 'disunited Kingdom'.[59] It was a political approach which later led Conservatives to dub the paper 'the Walworth Road Pravda'. Alastair Campbell, the *Mirror*'s political editor from 1989 to 1993, for once agreed: he described himself as a Labour propagandist rather than a detached journalist, and this proprietor as 'the man of Labour' whose commitment to the party cause was unshakable.[60]

Others have strongly doubted whether this approach represented Maxwell's true political beliefs. But even if one accepts that he was really 'a man of the most extreme reactionary views', an examination of the *Daily Mirror* between 1984 and 1991 only confirms how limited his political input into the paper was. Even the paper's brief employment of the right-wing controversialist George Gale illustrated the dominance of the paper's journalists, for when a general election seemed imminent, Maxwell bowed to pressure from Stott and Haines and sought to restrict Gale to the *Sunday Mirror*.

Gale refused and left.[61] More generally, despite the suspicion with which Maxwell was viewed, the traditional informal links between the paper and the Labour party continued much as before. For instance, whereas Cudlipp designed electoral publicity for Labour under Wilson, so the man he taught the art of newspaper design, Molloy, did the same for later Labour leaders, including Kinnock.[62]

The above evidence rather refutes allegations that the Mirror's support for Labour took on a tokenist character in the 1980s. The implicit contrast with a golden era of radicalism also suggests the romanticisation of a paper whose original decision to support Labour in the 1930s was little more than a marketing calculation that its appeal to a working-class audience meant that 'the politics had to be made to match.'[63] By 1945 the paper had a clearly developed social conscience, which was demonstrated in its powerful 'VOTE FOR HIM' anti-Tory campaign in the 1945 election. But one should not exaggerate either its extent or intensity. The 1947 *Royal Commission on the Press* came to the conclusion that far more prevalent than its broad pro-Labour sympathy was a style of political coverage which was 'often inadequate and tended to emphasise sensational rather than important news'. The paper went 'apolitical' in the aftermath of the 1951 election, with King observing at the height of affluence that they were 'moving right...because the country is moving right'. It was only opposition from Cudlipp which prevented the *Mirror* from supporting Suez.[64] Similarly, after the 1959 election, the results of which were cheered by the paper's Tory-supporting staff, Cudlipp dropped Dick Crossman's column with the explanation that 'the paper isn't going to be as pro-Labour as that'. The paper told readers that the emphasis was now on youth, gaiety, fun and 'finding the girl with the smartest autumn sparkle'.[65]

Again, large parts of the paper's increasing preoccupation with politics in the second half of the 1960s were devoted to King's apocalyptic warnings about the failings of Wilson's Labour government, which he strove to replace with a centrist coalition of businessmen in which he would be a leading figure. This was an action which had little to do with a crusade on behalf of the paper's readers, a 'stupid' mass of whom King was contemptuous. It was related more to King's frustration that he had not been offered a position commensurate with his abilities or status.[66] Later, the 1974 *Royal Commission on the Press* found that the *Mirror* devoted less space to foreign news than even the *Sun* and was marginally more anti-union than its rival in the coverage of industrial disputes.[67] In 1978–9, Pilger's support of the low paid in the 'Winter of Discontent' was dwarfed by coverage which was so anti-union that more people in the subsequent general election thought that the paper was biased on the Conservatives' behalf rather than to Labour. The *Sunday Mirror*, for example, produced a misleading story of a 'Supersparks' who allegedly earned £738 in one week. This was widely picked up by the Conservative tabloids, to counter excessive sympathy for the low-paid strikers.[68]

The paper ensured that its 'essential timidity was disguised with superficial audacity' by performing 'a series of pseudo radical charades'. The most notable of these was the famous rebuke of Khrushchev in 1960: 'MR K! (if you will pardon an olde English phrase) DON'T BE SO BLOODY RUDE!'.[69] This may have been a 'self-consciously daring' front-page of 'vigour and flair' but, as Raymond Williams observed, its most striking feature was not its intemperate rebuke but the archaic 'nervous parenthesis', which represented 'a kind of apology within an apology'.[70] All this was symbolic of a paper which often offered 'spiced puff' and the appearance of radicalism rather than its substance. The stance was concealed behind brash rhetoric and a frequent self-aggrandising posture, which at times seemed to have as much to do with placing the *Mirror* at the centre of political developments as conveying something of substance. So politically, too, the contrast between radicalism and reaction is misleading, and it could be argued that even the attention later given to Maxwell's all-year role as the nation's 'munificent Father Christmas' only represented a crude personalisation of the paper's sizable ego.[71]

This theme of continuity is also supported by an examination of the other, rather contradictory, allegation from the left about the *Mirror*'s political line in the 1980s – namely, that the paper adopted a sycophantic loyalty to the Labour leadership. Pilger suggests that 'Maxwell saw the *Mirror* as simply a Labour party organ that should publish smiling pictures of Neil Kinnock and laudatory articles. Before Maxwell, the *Mirror* never used to do that.'[72] But this claim again needs to be qualified. Firstly, the *Mirror* did periodically adopt a critical stance under Maxwell, notably on the subject of Labour's unilateral defence policy, about which there was a convenient coincidence between the views of the proprietor and the paper's tradition.[73]

If the *Mirror* was more loyal between 1984 and 1991, this may have been a result less of Maxwell's demand for such a stance than of the fact that under Kinnock the party was realigning itself with its own – and the *Mirror*'s – traditional viewpoint. More importantly, the paper's alignment must be seen in the context of a general increase in the partisanship of the tabloid press as a whole, dating back to the 1970s. The paper became more overtly loyal to Labour after Cudlipp's retirement in 1973; and its loyalty may also have been sharpened in reaction against the vicious anti-Labour campaign by the rest of the tabloids during the 1980s.[74] All that, moreover, predated 1984: the paper could hardly have been more loyal under Maxwell than it was to the party in the early 1980s. The loyalty initially continued, too, after the tycoon's death, as was demonstrated in the paper's 1992 election coverage – which was a virtual carbon copy of 1987.[75]

As for the paper's attitude to the Labour left, Benn's complaints, which in any case long predated Maxwell's arrival, are very similar to Bevan's attacks on the 'rancid' and 'hysterical' hostility of the *Mirror* to the Labour left in the 1950s. This hostility was well exemplified in a violent attack by Cudlipp, in 1952, on Bevan's 'vanity, arrogance and spleen'. Foot later condemned the article as 'the nearest the Britain of the 1950s saw to a McCarthyite essay in character assassination'. In this sense, then, it is difficult not to see Maxwell's personal opposition to the 'pestilential militant influence' as anything other than consistent with the *Mirror*'s tradition.[76]

Dumbing down

The allegations about the *Mirror*'s plunge down market under Maxwell, finally, also probably overstate his role. It is suggested that he 'made the *Mirror* cruder and started to imitate the *Sun*', because the paper proved 'increasingly unwilling to take politics seriously any more' (a claim symbolised by the loss of sophisticated journalists such as Pilger and Keith Waterhouse).[77] But again this has to be put into perspective. On one level it reflected the dominance of one part of the *Mirror*'s ambivalent response to the *Sun*'s successful downmarket drive in 1969. The *Mirror* developed a split personality, unsure whether to imitate its rival or seek to remain aloof. To the extent that the paper did move in the *Sun*'s direction under Maxwell, it also owned much to the instincts of Stott, the editor for most of this period; and it has to be seen also as part of a general shift down market by the entire British press during this period.[78] Moreover, to describe the Maxwell *Mirror* as a carbon copy of the *Sun* is an exaggeration. The paper's journalists and its readers certainly did not see the two as synonymous. Research conducted in April 1991 showed that whereas the *Sun* was given a lowly believability rating of 1.4 out of 5, the *Mirror's* rating at 2.5 was just below that of the mid-market tabloids and somewhere in the middle compared with the believability of the broadsheet press. One study in the late 1980s also found that *Sun* readers did not see the *Mirror* as an alternative, because it was perceived as too serious and lacked the frivolity and apolitical stance of its rival. The *Mirror* in the 1980s still retained an appeal to a very different constituency. Its readers were generally both Labour supporters and as interested in politics as readers of the middle-market newspapers; while *Sun* readers, by contrast, tended to be more politically apathetic and uncommitted to any party.[79]

The argument that Maxwell trivialised the *Mirror's* journalism is also perhaps the most selective of the allegations against him, when examined within the tradition of the paper and the popular press as a whole. Indeed the recent term 'dumbing down' is barely even a new name to describe a very old complaint: society was already said to have been 'levelled down' by the time Lord Salisbury condemned Northcliffe for designing one paper for people who could read but not think and another for those who could see but not read. Murdoch and Maxwell simply reinforced rather than caused what one celebrated journalist described as a 'gravitational force of decline in journalism', which was actually present long before their arrival.[80] Ironically, too, it was probably the *Mirror* rather than Murdoch which contributed most to the constant down-market adjustment which nearly all newspapers have made during the twentieth century. To quote one symbolic example, the *Mirror* headline which announced the sinking of the Titanic in 1912 was just half the size of a 1998 prediction by the *Guardian* of a minor cabinet reshuffle.[81] One of the reasons for this change was that in the second half of the 1930s the *Mirror* initiated a tabloid revolution, characterised by 'sledgehammer text' and 'piledriver headlines' of a kind not hitherto seen in the British daily press. As Francis Williams put it, a 'frenzied gusto of sensational stories about sex and crime' competed with human interest stories, strip cartoons, 'live' letters and sports coverage, to fill the paper.[82] It was Cudlipp who introduced the first nude into tabloid journalism shortly after becoming editor of the *Sunday Pictorial* in the late 1930s, and who was responsible for headlines such as 'Sir Vivian Fuchs Off to the Antarctic'. It is perhaps little wonder that he later declared himself an admirer of *Sun* editor Kelvin MacKenzie.[83]

Contemporary responses to this style of journalism anticipate more recent denunciations of the *Sun*. The *Mirror* helped 'lower the moral and intellectual standards of the country' through what Randolph Churchill described as a river of pornography and crime. On the left, *Tribune* offered its verdict on a daily magazine', which had carried off the prize of sensational journalism by omitting 'whole chunks of news'; the results being a more ignorant public and lower standards of journalism.[84] One concrete example was felt to be the paper's less than reverential coverage of the romance between Princess Margaret and Group Captain Peter Townsend. A readers' poll asking whether she should be allowed to marry the divorcee brought widespread condemnation for 'the cheapest kind of tenth rate gutter journalism'. This followed an even more famous instance in 1949, when the paper's editor, Sylvester Bolam, was jailed for three months for contempt of court. His crime was a 'scandalous and wicked' front page headline – 'THE VAMPIRE CONFESSES' – which convicted an alleged murderer without the trouble of a court trial as a monster guilty of 'sadistic murder, mutilation and the drinking of his victims' blood'. The episode provided a classic illustration that the *Mirror's* existence was, as King later conceded, 'primarily to provide entertainment'.[85]

This is not to deny that the *Mirror* had a serious side. But its effectiveness is debatable. Mass Observation's study in the late 1940s noted that a third of the paper's readers did not even know which party the paper supported. 29 per cent of readers liked the paper for its letters and a similar number for its cartoons; but just 3 per cent bought it for its political line, and only the same number bothered reading the editorials.[86] The *Mirror's* solution to postwar affluence by the 1960s, however, was to became more serious, less raucous and less strident, and to introduce such features as 'Mirrorscope', a four-page pull-out examining world affairs. Without doubt there is much to admire in the *Mirror* of the pre-*Sun* era, but how far this was what many readers actually admired is another question.

Mirrorscope's most visible impact, for instance, seemed to be on the London tubes, which were sometimes said to be littered ankle deep in discarded copies.[87] In some respects, it was the respectable, serious *Mirror* of the 1960s that was the aberration. Certainly far more central to the paper's history than its serious and impassioned journalism was its popularisation of sensational and trivial news. Murdoch simply took this one phenomenally successful step further – on the basis, in fact, of what he saw as an updated version of the *Mirror*'s formula of the 1940s and 1950s.[88]

The paper's subsequent circulation decline shows that even in this area too the evidence of a detrimental Maxwell effect is uncertain. During 1984 to 1991, the paper lost 19 per cent of its circulation, while the *Sun* lost 10 per cent. The bulk of this decline occurred in the first turbulent eighteen months of Maxwell's control. From 1985 sales stabilised and even rose slightly in a declining market. With the exception of Maxwell's innovative introduction of colour printing – his solitary triumph over Murdoch – it is difficult to dispute that the paper's performance from 1985 onwards was largely despite rather than because of him. But if Maxwell cannot be credited with the stabilisation of the paper's circulation, equally he can hardly be blamed for the previous long term decline, which had seen the paper lose more than one third of its five million sale in the 25 years up to 1984. The drop in circulation continued overall at much the same rate under his ownership as before, and it suffered an even faster fall after his death.[89]

Conclusion

There can be no doubt that Maxwell's ownership disastrously sullied the appearance of the *Mirror*, changing popular perceptions of the paper through its very identification with the corrupt tycoon. But although Maxwell 'repainted the bandwagon' underneath, at least in the three areas examined, there was in fact little significant change – or else, what change occurred was well within the traditions of the paper.[90] It is fitting that under the ownership of one of the century's biggest fraudsters, the image changed far more than the substance, and that the 'Max factor' proved to be largely cosmetic in effect. Maxwell was more a symbol of the end of a partly mythical golden era at the paper, and a convenient scapegoat.

He was not the true cause. Quite when the golden age existed, moreover, is difficult to establish. As Molloy, journalist at the *Mirror* for 30 years and editor between 1975 and 1985, puts it, the 'golden age' analysis seems essentially a nostalgia for the past:

> The golden periods are always false. I now understand from people that my editorship of the paper was a golden period of civilisation when the paper had the finest writers ... but at the time there was no question. Already people were thinking about a golden period of the fifties and the sixties and other people in the fifties and sixties were thinking about a golden period of the 1930s.[91]

Perhaps the best illustration of this was the reaction to the events at the paper in 1992–93, after the installation as chairman of David Montgomery. The man described by one journalist as a 'Thatcherite bastard' quickly lived up to this reputation. He savaged the paper by sacking three editors and 100 journalists and he replaced senior staff with ex-Murdoch journalists like himself. Campbell left amidst vocal Labour party protests about the dilution of the *Mirror's* centre-left political stance, while others resigned complaining about an atmosphere in which journalists were motivated by fear. Sales rapidly declined to a (temporary) all-time low, amidst allegations of a reduction of political coverage and a preference for *Sun*-style 'trivia, sensationalist reporting and sleaze'. According to one former *Mirror* journalist, the events signalled the effective death of the old *Daily Mirror*. It was now the serious, journalistically powerful and pro-Labour paper of the 1980s that was viewed with nostalgia and yearning.[92] Ironically, it almost seemed that another retrospective golden era of the *Mirror*, this time under Maxwell, was now emerging, amidst a cry from journalists and politicians: 'Come back Cap'n Bob, all is forgiven'.

Notes

1 *Royal Commission on the Press, 1947–1949 Report*, Cmd 7700 (London: HMSO 1949), p. 42.
2 Tom Bower, *Maxwell the Outsider* (London: Mandarin, 1998), pp. 358–78, 287; Roy Greenslade, 'Living with the Beast', *Sunday Times*, 8 December 1991.

3 *Daily Mirror*, 14 July 1984; *Playboy*, October 1991, interview: Maxwell; Bower, *Maxwell the Outsider*, p. 396.

4 John Pilger, *Hidden Agendas* (London: Vintage, 1998), pp. 410–35; Bruce Hanlin, 'Owners, Editors and Journalists' in Andrew Belsey and Ruth Chadwick, *Ethical Issues in Journalism and the Media* (London: Routledge, 1992), pp. 35–6; John Pilger, *Heroes* (London: Jonathan Cape, 1986), pp. 508–21.

5 Julian Critchley, *Some of Us* (London: John Murray, 1992), p. 188; *Guardian*, 28 December 1998.

6 Hanlin, 'Owners, Editors and Journalists', p. 35; Robert Edwards, *Goodbye Fleet Street* (London: Hodder & Stoughton, 1998), pp. 222–3; Roy Greenslade, *Maxwell's Fall* (London: Simon & Schuster, 1992), p. 109.

7 Edwards, *Goodbye Fleet Street*, pp. 236–48; author's interview with Geoffrey Goodman; Greenslade, *Maxwell's Fall*, pp. 101, 228, 270.

8 Ivan Rowan, 'The Costly Game of the Bingo Warriors', *Sunday Telegraph*, 3 September 1984, p. 6; Hugo Young, 'Maxwell the Megaphone', interview: Maxwell, *Guardian*, 5 March 1990; Pilger, *Heroes*, p. 508.

9 Bower, *Maxwell the Outsider*, pp. 388–94; *Private Eye*, Christmas 1986, p. 15; Keith Waterhouse, quoted in Bower, *Maxwell the Outsider*, p. 441; Elisabeth Maxwell, *A Mind of My Own: My Life with Robert Maxwell* (London: Pan, 1995), p. 639.

10 Judi Bevan, 'Holding Up the Mirror to Maxwell', interview: Maxwell, *Sunday Telegraph*, 14 April 1991; Bronwen Maddox and Jimmy Burns, 'Tell the Queen I'm Busy', *Financial Times*, 15 June 1992; for assessments of Maxwell's personality, see, for example, Greenslade, *Maxwell's Fall*, pp. 11–14; Russell Davies, *Foreign Body: the Secret Life of Robert Maxwell* (London: Bloomsbury, 1996) pp. 223–5.

11 Torin Douglas, 'Maxwell Moving to Dominate UK Media', *Marketing Week*, 31 January 1986; Pilger, *Hidden Agendas*, p. 423.

12 David Dugan, '"Forward with Britain" and Robert Maxwell', *Listener*, **114**, 18 July 1985, 7; Ian Aitken, 'Prince of Darkness', *London Review of Books*, 28 January 1994; Terry Eagleton, 'Looking After Number 23', *Times Higher Education Supplement*, 9 February 1990; Woodrow Wyatt, 'Maxwell: Tearaway Tycoon', *The Times*, 12 March 1998.

13 Young, 'Maxwell the Megaphone'; Richard Evans, 'Ebullient Send-Off for *The European* Thanks to Thatcher', *Independent*, 12 May 1990; *Daily Mirror*, 18 August 1984.

14 Michael Williams, 'Maxwell's Mirror', *New Society*, Vol. 69, No. 1135, 20 September 1984, p. 314; 'Why Kinnock May Not Like What He Sees in the Mirror, *Sunday Times*, 6 November 1988; Joe Haines, *Maxwell* (London: Futura, 1988), p. 399.

15 Bower, *Maxwell the Outsider*, p. 385; author's interview with Goodman.

16 Pilger, *Heroes*, p. 523–4; P. Thompson and A. Delano, *Maxwell: a Portrait of Power* (London: Corgi, 1991), pp. 14, 213; Pilger, *Heroes*, p. 516; Hanlin, 'Owners, Editors and Journalists', p. 35.

17 Williams, 'Maxwell's Mirror', p. 312; Dugan, 'Forward with Britain' and Robert Maxwell', p. 7.

18 Pilger, *Distant Voices* (London: Vintage, 1992), p. 71; author's interview with Goodman.
19 Pilger, *Distant Voices*, pp. 70–75; Pilger, *Heroes*, pp. 508–32.
20 'Cudlipp's Canons', *British Journalism Review*, 9(3), (1998), 28–9.
21 Ibid, p. 26; Matthew Engel, *Tickle the Public: One Hundred Years of the Popular Press* (London: Indigo, 1997), pp. 145–6; Philip Zec, 'There was an Old Woman in Stoke…', *British Journalism Review*, 4(3) (1993), 9–10; Michael Leapman, *Treacherous Estate: the Press after Fleet Street* (London: Hodder & Stoughton, 1992), p. 14; Engel, *Tickle the Public*, p. 146.
22 Pilger, *Heroes*, p. 528; Andy MacSmith, 'First Mate to Captain Bob', *Observer*, 23 October 1994; Frank Jaffa, *Maxwell Stories* (London: Robson Books, 1992) p. 190.
23 *Daily Mirror*, 6 November 1991; Austin Mitchell, 'The Great Betrayal', *Daily Mail*, 5 December 1991; *Sun*, 5 December 1991.
24 Williams, 'Maxwell's Mirror', p. 314.
25 Jeremy Tunstall, *Newspaper Power: the New National Press in Britain* (Oxford: Clarendon, 1997) pp. 129–30; author's interviews with Richard Stott, Mike Molloy, Joe Haines and Goodman.
26 Hunter Davies, 'How Clever to be Mr Jay', *Independent*, 21 April 1992; Pilger, *Hidden Agendas*, p. 434; author's interviews with Molloy and Goodman; Greenslade, *Maxwell's Fall*, p. 151.
27 Greenslade, *Maxwell's Fall*, p. 212; John Diamond, 'Why Greenslade's Mirror Cracked', *Guardian*, 22 April 1991; Jaffa, *Maxwell Stories*, p. 148.
28 Jaffa, *Maxwell Stories*, p. 152.
29 Geoffrey Goodman, *British Journalism Review*, 3(2) (1992), 57–8; author's interview with Molloy; Greenslade, *Maxwell's Fall*, pp. 11, 205–8.
30 Pilger, *Heroes*, p. 522.
31 Greenslade, *Maxwell's Fall*, p. 137; author's interviews with Molloy and Goodman; Nicholas Davies, *The Unknown Maxwell* (London: Pan, 1993), p. 55; Nicholas Coleridge, *Paper Tigers* (London: William Heinemann, 1993), pp. 505–6.
32 Author's interview with Molloy.
33 Ben Bagdikian, 'The Lords of the Global Village', *The Nation*, 12 June 1989, p. 805; Tom Bower, *Maxwell: The Final Verdict* (London: Harper Collins, 1995), pp. 92–3; Coleridge, *Paper Tigers*, p. 505; 'Conrad Black talks to Bill Hagerty', *British Journalism Review*, 9(2), (1998), p. 11.
34 Greenslade, *Maxwell's Fall*, p. 137; interview, Molloy.
35 Greenslade, *Maxwell's Fall*, p. 99; *Daily Mirror*, 17 November 1989; *Private Eye*, 8 December 1991, pp. 8. 15; Maggie Brown, 'After the Mirror, a Window of Opportunity', *Independent*, 23 February 1994.
36 Eve Pollard, *Sunday Mirror* editor, cited in *The Journals of Woodrow Wyatt: Volume One*, edited by Sarah Curtis (London: Macmillan, 1998), p. 620; author's interview with Molloy.
37 Greenslade, *Maxwell's Fall*, pp. 137–8.
38 Greenslade, *Maxwell's Fall*, p. 208.
39 Author's interview with Goodman.

40 Greenslade, *Maxwell's Fall*, pp. 109, 242–4; *Daily Mirror*, 14 January 1991; Diamond, 'Why Greenslade's Mirror Cracked'.

41 Bill Hagerty, 'More Shoeshop than Printshop', *British Journalism Review*, 7(3), (1997), pp. 72–4; author's interviews with Molloy and Goodman.

42 Hagerty, 'More Shoeshop than Printshop, pp. 72–4; author's interview with Molloy.

43 Francis Williams, *Dangerous Estate* (London: Readers Union, 1958), pp. 224–6; Cecil King, *Strictly Personal* (London: Weidenfeld & Nicolson, 1969), p. 104.

44 Hugh Cudlipp, 'The Humble Seeker After Knowledge', in Vivian Brodsky (ed.), *Fleet Street: the Inside Story of Journalism* (London: Macdonald, 1966), pp. 52, 56; Bower, *Maxwell the Outsider*, p. 386; author's interview with Molloy.

45 Author's interview with Goodman.

46 Author's interview with Molloy; Wyatt, 'Maxwell: Tearaway Tycoon'.

47 Author's interviews with Stott and Haines.

48 *Royal Commission on the Press, 1947–1949 Report*, p. 42; *Royal Commission on the Press, 1962: Minutes of Oral Evidence*, Vol. 1, Cmd 1812 (London: HMSO, 1962), pp. 189–91.

49 Author's interviews with Stott, Haines and Molloy.

50 Coleridge, *Paper Tigers*, p. 19.

51 Roy Greenslade, 'Sulks, Mischief and the Triumph of the Ego', *Guardian*, 11 January 1999.

52 *Daily Mirror*, 20 November 1981; *The Times*, 20 November 1981; author's interviews with Goodman, Haines and Molloy; Martin Harrop, 'The Press', in David Butler and Dennis Kavanagh, *The British General Election of 1983* (London: Macmillan, 1984), pp. 183, 189.

53 Young, 'Maxwell the Megaphone'; *Daily Mirror*, 1 October 1984.

54 Bower, *Maxwell the Outsider*, p. 372; Edwards, *Goodbye Fleet Street*, pp. 218–19.

55 Bower, *Maxwell the Outsider*, pp. 373–4; *Daily Mirror*, 6 July 1984; Edwards, *Goodbye Fleet Street*, p. 229; Bower, *Maxwell: the Final Verdict*, p. 224; author's interview with Molloy; Thompson and Delano, *Maxwell*, pp. 223, 14–15;

56 Author's interview with Haines and Stott.

57 *Daily Mirror*, 23, 24, 25, 26 July 1984; Edwards, *Goodbye Fleet Street*, p. 231; Tony Benn, *The End Of An Era: Diaries 1980–90* (London: Hutchinson, 1992), p. 364.

58 Young, 'Maxwell the Megaphone'; Martin Harrop, 'Press', in David Butler and Dennis Kavanagh, *The British General Election of 1987* (London: Macmillan, 1988), pp. 169–70; *Daily Mirror*, 9, 10 June 1987.

59 Harrop, ibid, p. 170; *Daily Mirror*, 14 October 1964, 1 June 1987.

60 *Daily Mirror*, 9 October 1991; John Mulholland, 'Labour's Mr Media', interview: Campbell, *Guardian*, 17 February 1997; Alastair Campbell, 'Maxwell, the Man of Labour', *Sunday Mirror*, 10 November 1991.

61 Pilger, quoted in Seamus Milne, *The Enemy Within: MI5, Maxwell and the Scargill Affair* (London: Verso, 1994), p. 177; P. Thompson and A. Delano, *Maxwell*, pp. 14, 213.

62 Janet Morgan (ed.), *The Backbench Diaries of Richard Crossman*, (London; Hamish Hamilton, 1981), pp. 714–15, 723; Pilger, *Hidden Agendas*, p. 403; author's interview with Molloy.

63 King, *Strictly Personal*, p. 101.

64 *Royal Commission on the Press, 1947–1949*, Cmd 7700 (London: HMSO, 1949), p. 358; Maurice Edelman, *The Mirror: a Political History* (London: Hamish Hamilton, 1966), p. 191; Tony Shaw, *Eden, Suez and the Mass Media: Propaganda and Persuasion during the Suez Crisis* (London: Tauris, 1996), p. 53.

65 *The Backbench Diaries of Richard Crossman*, pp. 798, 772; Francis Williams, 'Shattered Mirror', *New Statesman*, 17 October 1959, p. 496; *Daily Mirror* , 12–20 October 1959.

66 Hugh Cudlipp, *Walking on the Water* (London: Bodley Head, 1976), pp. 257–346; Denys Thompson (ed.), *Discrimination and Popular Culture* (London: Penguin, 1973), pp. 16, 81.

67 *Royal Commission on the Press: Analysis of Newspaper Content*, A Report by Denis McQuail, Cmd 6810-4 (London: HMSO, 1977, pp. 32, 213–14, 248.

68 Pilger, *Hidden Agendas*, p. 417; Peter Kellner and Robert Worcester, 'Electoral Perceptions of Media Stance', in Robert Worcester and Martin Harrop (eds), *Political Communications: the General Election Campaign of 1979* (London: George Allen & Unwin, 1982), pp. 58–9; *Sunday Mirror*, 28 January 1979; *Daily Mail, Daily Express, Sun*, 29, 30, January 1979.

69 Piers Brendon, *The Life and Death of the Press Barons* (London: Secker & Warburg, 1982), p. 212; *Daily Mirror*, 17 May 1960.

70 Keith Waterhouse, 'Excuse Me M'lord, Did I Hear You Murmur "F… off"?', *British Journalism Review*, 9(4), (1998), p. 17; Hugh Cudlipp, *At Your Peril* (London: Weidenfeld & Nicolson, 1962) p. 160c; Raymond Williams, 'The Face Behind the Mirror', *Observer*, 29 April 1962; Brendon, *The Life and Death of the Press Barons*, p. 213.

71 Williams, 'The Face Behind the Mirror'; Brendon, *The Life and Death of the Press Barons*, p. 212; A.C.H. Smith, *Paper Voices: the Popular Press and Social Change 1935–1965* (London: Chatto & Windus, 1965), pp. 178–89, 197–200; Davies, *Foreign Body*, p. 234.

72 Milne, *The Enemy Within*, p. 198.

73 See, for example, *Daily Mirror*, 22 June 1988.

74 Colin Seymour-Ure, *The British Press and Broadcasting since 1945* (Oxford: Blackwell, 1995), p. 222; James Thomas, 'Labour, the Tabloids, and the 1992 General Election', *Contemporary British History*, 12(2) (Summer 1998), pp. 87–90; author's interview with Molloy; Greenslade, 'Sulks, Mischief and the Triumph of the Ego'.

75 Martin Harrop and Margaret Scammell, 'A Tabloid War', in David Butler and Dennis Kavanagh, *The British General Election of 1992* (London: Macmillan, 1992), pp. 184–5.

76 *Daily Mirror*, 21 September 1981; Cudlipp, *At Your Peril*, pp. 128–30; Hugh Cudlipp, 'End the Bevan Myth', *Sunday Pictorial*, 28 September 1952; Michael Foot, *Aneurin Bevan: Volume Two, 1945–1960* (London: Davis-Poynter, 1973), pp. 378–9; *Daily Mirror*, 1 October 1984.

77 Author's interviews with Molloy and Julia Langdon, political editor, *Daily Mirror* 1984–9.

78 Molloy, quoted in Pilger, *Hidden Agendas*, p. 414; author's interview with Molloy; Brian MacArthur, 'New Readers, New Times', *The Times*, 3 February 1997; Leapman, *Treacherous Estate*, p. 181.

79 Andrew Gimson, 'Take Me to Your Leader Writer', *Spectator*, 6 June 1987, pp. 19–21; Steven Barnett, 'Sliding Down the Slippery Slope', *British Journalism Review* , 4(1) (1993), p. 69; Mark Pursehouse, 'Reading the Sun: Conflict in the Popular Press' (University of Birmingham: MPhil, 1989), pp. 36, 91, 116–17, 170; William Miller, *Media and Voters: the Audience, Content and Influence of Press and Television at the 1987 General Election* (Oxford: Clarendon, 1991), pp. 16, 191.

80 George Gissing, quoted in John Carey, *The Intellectuals and the Masses: Pride and Prejudice among the Literary Intelligentsia, 1880–1939* (London: Faber & Faber, 1992), p. 93; Tom Matthews, *The Sugar Pill: an Essay on Newspapers* (London: Victor Gollancz, 1957), p. 48; Bob Franklin, *Newszak and News Media* (London: Arnold, 1997), p. 242.

81 Keith Waterhouse, *Waterhouse on Newspaper Style* (London: Viking, 1989), p. 37; Ian Jack, Introduction, *The Granta Book of Reportage* (London: Granta, 1998), p. xiii.

82 Waterhouse, *Waterhouse on Newspaper Style*, pp. 32, 40; Williams, *Dangerous Estate*, p. 227.

83 Hugh Cudlipp, in Tony Gray (ed.) *Fleet Street Remembered* (London: Heinemann, 1990), pp. 118–21; Bill Grundy, *The Press Inside Out* (London: W.H. Allen, 1976), p. 26; Keith Waterhouse, 'In Search of the Sunday Papers', *British Journalism Review*, 9(3) (1998), p. 31.

84 Matthews, *The Sugar Pill*, pp. 151–2; Leapman, *Treacherous Estate*, p. 16; *Tribune*, 21 January 1949.

85 Cudlipp, *At Your Peril*, pp. 140–151; Matthews, *The Sugar Pill*, pp. 84–90; Engel, *Tickle the Public*, p. 176; *Daily Mirror*, 4 March 1949; Cecil King, *Without Fear or Fervour* (London: Sidgwick & Jackson, 1971), p. 198.

86 Matthews, *The Sugar Pill*, pp. 79, 82; Mass Observation, *The Press and its Readers: a Report* (London: Art & Technics, 1949), p. 124.

87 Cecil King, *The Future of the Press* (London: MacGibbon & Kee, 1967), pp. 63, 65; Bill Grundy, *The Press Inside Out*, p. 99.

88 Larry Lamb, *Sunrise* (London: Macmillan, 1989), pp. 5–6.

89 Brian MacArthur, 'Maxwell's Paper Chase', *The Times*, 6 November 1991; Colin Seymour-Ure, *The British Press and Broadcasting since 1945*, pp. 28–9.

90   Author's interview with Molloy.
91   Ibid.
92   *Socialist Worker*, 31 October 1992; *Guardian*, 17, 18 February 1993; *UK Press Gazette*, 8 March 1993; Gregor Gall, 'Looking in the Mirror: a Case Study of Industrial Relations in a National Newspaper', in Michael Bromley and Tom O'Malley, *A. Journalism Reader* (London: Routledge, 1997), pp. 233–46; John Diamond, 'Mirror Mirror Off the Wall', *Guardian*, 22 February 1993; Hagerty, 'More Shoeshop than Printshop', p. 74.

Index